TEACHING IN CONTEXT

TEACHING IN CONTEXT

The Social Side of Education Reform

Edited by
Esther Quintero

HARVARD EDUCATION PRESS
CAMBRIDGE, MASSACHUSETTS

Paperback ISBN 978-1-68253-037-5
Library Edition ISBN 978-1-68253-038-2

Library of Congress Cataloging-in-Publication Data

Names: Quintero, Esther, editor.
Title: Teaching in context : the social side of education reform / edited by
   Esther Quintero.
Description: Cambridge, Massachusetts : Harvard Education Press, [2017] |
   Includes bibliographical references and index.
Identifiers: LCCN 2016056260 | ISBN 9781682530375 (pbk.) |
   ISBN 9781682530382 (library edition)
Subjects: LCSH: Effective teaching—United States. | Teacher
   effectiveness—United States. | Teachers—Job satisfaction—United States.
   | School improvement programs—United States. | Education and
   state—United States. | Educational change—United States.
Classification: LCC LB2840 .T455 2017 | DDC 371.102—dc23
LC record available at https://lccn.loc.gov/2016056260

Published by Harvard Education Press,
an imprint of the Harvard Education Publishing Group

Harvard Education Press
8 Story Street
Cambridge, MA 02138

Cover Design: Ciano Design
Cover Graphic: iStock.com/KrulUA
The typefaces used in this book are Adobe Garamond Pro and ITC Legacy Sans

CONTENTS

Foreword

Moving Forward Together

Teaching is in trouble. And if teaching is in trouble, so is learning. Fulfilled learners don't come out of a system of frustrated and unfulfilled teachers. The proliferation of harmful working conditions and corrosive school cultures around American teachers is not a matter of assertion or opinion. As this important book repeatedly shows with large-scale and up-close evidence from the top researchers in the field, it is underpinned by hard evidence. The disturbing pattern of unstable, unsatisfying, and ineffective work cultures in American schools, particularly those that are supposed to serve children in poverty, can no longer be ignored or denied.

But things don't have to be this way. *Teaching in Context* takes a positive and hopeful approach in pointing to malleable factors and deliberate interventions that have improved working conditions and professional cultures for teachers. As a consequence, significant gains have been made for some of the poorest children in many US contexts. It is now time, with all that we know, to get these kinds of results on a nationwide scale. First, though, let's be clear about the problem.

Teachers in the United States have been suffering for too long from the fundamental problems that three of the founding thinkers of social thought depicted as the basic afflictions of the whole of society a century and more ago. In the 1920s, the German sociologist Max Weber diagnosed the greatest problem in society as being one of excessive *bureaucracy*. Bureaucracy, he said, began fifteen hundred years ago in China as a system of promotion and upward mobility based on civil service examinations and merit rather than aristocratic preference and patronage. But this impartial system of assignment and achievement turned into an "iron cage" of bureaucracy that stifled the human spirit and cast people into a state of disenchantment where the magic of life had been lost. His conservative French counterpart, Emile Durkheim, blamed society's ills on something he called *anomie,* or normlessness, when the basic principles of social regulation have collapsed, when agreed on and understood standards and codes of human conduct have disappeared. In an anomic society, everyone is morally on their own, with no limits to their actions.

The most infamous member of this classic trio of social thinkers, Karl Marx, along with his associate Friedrich Engels, pointed to a third problem. They argued that as a result of the exploitation of labor, the pervasive condition of capitalist societies was one of alienated labor, or *alienation*. Alienation, they said, occurred when people no longer created meaning and fulfilled themselves intrinsically through their work, having become estranged from themselves and their work because they were producing extrinsic results for others. In much more recent times, many writers who would not regard themselves at all as Marxists have found that alienation or disengagement remains all too common in modern working life. Indeed, Gallup polls find that high proportions of US workers are disengaged from their work.

Marx and Engels wanted a social revolution. By contrast, inspired by his travels across nineteenth-century America, the French social thinker Alexis de Tocqueville advocated for something else. The answer, he felt, was in "the arts" of democracy—in the capacity to argue, negotiate, and compromise—that were at the heart of the country's strong communities and public life. As educators in the state of Vermont recently put it to me, this was the Vermont way—to roll up one's sleeves and argue things out together.

Too many US teachers today are suffering from the triple jeopardy of bureaucracy, alienation, and anomie. And far too many educational reform efforts in the United States and elsewhere have actively contributed to these ills, with no overall benefit for young people's learning and development.

- *Bureaucracy* has burgeoned through the proliferation of standardized testing and the imposition of prescribed instruction on which more and more teachers' performance ratings have come to be based as a consequence of federal, "big government" policy.
- *Alienation* is everywhere, as disengaged and dissatisfied teachers leave the unsupportive and managerially toxic system with increasing frequency, so that the modal number (most commonly occurring number) of years in teaching in America has plummeted from well into double figures right down to one!
- The *anomie* of competitive individualism is everywhere. Individual teacher evaluation and the charter school movement have often pitted teachers and schools against one another in the same communities and sometimes even in the same buildings.

What has been the result of all this reform? In deadpan yet deadening prose, the US government's own evaluation of Race to the Top concludes that "it is not clear whether the RTTT grants improved student outcomes"!

So it is clearly time for another way, and this book shows how more than a few teachers, schools, and even states have already found one. As Esther Quintero points out in her informative interpretation of the findings reported in this book, ever since the early 1990s, there has been a consistent evidence base that teachers who work together collaboratively in a supportive environment where everyone expects that all students can succeed get better results, student for student, than do teachers who work in schools where they are mainly left to teach and plan on their own. The research findings reported in this book confirm these results and begin to give them more precision.

What *Teaching in Context* shows is not just that it is better to collaborate than not collaborate, but the contributions reveal that there are different ways of collaborating, not just one specific structure or program. Yet, not all these forms of collaboration are equally effective. Collaboration is not just correlated with greater student success, but some studies over time and as a result of specific interventions demonstrate that the relationship is a causal one. Deliberately designed processes such as inquiring into student learning or figuring out what interventions to make or supports to provide for particular students can be highly effective. Others that involve much talking and little doing may have little immediate benefit at all. Yet time has to be invested in building relationships and shared beliefs in and commitment to everyone's success, otherwise the deliberately designed processes can degenerate into the stilted routines of contrived collegiality. It is folly to think there is a magic method that can be hastily imposed on everyone to yield instant returns.

There also needs to be time and persistence to build cultures of mutual trust and support. Formal and informal, short-term and long-term, direct and indirect—it is how all the different forms of collaboration are joined into a single compelling narrative of improvement that matters in the end.

The Every Student Succeeds Act makes ample provision for evidence-based approaches in order to justify funding through different programs. There are few reforms more evidentially compelling than building up the social capital of the teaching force and providing the resources and support to do that, while taking away the distractions of relentless individual teacher evaluation. Too many reforms in the past decade and more have been driven by the interests of making capital gains from our children through the profits returned to charter school owners and the sales that are made from testing and technology products. We need to make an investment in a new kind of capital now in education—what Michael Fullan and

I call the *professional capital* of our teachers—and this includes social capital. How teachers are expected to work together is a defining condition of the job, and how well they are able to work together is a result of supportive working conditions, provisions of sufficient time, and the protections afforded by stable and effective leadership.

Albert Shanker, who gave his name to the institute from which this book springs, had a vision of teacher unions and the teaching profession that involved them promoting positive change as well as protecting teachers against reforms that were harmful to them and their students. This fine book and its vision of what can be achieved when teachers are expected, encouraged, and enabled to work together, is a fitting tribute to his memory.

—Andy Hargreaves
Brennan Chair in Education
Boston College

The Social Side of Education Reform

ESTHER QUINTERO

Over a decade ago, Anthony Bryk and Barbara Schneider identified a major obstacle to achieving sustained, systemwide school improvement in the United States: most reform efforts overlook the fact that "teachers must engage not only particular subjects and ideas about how to teach them, but also students, their parents, and professional colleagues." They noted that "important consequences play out in these daily social exchanges."[1]

The present volume is about the nature and impact of these social exchanges, with a specific focus on teachers' relationships with their peers and, to a lesser extent, with leaders and parents.[2] It shows how these exchanges influence important teacher and student outcomes (e.g., teacher retention and effectiveness, student achievement) as well as organizational aspects like school safety and school climate. Specifically, the chapters in this volume make the case that school contexts characterized by strong and stable relationships among adults are more conducive to the learning and improvement of adults *and* students and the system as a whole.

Teaching in Context brings together scholars from diverse fields. In surveying not only their own but others' research, these contributors show that teachers become better faster when they work in organizations that support them professionally—in schools and districts that purposefully strengthen the interpersonal and collective dimension of teachers' work through structures that allow them to work together, learn from each other, and coordinate their instruction for the benefit of all students.

This volume comes out of the realization that, while the research base for these ideas is ample, growing, and robust, the message has not reached the world of policy. It is possible that this body of knowledge, which goes back to the 1970s and 1980s, has not been disseminated as broadly as other scholarly work and that policy makers are simply not aware of this research, a situation this book looks to remedy.[3] Or it may be that some in policy circles perceive the idea that relationships matter to be too "touchy feely," a notion researchers in this volume challenge. Strong and trusting relationships—whether among teachers or between teachers and supervisors or teachers and students—are forged under conditions that have very little to do with being "buddies" and everything to do with clarity around goals and expectations, structures that facilitate focused conversations, and supports designed to improve. Another misperception is that interpersonal aspects of the profession are unmeasurable. Addressing this, the contributors capture the quality, frequency, and nature of teachers' professional relationships in a variety of sophisticated ways, such as by constructing measures derived from practitioners' answers to working conditions surveys, collecting social network data, conducting in-depth interviews, designing and validating ad hoc teacher and administrator surveys, or using time-use and other daily instruments. A final reason for why the social side of education reform has not been duly recognized by policy makers is that they may not perceive these findings to be actionable. And while there is some merit to that argument, John Papay and Matthew Kraft note that "although the collective and interpersonal nature of school contexts makes quick policy fixes unlikely to succeed, research suggests several concrete ways in which educators and policy makers can take on this challenge."

A shift in education policy is sorely needed. Policy does not sufficiently attend to, let alone leverage, the interpersonal aspects of teachers' work. Instead, the focus remains on technical and individual-level solutions. For example, policies aimed at improving teaching focus on identifying the most talented individuals (and dismissing those who are less able) and on increasing their individual abilities (through pay-for-performance, overhauling teacher preparation, etc.) In the meantime, most practitioners are largely missed by these remedies. Too many educators continue to work in isolation, focusing on their own students, interacting only intermittently and often minimally with colleagues and supervisors, and stagnating in (or about to leave) schools that were never set up to support them or promote their professional growth.

This inefficient approach to improvement is predicated on the idea of making the system better by increasing the quality of instruction one teacher at a time. A shift to targeting the organizational context could benefit teachers collectively and result in more sustained and sustainable improvement. For example, reforms centered on connecting educators and facilitating their learning from each other create a value that exceeds the sum of their individual talents, thereby transforming schools into *learning organizations*.

I do not take issue with existing policy instruments per se but, rather, with the way they are used. For instance, would performance incentives produce better results if administered at the school or team (not the individual) level? Would conventional professional development be more useful if it focused on the acquisition of relational skills such as giving and receiving feedback, facilitating team meetings, and so on? The evidence presented in this volume may call for a redirection of some existing instruments, but, more than anything, it calls for new approaches that finally put to use the knowledge we've gained over the years about how teachers get better at teaching. The chapters comprising *Teaching in Context* offer many practical suggestions and ideas for getting started on this policy re-design process.

Some of the studies in this volume use performance on stan-dardized tests as a way to gauge student learning and teacher effec-tiveness. While evidence shows that test scores are not the only way to measure success (of students or of adults), however partially or imperfectly, they do capture what students know about particular subjects. In addition, test scores are an outcome that policy makers pay attention to. But this volume focuses on the social *processes* that contribute to these outcomes, for, as Susan Rosenholtz has argued, "if we look only at the outputs of schools and not at the structures and processes influencing them, we will never learn why organiza-tions such as schools work, and how positive outcomes are brought about." The most important questions in the area of school effective-ness "are not methodological but conceptual—not *how* to measure effectiveness but *what* to measure."[4]

The answer that the contributors to this volume unanimously and resoundingly offer is that we need to pay attention to whether and how teachers' capacities are supported or constrained by their social-organizational context and the broader systems and commu-nities where schools are situated. *Teaching in Context* hopes to shift and lift a policy conversation that has become overly centered on drivers that are demonstrably insufficient for improvement.

SURVEYING THE VOLUME

The chapters in this book deliver a consistent story. This isn't because the contributors are all part of the same research groups, or because they look at the same data sources, or because they share a simi-lar methodological or disciplinary backgrounds. Some authors have worked with each other, but most have not. They draw on a mul-tiplicity of data sources from contexts across the United States, and they use a wide variety of research methods and represent disciplines from across the social sciences spectrum. The *Teaching in Context* story is consistent because of the degree to which the contributors' findings agree.

Interpersonal Features of School Context/Organization

In Chapter 1, "Developing Workplaces Where Teachers Stay, Improve, and Succeed," John Papay and Matthew Kraft highlight the critical role that teachers' workplace context plays in their career decisions, professional development, and instructional effectiveness through a discussion of a series of recent studies on the interpersonal features of the work environment This chapter challenges several common assumptions about teachers' preferences and how/when they grow professionally. First is the idea that teachers prefer to work in schools serving affluent students and avoid (or leave) schools serving poor and minority students. In Papay and Kraft's studies, teachers' working conditions "were much stronger predictors of teachers' career plans than were the demographic characteristics of students in these schools." Moreover, students in schools rated as most supportive by their teachers experienced larger test score gains than students in schools deemed to be less supportive by their teachers. A second assumption is that teacher ability is more or less fixed (teachers "plateau" after the first few years in the profession) and portable, or independent of teachers' work contexts. Papay and Kraft show that educators working in schools with strong professional environments continue to learn throughout their career and get better at much faster rates than colleagues working in schools characterized by a weaker professional environment.

But what do schools with strong professional contexts actually look like? Chapter 2, "Reaping Rewards for Students," examines a sample of schools that were able to support and develop their teachers and, as a result, experienced success with students. Authors Susan

Moore Johnson, Stephanie Reinhorn, and Nicole Simon synthesize findings from a series of studies that examine data from a comparative case study conducted in a large, urban district in Massachusetts. Researchers conducted in-depth interviews with 172 teachers and administrators from six schools that ranked high in the state's accountability system (despite serving high proportions of disadvantaged students) and operated under different policies and systems (e.g., public, charter, turnaround). Despite their differences, all schools had broad autonomy and "were remarkably similar in how they organized practices that affected teachers." The big takeaway from Chapter 2 is that successful schools must have intentional and interdependent procedures for selecting, supporting, and developing their teachers. As the authors explain, hiring tends to be last minute and rushed in most US schools. By contrast, schools in their study had information-rich hiring mechanisms which ensured that prospective teachers were well matched with their future colleagues and students. Evaluation in these schools was a real vehicle for improvement; teachers were observed often and received frequent, detailed feedback. Finally, teachers did not work in isolation but in well-organized, high-functioning teams. Importantly, school principals with the right skills and dispositions were critical in orchestrating these various personnel practices.

Human and *social capital* are terms that don't always resonate with practitioners or even policy makers; they can seem too abstract, divorced from what goes on in actual schools and even from one another. However, as Chapter 2 aptly illustrates, human and social capital are closely related and ever present in the daily operations of schools. Take hiring. The schools described by Johnson, Reinhorn, and Simon didn't just seek top talent; they sought out the *right* talent for their schools, searching for teachers who would identify with the school's mission and, crucially, work well with the existing faculty. As the authors explain, "Success for teams depended in part on effective hiring and evaluation, which assured teachers that their peers would be strong partners." But also, teams were instrumental for new hires: "No school reported deliberately creating teams to support new teachers' induction, although they served that purpose." In short, these schools recruited human capital that would continue to grow their social capital and, simultaneously, used their existing social capital to cultivate their newly acquired talent.

In Chapter 3, "Better Collaboration, Better Teaching," Matthew Ronfeldt zeroes in on one aspect of teachers' organizational context: collaboration in instructional teams. Ronfeldt provides a succinct but throughout review of the collaboration scholarship and then summarizes the results of two of his recent large-scale studies, explaining how they strengthen the case that teacher collaboration leads to better teaching. His first study, which examines collaboration in instructional teams across the large, urban Miami–Dade County school district, found that collaboration quality matters to teacher effectiveness and that that teachers improve faster in schools with better collaboration quality. Ronfeldt's second study found that teachers who learn to teach in schools with stronger collaboration are more effective once they complete their certification than are fellow teachers who learn to teach in schools with inferior collaborative cultures.

Chapter 3 provides an excellent overview of how the teacher collaboration research has advanced as a field, how scholars have become more certain that collaboration isn't just associated with instructional improvement but that it is responsible for it. As Ronfeldt explains, "It is unusual to find a body of evidence from a group of well-designed studies that all seem to point to the same general conclusion."

Relationships and the Systems Where Teachers Work

Effective teamwork, collaboration, and, more broadly, high-quality collegial interactions characterize schools that have strong social capital. In Chapter 4, "The Social Side of Capability," James P. Spillane, Megan Hopkins, Tracy M. Sweet, and Matthew Shirrell provide a broad overview of the concept of social capital and synthesize what they have learned through a series of recent investigations about the factors that influence the formation of social ties among staff within and across schools.

Chapter 4 leads with two important ideas. First, social relations don't just happen by chance. Nurturing social capital requires intentional, coordinated, and systemic strategies to ensure that high-quality professional interactions take place. Second, we know from decades of sociological research that individuals tend to associate with those who are like them. In this particular context, however, Spillane and colleagues found that social relations among educators are more strongly shaped by aspects of the infrastructure (e.g., roles and job titles, organizational routines, scheduling, spatial arrangements) than by individual characteristics (e.g., race, gender). This is good news, because only these aspects can be adjusted to promote social interactions and organizational learning. The authors contend that "system and school leaders can influence who talks to whom about instruction" by making strategic staff decisions that elevate the influence of more expert teachers. The end goal of such "engineering" is to maximize (at both the school and system levels) exposure to expert teachers, knowledge diffusion, and coordination throughout the school organization and district.

According to Carrie Leana and Frits Pil in Chapter 5, despite extensive evidence that social capital is a core component of school success, it remains "an untapped resource for educational improvement." The authors report on their research on organizational performance across a wide range of contexts (auto plants, nursing homes), including public schools. Time and again they found that interpersonal aspects of the work are critical to the success of any type of organization. They undertook extensive large-scale studies in several urban districts across the United States, including Pittsburgh, Nashville, Providence, and New York City. In one of their studies they collected data from teachers, principals, students, and parents and used them to quantify the quality of communication, the degree of trust present in schools, and the extent to which staff had a shared vision—three core components of social capital. Leana and Pil found that student performance increased dramatically in schools which had high levels of social capital. In a later study, Leana and Pil followed more than 1,000 teachers in 239 grade teams, and linked teacher reports of their professional conversations about math to the growth in math achievement scores of their 24,187 students. When math-centered conversations were more frequent in grade-level teams, student performance improved significantly.

As Chapters 1–5 suggest, leaders are key orchestrators of organizational and system change. But what happens when leaders are in perpetual flux? In Chapter 6, "The Social Cost of Leadership Churn," Alan J. Daly, Kara S. Finnigan, and Yi-Hwa Liou review what little research exists on leadership churn, including their new study of 257 central office and site leaders of a large urban district. While previous studies have primarily focused on leadership departures at the top level, Daly, Finnigan, and Liou focus on leaders at the system *and* school levels, examining their movement in and out of the district for a period of three years. They found that leaders who were most central in the district's expertise network, as well as those who more often acted as brokers, were also more likely to leave the district during the period of the study. Excessive levels of churn can make systems vulnerable, disrupting social relations that are critical for improvement. In short, to ensure change, we need stable relationships.

In Chapter 7, "How the Organization of Schools and Local Communities Shape Educational Improvement," Elaine Allensworth looks beyond the benefits of high-quality relationships among staff within and across schools to the larger community in which schools are situated: "relationships among members of a school community—teachers, leaders, students, and families—whether strong or weak, good or bad, influence the likelihood that students will learn, teaching will improve, and school leaders will reach their goals."

She synthesizes some of the influential research conducted by the Chicago Consortium for School Research, which in the mid-1990s set out to investigate why some Chicago schools improved dramatically after decentralization while others stayed the same or got worse. A team composed of researchers and practitioners developed a list of five elements that seemed crucial for schools to improve. Importantly, the team found that strong relationships are the common thread holding together the five components. This framework was refined by the Consortium through an extensive study that culminated in the book *Organizing Schools for Improvement.* This work firmly establishes that schools strong in these five components are highly likely to improve, while those that are not stagnate or get worse.

Chapter 7 zeroes in on the importance of parent-community ties. In their investigations, Allensworth and her research colleagues found that teacher-parent collaboration was a strong predictor of a safer and more orderly climate, of increased feelings of efficacy among teachers, and of teacher retention. While neighborhoods influenced school climate, much of what accounted for the large differences in safety among schools had everything to do with the ways in which parents, teachers, and students collaborated with one another in those schools.

Moving Ideas into Action

Pulling together the volume's themes, Joshua P. Starr makes the case in Chapter 8, "Organizing Adult Learning for Adaptive Change Management," that *adult,* not student, learning is the biggest challenge facing American public education today. In the United States, professional learning isn't typically viewed as the vehicle for student learning. Thus, schools and school systems are not really organized around this goal and for this purpose. In fact, Starr notes, suggesting a focus on adults is often received with skepticism at best. Nonetheless, he believes that the primary responsibility of leaders seeking to improve student achievement is to organize systems for adults to learn from one another.

Starr reflects on various key pillars sustaining adult learning, including the importance of attending to measures beyond student achievement, such as employee engagement and turnover, which can provide sense of the quality of a school's learning environment and culture; training and supporting school leaders in incorporating these metrics in how they manage and support their staff; and scaling-up collaborative structures by thinking carefully about scheduling, resources, getting stakeholders onboard, and so on. In short, little learning is likely to occur within schools characterized by distrust and isolation; thus, leaders should be responsible (and accountable) for monitoring these aspects and using these metrics for improvement.

Reforms often falter at the implementation stage because they overlook the fact that social dynamics influence the speed, depth and success with which any new idea is implemented.[5] And the conventional approach to connecting research with practice has not made things any better. Traditionally, this relationship has been very one-sided, with the expectation being that educators unquestioningly embrace and put into action the knowledge generated by academics. In Chapter 9, "Research-Practice Partnerships and ESSA," William Penuel and Caitlin Farrell make the case for a more productive way of relating research, policy, and practice—a timely issue given the continued commitment to the use of research in policy reflected by the Every Student Succeeds Act (ESSA). Penuel and Farrell focus on research practice partnerships (RPPs), collaborations between researchers and practitioners where they jointly set the agenda and work together in authentic, long-term partnerships. According to the authors, RPPs are an excellent vehicle for ensuring productive evidence use because they address two common problems associated with the research *into* practice mind-set: the perception among practitioners that most research doesn't really respond to their pressing needs and, related, the fact that many reforms do not consider the local context in which they will be implemented. In short, RPPs create more opportunities for conversations among researchers, practitioners, and other stakeholders, thereby ensuring that research is relevant to its intended beneficiaries and that proper attention is paid to the social and contextual dimensions of evidence use, policy implementation, and change. Finally, Penuel and Farrell offer a timely analysis of the various roles RPPs are positioned to play to help realize ESSA's vision of evidence-based policy making.

While Chapters 8 and 9 focus primarily on the practical side of putting the volume's ideas into action, all the chapters offer evidence-based suggestions for policy and practice. In the Conclusion I offer a synthesis of these recommendations, providing a roadmap of how to move ahead systematically in realizing the level of attention social-relational aspects deserve in the improvement of teaching and learning.

CONCLUDING THOUGHTS

In the United States, debates over teacher preparation, certification, and evaluation demonstrate a relentless focus on improving teaching by augmenting the skills and qualifications of individual teachers. While these proposals seek to influence the teacher workforce as a whole, they fail to focus on the school organization or system— that is, on the work processes characterizing schools, roles people enact, social interactions, organizational norms and beliefs, and, importantly, how all of it comes together. Current policy proposals can be said to focus on "schools not as professional organizations, but as organizations of professional individuals."[6] These are two very different things, just like "consulting a series of specialized physicians separately constitutes a very different experience for that patient than consulting a team of coordinated physicians working together."[7]

Nothing in this volume suggests that teachers' individual human capital isn't important to educational progress, or that if we improve the contexts of teachers' work major structural problems such as poverty and inequality will cease to matter. However, the contributors argue and demonstrate that when schools and school systems prioritize strengthening the interpersonal aspects of teaching and learning, even schools serving low-income students can attract, retain, and develop skillful, stable faculties and achieve good academic results. We cannot ignore this evidence any longer. There seems to be increasing interest in these ideas, but it also tends to be thin, and conversations quickly pivot to "well, *both* context and individual matter." Of course, this is right. But what this statement obscures is that one side has received more attention than the other; it is now time for a balanced approach. Moreover, scholarship in the context matters camp incorporates the human capital perspective (Chapters 2 and 5 are perfect illustrations). The same cannot be said about the human capital perspective, which often disregards the social-organizational dimension.

As Spillane and colleagues explain, "Social capital can help expand our understanding of human capital, in particular the development of human capital in organizations and systems. Moreover, we suspect that scholarship at the intersection of social capital and human capital will generate new insights into capability for instruction and instructional improvement in schools and school systems."

So instead of holding on to the familiar or throwing up our hands claiming that if everything matters, then anything goes in policy, let's rise to this challenge and continue to produce scholarship and policy proposals at this intersection. Let's lift our gaze above frameworks and solutions focused on assessing and augmenting the qualities *of* individuals and embrace an equal focus on attending to and growing the value that can be created *among* them. This will not only benefit educators and the teaching profession but also America's students.

CHAPTER 1

Developing Workplaces Where Teachers Stay, Improve, and Succeed

Recent Evidence on the Importance of School Climate for Teacher Success

JOHN P. PAPAY AND MATTHEW A. KRAFT

One of the strongest lessons from the past decade of education research is a broad, scholarly consensus that teachers have large effects on students' learning and that some teachers are far more effective than others.[1] This research has been interpreted to mean that improving the American educational system at scale requires a policy focus on attracting and retaining "high-quality" individuals to teach the nation's students. We argue that this singular policy direction is a misinterpretation of the literature and that policy makers—and students—would be better served by a recognition of how teachers are supported or constrained by the organizational contexts (or professional environments) in which they teach.

Clearly, individual teachers play a primary role in shaping the educational experiences of students in schools. However, researchers and policy makers tend to ascribe teachers' career decisions to the students they teach rather than the conditions in which they work. They often treat teachers as if their effectiveness is mostly fixed, portable, and independent of the school context. An emerging body of research documents the limitations of these perspectives, show-ing that the contexts in which teachers work profoundly shape their job decisions and effectiveness.[2] Teachers who work in support-ive contexts stay in the classroom longer, improve at greater rates, and experience more success in the classroom than their peers in less-supportive environments.

In this chapter, we review the growing evidence about the im-portance of the professional environment in schools and describe recent quantitative studies that document how context influences teachers' career decisions, their effectiveness in the classroom, and their development. Throughout, we also provide examples from a recent large-scale qualitative study on which we collaborated with Susan Moore Johnson and colleagues as part of The Project on the Next Generation of Teachers at Harvard University. This study in-volved in-depth case studies documenting teachers' experiences working in six high-poverty schools in a large urban school district. These schools were quite varied in their approach to and success with engaging the high-poverty students they taught.[3] Throughout this chapter, we draw on interviews with a diverse set of ninety-five teachers and administrators whose stories validate and instantiate the emerging quantitative findings. We end by highlighting some prom-ising interventions for improving elements of the school context and conclude with a discussion of the implications of this emerging body of research for policy and practice.

DEFINING SCHOOL CONTEXT

Schools are complex organizations. A long history of detailed qual-itative research has documented the constellation of organizational features that shape teachers' and students' daily experiences.[4] We use *context* or *climate* to refer broadly to the environment in which the teacher works. These words have many meanings in the field of education. While we recognize that school climate can have direct influences on students—for example, students are better able to learn if they are in a safe environment—for our discussion we focus on how features of the organizational climate influence the adults in the building, thereby affecting students through their influence on teachers.

While the contexts in which teachers work are influenced in part by district and even state policies (such as standards and accountability), teachers' day-to-day experiences are shaped more directly at the school level as well as in micro contexts that arise within schools (such as grade-level or subject-area teams). Thus, as we define it, context refers broadly to teachers' professional environment, including policy (such as class sizes and salaries), traditional working conditions (such as facilities and textbooks), and more interpersonal features of the work environment (such as relationships with colleagues, collaboration with teams, and principal leadership).

Importantly, context is not a fixed feature of a school, nor is it unilaterally imposed by building-level administrators. Instead, teachers both work in the context and co-construct it with school leaders through their collective actions. Principals and other leaders help shape this climate through the policies they adopt and in the way they marshal collective action to promote (or not) a supportive school environment. In this way, the adults in the building have agency over the contexts in which they work. However, the nature of this process—whereby multiple actors with potentially differing priorities co-construct the school context—can make efforts to change the context difficult to achieve and sustain.

Scholarly understanding of the importance of school context has grown in recent years as large-scale teacher surveys have provided researchers with new data to quantify these organizational features. The availability of Race to the Top funds and an emphasis on measuring school culture led many states and school districts to adopt or develop their own surveys to measure working conditions in schools. For example, these surveys include the New Teacher Center's Teaching, Empowering, Learning and Leading (TELL) survey, TNTP's Insight Survey, the University of Chicago Consortium on School Research's (CCSR) 5 Essential Supports Survey, and a range of state and local district surveys designed to measure school working conditions (such as New York City's School Survey and Tennessee's Teacher Educator Survey or Boston Public Schools' School Climate Survey). While such surveys have been valuable for policy, they have also provided a treasure trove of information for researchers seeking to understand the effect of school context on teachers.

SCHOOL CONTEXT AND TEACHER TURNOVER

School climate survey data have shed new light on important questions about teachers' career decisions and their effectiveness. For example, in the 1980s and 1990s researchers consistently found that teacher turnover was higher in schools that served larger populations of low-income and minority students.[5] This finding, which has been interpreted frequently as illustrating that teachers' prefer to teach higher performing, whiter, and wealthier students, has led to policy prescriptions such as paying teachers "combat pay" to work in hard-to-staff schools.

However, more recent analysis, replicated in a wide range of districts, reveals that the high rates of teacher turnover observed in such schools are largely explained by the poor working conditions in these schools rather than the students they serve. Understanding the determinants of teacher turnover, and why turnover rates differ across schools and school districts, is important for policy makers. Large urban school districts experience relatively high rates of teacher turnover, and turnover is costly both for schools and students.[6] In addition to the substantial financial costs of replacing large numbers of teachers, turnover has long-term, negative consequences for teachers and students, especially those who live in low-income communities.[7]

In a recent study in Massachusetts, we documented the relationship between teacher working conditions and turnover using a statewide teacher survey.[8] As expected, we found that teachers reported less supportive working conditions in schools that served high proportions of low-income and minority students. This echoes detailed ethnographic research and interview studies documenting the challenging environments in which urban teachers often teach.[9] We also found much higher levels of reported teacher turnover in these schools.

However, we found that the working conditions in the schools were much stronger predictors of teachers' career plans than were the demographic characteristics of students in these schools. In fact, accounting for differences in the quality of teachers' working environments greatly diminishes the relationship between student demographics and teacher turnover. By contrast, the relationships between working conditions and turnover were essentially unchanged after controlling for student characteristics, suggesting that unsupportive conditions lead to turnover in a wide range of school settings. We document this pattern in figure 1.1, which demonstrates how in Massachusetts teachers are over three times more likely to report intentions to transfer away from a school with poor working conditions (bottom percentiles, on the left) than from one with strong working conditions (top percentiles, on the right) even after controlling for a range of student, teacher, and school characteristics. This finding has been replicated in a wide range of districts and states, including California, North Carolina, New York City, and Chicago.[10]

Schools with unsupportive working environments struggle to retain teachers, which leads to what Richard Ingersoll terms the "revolving door." Turnover then contributes to organizational instability and potentially reinforces a cycle of poor working conditions

FIGURE 1.1 The probability that Massachusetts teachers intend to transfer from their school by percentile of working conditions with predicted relationship overlaid.

and teacher turnover in these schools.[11] Furthermore, what appear to matter most to teachers about the contexts in which they work are not the traditional working conditions policy makers often think of, such as modern facilities and well equipped classrooms. Instead, aspects that are difficult to observe and measure, such as the quality of relationships and collaboration among staff, the responsiveness of school administrators, and the academic and behavioral expectations for students, appear to be most influential.[12] Several studies have documented how the quality of leadership in a school and the degree to which teachers feel supported by administrators are central to teachers' career decisions.[13] Quantitative studies, however, are limited in the degree to which they can isolate the relative importance of specific school context features given the measurement challenges associated with self-reported survey data and the interrelated nature of these features. Qualitative studies help illustrate the specific ways in which these features shape teachers' experiences and career decisions.

Our study revealed numerous examples of teachers, explicitly or implicitly, tying their career decisions to the professional environment in the school. For example, at a large, comprehensive high school, several teachers we interviewed said they were planning to transfer to another district school, one that served a relatively similar population of students, because of their current school's lack of a systematic response to student behavior. As one teacher explained, "Most of the teachers deal with things independently," causing them to spend "so much time handling discipline issues." Another agreed, saying, "I'm ready to teach. I'm ready to not worry about discipline." One spoke for herself and two colleagues, all of whom were discussing plans to transfer: "I know personally that the three of us don't feel supported by the [principal]. I feel like we're not making a difference because the behavior is so bad [that] the teaching is not happening." These teachers were not seeking to leave the students; on the contrary, they expressed that they were attached to their current school largely because of the students. Rather, they were planning to leave because of a lack of institutional support for their work.

SCHOOL CONTEXT AND TEACHER EFFECTIVENESS

The same unsupportive working environments that may motivate teachers to leave a school also constrain their ability to be effective with students. Although often treated as a fully portable characteristic of an individual teacher, teacher effectiveness is supported or constrained by the environment in which teachers work. For example, the teachers described above clearly noted that they felt less effective in the classroom than they would have had the school developed a more orderly environment for learning. One can view the impacts of many educational interventions (such as curricula, school structure, or student behavior policies) as operating, at least in part, through improved teacher effectiveness given that these efforts develop the conditions for success in the classroom.

Survey data provide additional opportunities to examine the relationship between context and teacher (or school) effectiveness. Using rich survey data on school climates from CCSR's 5 Essential School Survey, Bryk and colleagues show that Chicago schools with stronger and more supportive work contexts experienced substantial improvements in student achievement.[14] Our work confirms this result. We examined the relationship between school context and student achievement in Massachusetts and found that schools with more supportive environments experienced larger gains in student test scores than schools with poor working conditions.[15] These patterns held even when we accounted for differences in many observable students and teacher characteristics and compared schools to only those within the same district. Ladd showed quite similar results in her study of working conditions in North Carolina.[16]

More recently, Kraft, Marinell, and Yee examined public middle schools in New York City over the course of five years and found that schools which experienced improvements in organizational culture—particularly in school safety and academic expectations—experienced corresponding improvements in student achievement.[17] The authors' analyses of changes in organizational contexts over time eliminate many of the primary threats to validity faced by previous cross-sectional analyses. In other words, it is not simply that higher performing schools report better organizational contexts; instead, when the reported context improves, student performance does too. Together these studies suggest that when schools strengthen the organizational contexts in which teachers work, teachers are more likely to remain in these schools and students appear to learn at greater rates.

One specific example comes in efforts to increase student attendance. Students learn more when they attend school more consistently. If schools can promote student attendance, they can improve the effectiveness of teachers in supporting their students' learning. When we interviewed teachers at a district-sponsored charter high school that enrolled predominantly low-income minority students, we heard about the value of the school's robust approach to student support. The school's staff included two full-time counselors and a dean of discipline dedicated to ensuring that students had access to appropriate social-emotional supports. These efforts helped create a safe environment where students wanted to be and felt supported in their learning.

For one teacher we interviewed, this environment stood in stark contrast to the school where she had taught previously, a school that served a very similar student population. She explained:

> While I was teaching at [my old school], it was very challenging because I was working with a lot of kids that were court-involved, and one day I would have thirty-two students in my classroom and the next day that number [was] down to twenty. And as I tried to get to know the kids better, I'd find that a lot of them are in and out of jail, or in and out of DUIs, or there were many issues that were interfering with their learning. And some of them lost interest in learning anything that I had to present because, well, the next day they had to appear in front of a judge and chances are they were going to be away for a while.

She noted that at her current school "we have the same group of kids," but with "the support that is in place . . . we give the kids a certain environment that they want to come back to, even though they may have a court date coming up . . . It's a positive environment for them to be, so they keep coming."

It is reasonable to infer that had this teacher continued to teach at her previous school, she would have been less effective in the classroom—not because she had changed or the students were different, but because the context provided an environment that supported effective classroom instruction. This is just one of many ways context can play a direct role in promoting student achievement and teacher effectiveness.

SCHOOL CONTEXT AND TEACHER DEVELOPMENT

In supportive schools, teachers not only tend to stay and be more effective in their classrooms, but they also improve at much greater rates over time. In a recent study, we tracked teachers in Charlotte-Mecklenburg Schools for up to ten years and examined how their individual effectiveness (as measured by contributions to student achievement) changed over time.[18] As shown in figure 1.2, we found that, over ten years, teachers working in schools with strong professional environments improved 38 percent more than teachers in schools with weak professional environments. Here we used six measures drawn from teacher surveys to characterize the environment: consistent order and discipline, opportunities for peer collaboration, supportive principal leadership, effective professional development, a school culture characterized by trust, and a fair teacher evaluation process providing meaningful feedback. More recently, Ronfeldt and colleagues used a similar research design to show that teachers in Miami-Dade County Public Schools improved at substantially faster rates in schools where effective collaboration took place through instructional teams.[19]

FIGURE 1.2 Predicted returns to teaching experience across schools with strong, average, and weak professional environments.

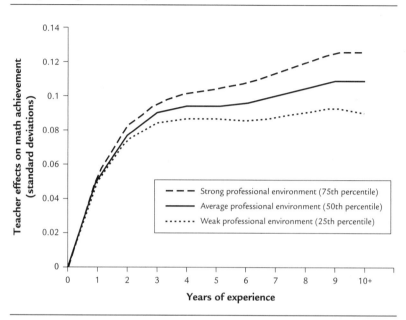

In the schools we studied, teachers reported that instructional teams supported their professional growth when teams were well structured and aligned with their own priorities.[20] Teachers met regularly in instruction-focused teams in all of the schools we studied. However, the degree to which organizational efforts to promote professional growth through teams depended on how well this time was used. For example, in one elementary school teachers met in grade-level teams designed to explore and support new instructional approaches. Teachers in these teams regularly tried out new approaches and used video and peer observations to provide feedback and refine practice. As one teacher noted, "We all kind of give each other feedback . . . we'll talk about what strategies we used, what we could do to improve it." This ongoing and targeted feedback led teachers to report that their instruction improved and they became more effective teachers.

SOME PROMISING INTERVENTIONS TO IMPROVE THE SCHOOL CONTEXT

These findings, and a growing body of evidence, make clear that the school context matters a great deal for teachers and, as a result, their students. Furthermore, school contexts are not set in stone; working conditions in schools can improve over time, and teachers are responsive to these changes.[21] However, simply saying that contexts matter and can change does not give policy makers and practitioners clear guidance about how to strengthen organizational practices in schools. Although the collective and interpersonal nature of school contexts makes quick policy fixes unlikely to succeed, research suggests several concrete ways in which educators and policy makers can take on this challenge.

We discuss four evidence-based practices that hold promise for improving school contexts and thereby boosting teacher effectiveness: leveraging colleagues to promote instructional improvement; developing effective behavioral supports; setting high expectations for learners; and engaging parents actively in students' education. The evidence suggests that if implemented well, all of these practices can promote teacher development and success. Importantly, the effectiveness of these supports rests on the school leader. There may also be synergistic effects of adopting policies that attempt to address these approaches together given that these efforts are all interrelated.

Leveraging Colleagues to Promote Instructional Improvement

One feature of the professional environment in schools that consistently seems to matter is the nature of collaborative relationships among colleagues.[22] There are many types of models of teacher collaboration (teacher teams, professional learning communities, peer observation models, etc.) that have demonstrated benefits for teachers' instructional practice when implemented well. We describe two examples that hold promise to improve classroom instruction: well-designed teacher teams that collaborate to coordinate instruction across students and solve common problems and efforts to have peer teachers provide instructional feedback to each other and learn from each other's practice.

In our case studies of high-poverty urban schools, nearly all of the teachers we interviewed talked about their regular participation in teacher teams.[23] This reflects a national trend toward increased collaboration and teamwork in schools, an effort to break down the "egg crate" model of teachers operating autonomously within their own classrooms.[24] However, while ubiquitous in the district we studied, teams functioned very differently across the schools we examined, with important implications for their influence on teacher effectiveness. At three of the schools, teacher teams were central to coordinating instruction across students and classrooms and served as critical professional learning opportunities for participants. At three others, teams were simply administrative hurdles that took time away from other, more productive, instructional activities—a model Hargreaves calls "contrived collegiality" because it has no real benefit for teachers or students.[25]

We found that for teams to be an effective approach to promote individual and organizational learning, teachers needed both guidance and support in creating effective team structures and flexibility in tackling the problems of practice the team was focused on. Here, principals were central to the success of these teams; they "were active in setting worthy purposes, encouraging learning through collaboration, and ensuring that teachers could safely express opposing views or explore new approaches."[26] Within such structures, teachers found their collaborative work meaningful and productive.

A second example of the role of collaboration in promoting instructional improvement comes from the Instructional Partnership Initiative (IPI) in Tennessee, an intervention designed to develop data-driven instructional partnerships that leverage professional expertise within the schools. This program uses indicator-level teacher evaluation data to pair teachers who have low scores in certain areas of instructional practice with peer teachers in the same school who have demonstrated a history of success in those same areas. For example, a teacher who struggles in managing student behavior and instructional planning might be paired with a colleague who excels in those areas. The teachers are encouraged to work together throughout the year to refine these practices. The effort is explicitly framed as a collaborative partnership (not coaching or mentoring). Partnered teachers are encouraged to examine each other's evaluation results, observe each other teaching in the classroom, discuss improvement strategies, and follow up with each other's commitments throughout the school year.

This intervention has proven quite effective at increasing teacher effectiveness, as measured by their students' test scores. In 2013–14, a small randomized experiment compared the outcomes of treatment schools that received the IPI to control schools that did not.[27] At the end of the school year, the average student in an IPI treatment school scored 0.06 standard deviations higher on math and reading/language arts tests than she would have in a control school, regardless of whether her teacher participated in a partnership. The gains are larger among the lower performing teachers; for these teachers, the IPI improved students' scores by 0.12 standard deviations. This is a large effect, roughly equivalent to the difference between being assigned to a median teacher instead of a bottom-quartile teacher.

Both of these examples document how one key feature of the organizational context—the nature of collaboration among colleagues—can promote teacher effectiveness and teacher improvement. When colleagues work together and learn from each other in well-structured collaborative activities, they can coordinate across students and classrooms, improve their instructional skills, and serve students more effectively.

Developing Effective Behavioral Supports

Teachers' work environments are shaped not only by the adults in the building and the facilities, but also by the needs that their students bring with them when they walk through the school doors.[28] As part of our study of high-poverty urban schools, we found that schools had quite different reactions to the uncertainty that minority youth from low-income families brought with them into school. When schools worked to provide teachers with support and guidance for engaging with these students' needs, teachers were better able to enjoy success in their classrooms.

Across the schools we studied, teachers spoke about how specific supports facilitated their ability to succeed with their students. Teachers in several schools described the value of creating strong environments for learning by providing support services to attend to students' social and emotional needs. They acknowledged that students brought many needs to the classroom, only some of which they were equipped to handle. Thus, teachers valued and thought their students benefited from these outside-of-class supports.

In the schools we studied, two quite different examples stand out. In one school, the principal had established a formal Student Support Team comprised of teachers and administrators who met weekly to discuss student issues. For each case, the team developed a set of recommendations that it asked teachers and, in some cases, parents to follow. In another school, administrative positions filled a very similar role. Rather than relying on a more collaborative team to handle these responsibilities, the school had a three-member Student Support Department, headed by a dean of discipline. These counselors worked not only on discipline issues but on broader social-emotional supports for students who were struggling. Despite the differences in how these student supports were delivered, teachers at both schools regularly described the services as critical resources for facilitating effective instruction.

Setting High Expectations for Learners

Evidence of the importance of teacher expectations for student achievement dates back to Rosenthal and Jacobson's study of the Pygmalion effect.[29] Many experimental studies have since replicated their seminal finding that teachers' beliefs about their students' abilities affect student learning.[30] More recently, studies examining variation in charter school effects have found that a culture of high expectations is likely a key ingredient in the success of high performing charter schools.[31] Studies also suggest that schools can work to collectively raise expectations for students. As Kraft, Marinell, and Yee show, schools where teachers raise their academic expectations for students experience corresponding increases in student achievement.[32]

However, simply articulating high expectations for students or decorating the hallways with college banners is unlikely to result in meaningful changes if these efforts are inauthentic, uncoordinated, or uncoupled from intensive student supports. Teachers need to not only hold high standards for student learning but to believe that all students can achieve those standards with appropriate support. High expectations matter, particularly when they come from someone students feel knows them and cares about them. In this way, developing strong relationships with students helps make a teacher's high expectations more credible. At the same time, these expectations must be upheld by all teachers rather than just a few. A student who is uplifted by a teacher's belief in her ability to do excellent work might easily lose self-confidence if she perceives that the teacher of her next class holds her to a lower standard than her classmates. Thus, students benefit most when there is a school-wide culture of high expectations.

A key complement to creating this culture of high expectations involves providing the necessary supports, both academic and social-emotional, to enable students to meet these rigorous standards. Many of the teachers we spoke with in low-income urban public schools felt they were able to hold students to high expectations because they could also count on the organizational supports at their school to provide students with the type of services and coordinated support they could not provide on their own. These services were both academic (additional instructional time or resources for specific students) and socio-emotional (services designed to attend to students' needs beyond core academic instruction). As one elementary school teacher explained, teachers and the school could not ignore students' personal experiences outside the school, which in some instances included living in abusive homes, foster homes, or homeless shelters: "They say you shouldn't take that into consideration, [that] we need to have high expectations, and yes we do. But still that needs to be addressed." Teachers' high expectations for students at the school were authentic because they were able to help students work toward meeting these standards with the assistance of student support teams and counseling services. Teachers were not required simply to go it alone.

Engaging Parents Actively in Students' Education

The important role that parents play in shaping students' experiences in school and supporting their success cannot be overstated. Parents affect the school context indirectly through their influence on students as well as directly via their interactions with teachers and engagement with the school. The teachers at the schools we studied consistently described how traditional attempts to engage parents only through open houses, back-to-school nights, and online grade books were often insufficient. In one teacher's words, these "push rather than pull" efforts did little to draw parents into the school or convey that they have invaluable insights into their child's experience that would help teachers be more effective. Instead, schools can facilitate stronger parental engagement and support through two primary avenues: by making active outreach to parents a schoolwide priority and dedicating resources to these efforts and by establishing clear expectations and effective support for teacher-parent communication.

Evidence suggests that schoolwide efforts to engage parents as active partners in students' education can benefit both teachers and students.[33] For example, Grand Rapids (Michigan) Public Schools have reduced chronic absenteeism by half through coordinated efforts to increase communication with parents when absences occur, to educate parents about the consequences of chronic absenteeism for student learning, and to enlist parents and community organizations in support of the district's attendance goals.[34] In several of the schools we studied, teachers described a range of nontraditional efforts their schools initiated to connect with parents. One school had a dedicated family outreach coordinator who offered Parent Nights, with classes designed to familiarize parents with the curriculum and make them more confident in their ability to support their children's academic and social-emotional learning needs. Administrators at another school worked to accommodate parents' demanding schedules by holding open houses and parent meetings at off-site locations, given that many students' neighborhoods were far from the school. Teachers saw these efforts as important supports that helped engage parents more actively in their child's learning and open lines of communication between parents and teachers.

School leadership teams also have a key role to play in establishing schoolwide norms and supports for teachers' efforts to connect with parents. Teachers face a range of barriers when attempting to communicate with parents, including the frequently out-of-date parent contact information, language barriers, and the lack of non-instructional time to make contact during the school day. Without formal expectations combined with sufficient time and the necessary communication infrastructure, teachers' may take a passive approach to communication as they shift their attention to other tasks. Efforts to establish communication norms and reduce barriers to communication can increase parent-teacher communication substantially and raise students' performance in school. Several randomized trials document how frequent communication with parents, often facilitated by automated or very brief personalized text messages, enhanced student engagement in school, improved attendance, and raised achievement.[35] When schools and teachers work to engage parents, they are also promoting a schooling environment where parents support both teachers and students to succeed.

CONCLUSION

Analyses of large-scale teacher surveys confirm what educators and qualitative researchers have long known: school contexts matter. We hope the new evidence summarized here will push public debate and policy about education reform to recognize and be responsive to this reality of working in schools. Of course, saying that context matters does not mean that the skills and aptitudes of individual teachers do not. Clearly, US schools need to work hard to recruit the most skilled and able candidates possible. However, our reading of the research suggests that policy makers cannot continue to focus so narrowly on the individual. Instead, effective teacher policy will require attending to the organizational context of the schools in which teachers work and the interpersonal relationships that form the basis for this context.

We have identified several key supports that show promise in sustaining supportive work environments. Importantly, these features do not exist in isolation; there are likely important complementarities and synergies that exist when schools attend to several of these dimensions at once. Furthermore, school principals play a key role in establishing productive professional environments in schools.[36] They are the ones who establish these organizational supports and build schoolwide cultures. Hiring principals who have the ability to identify organizational weaknesses, establish schoolwide systems to support teachers and students, and galvanize the collective buy-in and involvement of all teachers is a central lever for improving the teaching and learning environment.

The proliferation of school climate surveys in recent years has not only facilitated this research documenting the importance of school context but also afforded new opportunities to inform school improvement efforts. These surveys provide rich data on schools' organizational strengths and areas for improvement. For example, school context reports could provide building principals with important feedback on their organizational leadership, and such reports could help school and district leaders identify and target efforts toward strengthening specific organizational weaknesses in their schools. In short, these data are rich, and the opportunities to use them are great. Of course, as with any measure, incorporating school context surveys into accountability systems may undermine their value and lead to biased results if teachers, students, and parents feel pressure to rate their school favorably.

We conclude where we began, arguing that policy makers should focus as much attention on developing supportive work environments as they give to staffing their schools with effective teachers. There are two central reasons why we believe this focus on the organizational climate in which a teacher works is important. First, the school context influences how effective a teacher is with her students, her career decisions, and her development throughout her career. Teachers are more effective, more likely to stay, and improve at greater rates in supportive working environments. But, more broadly, this organizational perspective will bear fruit because education itself is necessarily an interpersonal and organizational endeavor. Students move across classrooms and teachers as they move from subject to subject and grade to grade throughout their schooling. Attending to the school context, rather than simply the classroom, will help policy makers frame the challenge of ensuring student success more accurately, focusing attention on improving students' learning trajectories across their schooling experiences and not simply their learning in an isolated classroom. The types of coordination and continuity supported by strong work environments will help promote sustained student learning throughout their schooling.

CHAPTER 2

Reaping Rewards for Students

How Successful Urban Schools Systematically Invest in Teachers

SUSAN MOORE JOHNSON, STEFANIE K.
REINHORN, AND NICOLE S. SIMON

Since 2000, policy makers have adopted strategies for improving the quality of teachers while largely ignoring the school context in which those teachers work. Scholars have documented not only the importance of the individual teacher in students' learning but also the crucial role that the school context plays in teachers' and students' success.[1] Overlooking the teachers' workplace has had serious consequences for students from high-minority, high-poverty urban communities, who all too often are shortchanged by dysfunctional schools that fail to attract, support, and retain effective teachers.[2] A thorough review of recent research finds that it is those schools, not their students, that teachers flee.[3]

In assessing their schools, teachers are most concerned about their principal's leadership, their relationships with colleagues, and their school's culture.[4] Our earlier analysis of a Massachusetts survey of working conditions showed that teachers in schools that received high marks on these factors were more satisfied and planned to stay longer than those in schools receiving low marks. Notably, among schools that served demographically similar students, those rated more favorably by teachers also demonstrated higher rates of learning for students. Therefore, positive work environments are associated with greater satisfaction and higher retention for teachers and better learning for students.

Strong evidence from this study and others (many reviewed by Kraft and Papay in Chapter 1) highlights the promise of improving students' learning by investing in the school as a workplace for teachers. (We use the term *workplace* to refer to a wide range of factors that create the context for teachers' work, including organizational features, such as teachers' roles and opportunities for leadership, and social factors, such as teachers' relationships with colleagues and parents.[5]) However, it is not always obvious what to do with what we know. For example, we know that teachers respond favorably when their principal is a good manager and effective leader; when colleagues are skilled, committed, and collaborative; and when the school's culture is respectful, orderly, and focused on teaching and learning.[6] However, it is less clear how administrators and teachers can establish those conditions, particularly in high-poverty settings or in a school that experiences repeated failure. Many informative studies focus on particular human capital practices, such as pay, teacher induction, or professional development, yet few consider the school as a whole, an approach that could explain how the practices that matter to teachers combine and interact.[7]

We designed this study to address this need for more detailed school-based analyses of teachers' experiences and the factors that support them in their work. It grows out of extensive research conducted over the past eighteen years at The Project on the Next Generation of Teachers at Harvard University. Recently, we have sought to understand teachers' experiences in the most challenging school contexts—those serving low-income, high-minority urban communities.[8] In 2011–12 we studied a sample of six schools that had different levels of student achievement and identified some promising practices in the more successful schools. For the current study we focused only on successful urban schools, hoping to learn more about what works in schools that serve students well. Although these schools differed notably in what and how they taught students, they were remarkably similar in how they organized the workplace for teachers. Across the schools, we found the following human capital systems to be prominent, interdependent, and mutually reinforcing:

- A two-way, information-rich hiring process provided prospective teachers with a good preview of what it would be like to work in the school, while enabling administrators and current teachers to judge whether an applicant was a good match for their school.[9]
- An evaluation system focused on teachers' continuous development by providing frequent classroom observations with rapid feedback and summative assessments that grew out of that formative process.
- Collaborative teams of teachers met regularly to support individuals' instruction and contribute to the school's overall improvement.

When these systems for hiring, evaluation, and teams worked in concert, they led to a more coherent school with increased capacity to effectively educate all its students. As James Coleman explained in 1988, the organization benefits when the human capital of individuals is transformed by social capital.[10] In this case, that social capital was enacted by administrators and teachers together as they hired staff, participated in supervision and evaluation, and conducted collaborative team meetings.

ONE CITY, DIFFERENT POLICIES

Despite being located within the same large city, the six schools were subject to different policies, which created varied opportunities and constraints on their efforts to improve. We found that several federal, state, and local policies enabled some schools to create and maintain stronger, more responsive systems than others.

Our sample includes six elementary and middle schools, all located in Walker City, Massachusetts.[11] These schools served high-poverty students (70 percent or more eligible for free or reduced-price lunch), most being students of color (table 2.1). The state had previously intervened in three of these schools because of poor performance, but when we conducted this study in 2014, all had achieved the highest rating in the state's accountability system and were widely viewed as high performing.

Despite their proximity, each of the schools functioned in a distinct policy context:

- *One traditional district school*: Dickinson Elementary was a neighborhood school within the Walker City School District (WCSD). Dickinson had no extra resources or special autonomies and was subject to all relevant federal, state, and local policies, including the teachers' contract.

- *Two turnaround schools*: State officials had taken over Fitzgerald Elementary and Hurston PreK–8 several years earlier for persistently poor performance. At the time, Hurston was functioning as a WCSD pilot school, which meant that it had broad autonomy over staffing, curriculum, budget, and schedule. Nonetheless, the school was failing. Consistent with Race to the Top regulations, the district appointed new principals at both schools who then could rehire up to 50 percent of the current teachers, although they retained only 40 percent and 20 percent, respectively. Additional teachers recruited from other WCSD schools or hired from elsewhere completed the staff. Therefore, most teachers in these two schools had joined their school recently. (Dickinson, by contrast, had never experienced

TABLE 2.1 Selected characteristics of six sample schools

School name	School type	Grades	Estimated enrollment	% Low-income students	% African American or black students	% Hispanic or Latino students	% Other nonwhite students	% White students
Dickinson Elementary	Traditional district	PreK–5	370	76	4	85	2	9
Fitzgerald Elementary	District—Former turnaround	PreK–5	390	85	70	25	3	2
Hurston PreK–8	District—Former turnaround	PreK–8	800	75	41	54	4	1
Kincaid Charter Middle	Charter—Restart of district school	6–8	475	88	50	30	10	10
Naylor Charter K–8	Charter	K–8	500	82	70	24	5	1
Rodriguez Charter PreK–8	Charter	PreK–8	420	72	55	20	7	18

Note: Percentages are approximated for confidentiality purposes.

such zero-based hiring.) As turnaround schools, Fitzgerald and Hurston received additional resources from federal School Improvement Grants (SIGs), which they used to expand their teachers' workday, students' learning time, professional development, and administrative supports. Both the autonomies associated with being a turnaround school and SIG funding ended when the schools successfully exited turnaround. In order to continue exercising some of the autonomy they had during turnaround, Hurston reverted to being a pilot school in WCSD and Fitzgerald became a state Innovation School.

- *Two state charter schools:* Naylor Charter K–8 and Rodriguez Charter PreK–8 were established ten and twenty years earlier, respectively, under the state's charter school law. Each was responsible to its own board. Neither was subject to state or local policies restricting hiring or transfer, but both did have to administer the state's annual tests and meet both state accountability standards and requirements for teacher evaluation.

- *One restart school:* Kincaid Charter Middle, functioned as an in-district charter school run by the Kincaid Charter Management Organization (CMO), appointed by the state to restart the school in 2011. The CMO appointed all new administrators and an entirely new teaching staff, although it continued to serve the same students. Because Kincaid was a restart school, its principal had broad autonomy in scheduling, curriculum, and staffing, much as other charter schools had. The salary scale of the WCSD teachers' contract remained in effect, but other work rules did not apply.

Across the six schools, we interviewed 142 teachers and administrators about a wide range of practices affecting teachers and their work (see table 2.2). In each school we interviewed a sample of teachers with a range of experience, including novices (1–3 years),

TABLE 2.2 Number of interviewees at each school

School name	Administrators	Nonteaching staff	Teachers in training	Teachers	% of total teachers in the school interviewed
Dickinson Elementary	1	2	n/a	15	56
Fitzgerald Elementary	2	2	n/a	14	47
Hurston PreK–8	4	5	n/a	21	31
Kincaid Charter Middle	5	5	2	15	38
Naylor Charter K–8	2	3	3	16	46
Rodriguez Charter PreK–8	3	3	3	16	36

Notes: Administrators include directors of CMOs and school-based administrators who directly supervise teachers. Nonteaching staff includes instructional coaches, parent coordinators, data leaders, recruitment officers, deans of discipline, and other administrators who do not teach students and do not supervise teachers.

TABLE 2.3 Total teachers interviewed at each school and years of experience

School	Novice* (1–3 years)	2nd stage (4–10 years)	Veteran (11+ years)
Dickinson Elementary	3	5	7
Fitzgerald Elementary	1	11	2
Hurston PreK–8	6	11	4
Kincaid Charter Middle	4	11	0
Naylor Charter K–8	7	7	2
Rodriguez Charter PreK–8	1	9	6
Totals	**22**	**54**	**21**

Note: Does not include teachers in training.

second-stage teachers (4–10 years), and veterans (11+ years) (see table 2.3). We also collected and reviewed relevant documents, such as memoranda, contracts, and evaluation documents. During our school visits, we informally observed in offices, classrooms, hallways, and cafeterias throughout the school. We recorded and transcribed all the interviews and coded them for analysis (see the appendix).

THREE KEY HUMAN CAPITAL SYSTEMS

In analyzing teachers' and administrators' responses within and across schools, three systems for improving human capital of the teaching staff stood out—hiring, evaluation, and collaborative teams. Combined, these systems ensured that teachers were well matched with the school, received the ongoing support they needed, and contributed to greater coherence throughout the school, all to the benefit of students.

Hiring

Traditional hiring in many schools is typically "late, rushed, and information-poor."[12] Due to many internal and external factors (bureaucratic procedures, delayed budget approval, prolonged transfer processes), urban schools enrolling high-poverty students often fail to recruit and hire teachers in a timely way.[13] As a result, they frequently lose their most promising candidates to suburban schools. Because hiring often happens during the summer, many new teachers assume their position knowing little about their school and its expectations, while their principal and colleagues know virtually nothing about their accomplishments, potential, and needs.

Historically, large, urban districts relied on centralized hiring to achieve efficiency and ensure fairness for both schools and teachers. After recruiting and selecting teachers, central administrators then assigned them to vacancies in the schools. Over the past two decades, it has become clear that school communities differ and that teachers have unique interests and expertise, which fit better in some schools and programs than others. Schools today have much more autonomy to hire and transfer teachers, and teachers have more say in where they teach. Nationally, over 90 percent of principals report that they now have extensive autonomy in hiring, although many teachers still view the hiring process as inadequate.[14]

Every school we studied had a remarkably robust process for selecting teachers. Each used a set of carefully sequenced steps, such as reviewing resumes and cover letters, conducting a preinterview screening by phone, interviewing the candidate, observing the candidate teach, and interacting with the candidate during a school visit. Administrators and teachers explained how this provided both their school and the prospective teacher the information they needed to make a well-informed decision. The process of achieving a good match between the candidate and the school was widely viewed as the bedrock of these schools' strategies for improvement. Principals recognized that their school was not the right place for every teacher. In describing her school's applicant pool, a Rodriguez administrator said, "Some are a good fit for Rodriguez. Others are great teachers, but we are not perfect for them and they are not perfect for us."

Although the particulars varied, these schools considered similar elements of fit. First teachers had to embrace their school's mission. Fitzgerald's principal said that the school's primary decision rule in hiring was whether candidates shared the school's "belief system." That is, did they think that "children who are African American or Latino and poor could learn?" She was explicit with applicants: "We're on a mission, and if you don't see yourself as fitting in here, we welcome you to go somewhere else."

Second, the schools sought teachers who would reinforce and advance their priorities in curriculum and instruction. At Fitzgerald and Rodriguez, teachers were expected to develop complex, project-based learning experiences for students. At Hurston and Dickinson, the arts were a priority, because, as Dickinson's principal explained, a strong arts program is key to providing students with an education on par with their suburban peers' experience. Prospective teachers at Naylor and Kincaid were expected to provide teacher-centered, data-driven instruction.

Third, schools sought candidates who endorsed their professional norms, teachers who exhibited what many called a "growth mind-set"—an unwavering commitment to improving their craft.[15] An administrator at Hurston said teachers had to "be willing to constantly reassess, reinvent and really be creative," a view expressed often by other teachers and administrators. Further, all schools expected teachers to collaborate with peers regularly about how they were educating their students and what they might do better.

Finally, the schools—which ranged from traditional to progressive, with an organizational culture and rules to match—expected teachers to uphold and reinforce their requirements and norms. Teachers seeking a position at Kincaid had to be comfortable enforcing a strict dress code, and those applying to Hurston had to view parents as partners. All schools expected teachers throughout the school to support an orderly environment focused on learning.

Although many principals believe that professional references and a thorough interview provide all the evidence they need to make a sound hiring decision, these schools also required candidates to teach a demonstration lesson, showing that they knew their subject and could establish order and rapport with the school's students. Several administrators also wanted to see how candidates responded to feedback about the lesson. What did they think went well or not so well? Were they open to advice, and could they learn from it? One principal said she listened for whether applicants took personal responsibility for shortcomings in a lesson or, instead, subtly blamed students.

Some teachers we interviewed suggested that the experience of receiving feedback following a demonstration lesson had convinced them they wanted to teach at that school. A Naylor teacher observed that the lesson debrief provided "a great preview of what it would be like to work [there]," noting that it "was exactly the same tone and intent as my [current] weekly debriefs with my principal after she observes me." Principals and teachers agreed that investing time and resources in hiring made sense because those decisions had serious, long-term consequences for students and teachers alike.

Beyond setting licensing requirements, state policy had no direct, ongoing effect on hiring. Local WCSD policy gave district schools, such as Dickinson, the right to choose their new teachers but required them to comply with the district's hiring schedule and to ask a uniform set of interview questions. In-district and state charter schools had full autonomy under state law to recruit teachers and tailor the steps of their process to meet their needs. Of the relevant policies, the state accountability regulations for turnaround and restart schools had the greatest effect on staffing, but most of that took place before our 2014 study.

The benefits of a deliberate and thorough hiring process are unmistakable. Individual teachers, their colleagues, and the school's students all stand to benefit when a new hire is a good match for the school's expectations, norms, and practices. Many urban school leaders may not have the same level of resources or discretion in hiring that most of these principals had; yet, in 90 percent of US public schools, principals have the right to select teachers. This suggests that many do not exercise the autonomy available to them. If principals are to make the most of hiring, they must recognize the importance of well-informed decisions and give hiring priority among their many responsibilities. This means moving ahead purposefully when hiring opens and then investing the time it takes to conduct thorough interviews with candidates that clearly convey the school's mission, expectations, and supports for new teachers. Although it takes precious time to arrange and debrief candidates' demonstration lessons, there is no substitute for watching a prospective teacher at work with students. By engaging current teachers in recruiting, assessing, and selecting their future colleagues, principals can ensure that the teachers they hire will be engaged from the start in the professional life of the school.

Teacher Evaluation

A thorough and successful hiring process aimed to ensure both that new teachers were committed to its mission and professional norms and that they were competent instructors. However, that was only one part of these schools' strategy for increasing human capital; two additional systems—evaluation and collaborative teams—extended further support for all teachers.

Until very recently, teacher evaluation in most urban schools was largely a bureaucratic process with few consequences and little perceived value.[16] However, in response to strong evidence about the shortcomings of traditional teacher evaluation, forty-two states recently adopted new standards-based evaluations. The Massachusetts policy, which applied to all schools we studied, was intended to promote both continuous improvement and, if a teacher did not improve sufficiently, a clear path to dismissal.

Because the principals of these schools had invested so much in hiring their teachers, they approached evaluation primarily as an opportunity to develop them rather than hold them accountable or build a case for their dismissal. The head of Naylor's CMO explained that the school's mission and teacher development were entwined: "We do believe that our whole mission is to be a human capital organization. We are here to develop our kids. We are here to develop our teachers. We are here to develop our administrators. This is what we do and what we're all about." As a result, she said, administrators concentrated their time observing instruction and providing feedback: "We think that the most transformational thing is just being in people's classrooms, talking with them afterwards."

All schools we studied met or exceeded the state requirements for observations. Many teachers described an intense cycle of observation, followed soon by written or oral critique and recommendations for improvement. Approximately 40 percent of the teachers we interviewed said they were observed and received feedback at least twice each month; approximately 20 percent estimated that this occurred for them five to ten times per year; and the final 40 percent estimated that they had been observed one to four times per year, as the state required.

Teachers widely endorsed regular observations and feedback, using phrases such as "hugely helpful" or "super supported." Across schools, novice teachers and new hires were observed most often, and many experienced teachers said they wanted more frequent observations. One Naylor teacher, in her seventh year of teaching, viewed the feedback as a highlight of her job: "I constantly feel like I'm getting better." A Kincaid teacher with six years' experience said that she had become "a drastically better teacher" during her three years at the school.

These efforts to develop teachers fed directly into the summative evaluation process, which included midyear and end-of-year meetings to discuss the teachers' ratings on the evaluation rubric and their progress in meeting designated goals. As Hurston's K–8 principal explained, "I think evaluation without ongoing supervision is meaningless. It becomes only the way that you terminate employment. We need to be in classrooms all the time, giving feedback, asking questions, pushing people. And then all of that just gets rolled into an evaluation. No surprises."

A small number of teachers in several schools were on official improvement plans, which included goals they had to meet to keep their job. Teachers realized that formal evaluation could be used to inform employment decisions but did not suggest that falling short of the top rating would put them on the path to dismissal. Virtually all said that the formal evaluation process provided an accurate assessment of their practice and, with only a few exceptions, suggested that they were beneficiaries, not casualties, of evaluation.

Despite its value, implementing evaluation came with challenges, especially in district schools with few resources and little flexibility. The most common concerns were about subject-based mismatches between evaluator and teacher and the demands that the process placed on evaluators' scarce time. Teachers repeatedly praised their principals as instructional experts who could identify strengths and shortcomings in their lesson and suggest how to improve it. However, they also often mentioned that their evaluator lacked experience teaching their particular subject and, therefore, could not offer subject-specific recommendations. A middle school math teacher at Hurston, who called her evaluator's comments "affirming," found her math colleague's feedback more helpful because "he just knows more about the content." A history teacher at Kincaid who was supervised by a former English teacher said that his feedback often focused on how to teach writing through history but neglected the "nitty-gritty of history." At Fitzgerald and Kincaid, teachers of students with special needs expressed concern that their supervisors lacked experience in special education.

Principals in four schools talked about the daunting demands of conducting frequent observations and providing detailed feedback for all teachers. Most evaluators had fifteen to twenty teachers to supervise, but some had even more. A Rodriguez administrator said, "I have twenty people I evaluate and supervise, and it feels like too many to me. I'm always thinking, 'Oh, I haven't been there for so long!'" Notably, three schools (Naylor, Kincaid, and Hurston) had sufficient resources available from fund-raising or SIGs to expand their administrative teams so that the principal and other instructional administrators could observe and meet with teachers while other staff members handled responsibilities such as student discipline, building maintenance, or budgeting. The director of operations at Hurston explained, "My role has been to block and tackle so that [the evaluators] can spend their time in the classroom coaching teachers and [attending] team meetings."

In addition to setting requirements for observations and assessments, state officials provided schools and districts with a model system and templates for its activities. Principals found those useful but struggled to address the challenges of subject mismatch and insufficient time. Ironically, turnaround schools that had used grants to increase their administrative team so that they could observe more frequently had to cut back after losing state funding when they successfully exited turnaround.

Although public commentary about teacher evaluation often focuses on whether weak teachers can be fired, these schools invested in developing rather than dismissing their teachers. Because the principals were highly respected as instructors, teachers welcomed their feedback and often asked for more. Their experiences suggest strongly that frequent observations with feedback are well worth the investment of administrators' time, even though it may be difficult to arrange. If evaluators must also manage school operations and discipline, they will not be able to visit classes regularly. Therefore, hiring additional administrators and, reorganizing the responsibilities of current administrators can increase the likelihood that teachers' instructional practice gets the close attention it deserves. Although these schools did not rely on exemplary teachers as peer evaluators, doing so might be a very wise use of the school's human resources to ensure better matches and subject-specific recommendations for teachers.

Collaborative Teams

The intensive process of screening and hiring teachers ensured that teachers in these schools had the commitment and will to succeed, while an evaluation process with frequent observations with feedback contributed to teachers' continuous development. Both hiring and evaluation focused primarily on the individual teacher. However, the principals we interviewed also saw the importance of promoting collaboration among teachers in order to achieve coherence in improvement efforts throughout the school. This could not be done one teacher at a time but instead required an organizational strategy so that teachers could learn from one another while adjusting and integrating their practice.

Teachers have long reported that they value their colleagues, and evidence shows that systematic collaboration not only supports and sustains individual teachers but also leads to improved learning for students.[17] Since 2000, teacher teams, or professional learning communities, have rapidly emerged as a means to manage and support collaboration among teachers, especially those in urban schools. Accountability policies requiring schools to succeed with all subgroups of students have shown teachers that they have a stake in both their own and their colleagues' success.[18] Teams provide forums where the school's social capital increases its human capital. Teams are meant to decrease professional isolation, promote teachers' ongoing development, and substantially reduce well-documented variation in teachers' effectiveness within schools.[19] When teams work well, teachers with different skills, areas of expertise, and levels of experience not only report that they find support for their own instruction, but they learn how to contribute to the success of their school.[20] However, many teachers give their teams mixed reviews. They experience many competing demands for their scarce nonteaching time and often find that uncertainty about why they are meeting and what they are supposed to accomplish compromises the effectiveness of their team.[21]

Being familiar with these challenges and the difficulty many schools have in scheduling time for teams, we were surprised to find that five of the six schools we studied invested heavily in teams as a strategy for improvement. In those five schools, teachers and administrators strongly endorsed their teams. For example, when we asked an experienced Fitzgerald teacher where she went for teaching support, she quickly responded, "My team members." When we probed about the kinds of support she might seek, she answered, "Everything, every day, many times." Her principal reflected on her school's rapid improvement during turnaround: "I would say a lot of our success is because we really work at teams. The primary unit is the grade-level team . . . It's really like you are married to your team." Similarly, an administrator at Kincaid characterized the team as the teacher's "first line of defense." Virtually none of the teachers we interviewed in these schools suggested that team meetings lacked purpose, wasted their time, or were hijacked by administrators.

Teams had two areas of focus, both of which teachers saw as crucial to their success: academic content and the student cohort. A Kincaid teacher described his school's team assignments: "You basically are always part of two teams. You're part of a cultural [cohort] team, and you're part of a department [content] team. Your department team teachers will never teach together, but you will plan [instruction] together. On your cohort team, you never teach the same subjects, but you all teach the same kids."

Content teams were composed of either primary grade-level teachers who taught in self-contained classes or teachers in upper-elementary or middle school who taught one subject to several classes. Some teams included teachers of special education or English as a second language, who co-taught regularly in an inclusion class.

Hurston's elementary teachers met in grade-level teams to plan the sequence of topics and competencies they would all teach; this then guided their decisions about curriculum units and daily lesson plans. Experienced and new teachers routinely said that their content teams reduced the uncertainty about what and how to teach. A Kincaid history teacher with nearly a decade of experience summed up the benefits: "[It has] helped turn the job of curriculum design into a much more manageable beast." All schools dedicated time for content teams to analyze data about students' learning in order to gauge the effectiveness of their instruction.

At three schools—Kincaid, Fitzgerald, and Naylor—teachers also shared responsibility for lesson plans. Teachers did not simply exchange and use their colleagues' prepared lessons; they first critiqued and revised them. Although some teachers identified drawbacks in team-based lesson planning—for example, the time it took to consider everyone's views or an individual's obligation to teach a lesson she did not love—their overall response was very positive.

Cohort team meetings were dedicated to ensuring that students could and would do their part as learners. Teachers systematically discussed the needs of individual students within their grade-level cohort, reviewed the group's behavior, and strengthened aspects of its culture. By focusing on the academic and personal well-being of individual students, teachers could identify those having difficulty in several classes and intervene to get them back on track. Hurston's middle school cohort teams met with relevant student support staff each week (the dean of discipline, grade-level counselor, and representatives of the afterschool program) and reviewed individual students' needs and progress, sometimes inviting a student's parents to join them. During cohort team meetings, teachers also took stock of their students' behavior, often discussing how to consistently enforce the school's expectations. Cohort teams also created new activities and incentives to motivate their students to invest in learning.

Success for teams depended in part on effective hiring and evaluation, which assured teachers that their peers would be strong partners. One teacher called her colleagues "rock solid," a judgment echoed by others. In this way, systematic human capital practices fostered social capital throughout the school. Participants identified other factors that they said contributed to their teams' success.

First, principals remained actively engaged in the work of teams, at a minimum vouching for their importance and monitoring their deliberations. No principal formed teams and then left them to find their way. Several attended meetings often, although Dickinson's principal alone regularly chaired her school's team meetings.

Second, team time was carefully scheduled and never preempted by other programs or priorities. A Hurston teacher said, "We now have schedules that are like a dream. It's arranged so that our content and grade-level [cohort] meetings are two consecutive hours a week. That uninterrupted time is so precious that we can actually get a whole lot of work done." Although each school dedicated blocks of time for team meetings, practices varied widely across the sample, depending largely on the amount of time available during the teachers' workday and the extent to which the principal could decide how that time was used. Of the schools we studied, Dickinson had the least time dedicated to team meetings, and Naylor had the most.

Although attending meetings increased the demands on teachers, it came with significant professional payoff. Teachers widely viewed team time as time well spent.

Third, in the turnaround and restart schools (Hurston, Fitzgerald, and Kincaid), teacher leaders facilitated teams. Hurston further had assigned a full-time administrator to supervise the facilitators' work. With very few exceptions, teachers praised their team leaders. For their part, team leaders appreciated the chance to develop new skills and expand their influence. However, on exiting turnaround, the funds that supported the facilitators' $6,000 stipends disappeared, and principals were left to find new funding or make the assignment voluntary.

We conclude that, in the right context and with the right supports, teachers welcome collaboration and thrive as team members. In these schools, teams augmented and reinforced collaboration among teachers, which led to greater instructional coherence within grade levels and subject areas throughout the school. Teachers also observed each other's instruction, supplementing evaluators' observations and feedback. Teachers widely credited their teams for their students' success and their school's improvement, and some said that they wanted to stay at their school because of its steady support for teams.

No school reported deliberately creating teams to support new teachers' induction, although they served that purpose. Novices quickly became fully engaged with their peers in deciding what and how to teach. Rather than waiting for intermittent help from a mentor, whose interests and pedagogical style might differ from their own, novices could observe others' classes, be observed, and get feedback as part of their team's routines. A principal could confidently promise applicants ongoing support from team colleagues.

These schools' success in creating and sustaining effective teams was not accidental. Principals who seek to achieve similar results must convey a clear and worthy purpose before asking teachers to commit so much time to team meetings. Then they must schedule that time and ensure that it takes priority over all other activities. Teacher leaders can make important contributions as facilitators who ensure that teams work well. However, these schools' experiences suggest that teacher leaders are likely to be more effective in that role if they are carefully chosen, well supervised, and compensated for their responsibilities. Even with the best facilitators, principals should remain informed about and engaged in the teams' ongoing work, bringing to bear their broader understanding of the school's program and the students' needs.

DISCUSSION AND IMPLICATIONS

All six schools we studied had a purposeful, interdependent set of approaches for selecting, supporting, and developing their teachers. Ambitious hiring procedures ensured that teachers were well matched with their school. From their first encounter, applicants knew that they would be expected to commit to the school's mission and norms and to collaborate with colleagues. Most prospective teachers had to demonstrate their instructional competence and debrief their lesson with the principal and, sometimes, teachers. Throughout our interviews, teachers repeatedly expressed confidence that this thorough hiring process meant that they could count on their colleagues.

Also, because administrators observed teachers' instruction often and discussed written feedback in face-to-face meetings, most teachers had ready access to critique and advice. This close attention to individuals' development was then supplemented by teachers' experience on teams, where they coordinated their planning and instruction, reflected on their students' performance, and devised new approaches for improving performance of their grade level or department. The work of these teams contributed to a more deliberate and coherent schoolwide program.

Federal and state policies affected these schools' practices, although that effect was more indirect than direct. For example, beyond setting licensing requirements for teachers, the state did not intervene in hiring. However, provisions of state accountability laws had substantially affected staffing of three schools several years prior to our study. Also, state charter laws granted two schools autonomy in hiring and dismissing teachers. More direct effects of Massachusetts policy were apparent in the state's new evaluation policy. However, interviews made it clear that the policy reinforced, rather than changed, the priorities of these principals, who already were committed to developing their teachers through observations and feedback. By adding elements to the process, such as asking teachers to set goals and provide artifacts of their progress, state officials increased the depth of evaluation.[22] No federal, state, or local policy called for creating or supporting instructional teams, although accountability policies that called for schools to demonstrate progress with all subgroups of students provided a new incentive for teachers to learn what their colleagues were teaching and to adjust their own instruction in response.

Policy indirectly affected most schools' practices by increasing their autonomy and resources. All but Dickinson had been granted substantial discretion over a range of practices as a result of being a charter school or having been assigned to turnaround or restart status. Following turnaround, Hurston and Fitzgerald managed to retain much of that flexibility by reverting to pilot school status or becoming a state Innovation School. The autonomy that these five schools enjoyed gave their principals considerable discretion over who taught in their school and how teachers' time was used, which they relied on to strengthen staffing and the work of teams. Dickinson's principal, by contrast, worked within (and sometimes around) the district's requirements for hiring and contractual constraints on allocating teachers' time, which meant that Dickinson's teams met only once weekly, although many teachers said that they convened on their own more often. Dickinson's principal coped with limitations on her autonomy due to these constraints, although she would have preferred having more discretion.

Policy also positively affected these schools by providing additional resources to turnaround and restart schools, while local charter school boards raised funds beyond their state allocation. The schools that received extra funding used it to invest in hiring, to expand their administrative team, and to fund supplementary time for teachers to collaborate—all of which contributed to a better school.

Just as we could observe the benefits of additional resources invested in these key practices, we could see how schools struggled when resources disappeared as a result of the school's success. Once it exited turnaround, Hurston cut the number of team facilitators and relied on local foundation funding to provide smaller stipends. At Fitzgerald, teacher leaders no longer received extra pay for their work, raising questions about whether voluntary roles for facilitators would be viable over time. Both schools were engaged in reducing their administrative teams in 2014, which meant that principals and other administrators with instructional responsibility had less time to spend with teachers.

TAKING ACTION

During our study, evidence emerged about the effects of policy on the progress and accomplishments of these schools. Our data suggest that the schools placed in turnaround or restart benefited primarily from being assigned principals who were skilled in instructional leadership and organizational change. Those principals created systems for hiring, supporting, and coordinating the work of teachers. Notably, the state's role in expanding discretion and resources for improvement played a powerful role in what these principals could achieve.

Their experiences suggest that in order for a school to assemble a staff of fully qualified, highly motivated, well-matched teachers, principals must be able to conduct school-based hiring. This does not mean, however, that those in the district's human resource office should step aside during the hiring process, for they can contribute by recruiting and screening candidates so that principals and their hiring teams can move quickly to identify and consider promising applicants. Local and state legislators can do their part by approving education budgets early so that urban schools can offer contracts at the same time as their suburban counterparts.

With additional resources, these schools could implement a thorough hiring process, expand their administrative team, and compensate teachers for additional time spent participating on teams and facilitating them. However, for the turnaround schools we studied, academic success triggered the loss of those funds. Viewing turnaround as a short-term process that can be both initiated and sustained with an infusion of temporary resources is misguided. Policy makers must recognize that the needs of urban schools often surpass those of suburban schools. When school leaders use additional resources wisely to deepen and expand successful programs, they should not be expected to suddenly do without. If the society is serious about ensuring that all students are well educated, extra investments in high-poverty schools must be ongoing so that effective practices endure.

This study has many lessons for practice embedded in the details of these schools' successful approaches to hiring, evaluation, and teams. In addition, these cases suggest that a school's fate is determined largely by its principal. The principals of all the schools we studied were widely viewed as instructional leaders and effective managers who could engage teachers and other administrators in the difficult, yet meaningful work of urban school reform. Our findings suggest that principals should have substantial say in who their teachers are, how they are supported and evaluated, and how they collaborate. Yet it also is clear that simply granting more authority to the principal will not guarantee improvement. To state the obvious: it all depends on who the principal is and what the principal does. Despite their extensive autonomy and extra resources, many charter schools fail to accomplish what all these schools did. Notably, Hurston had been a pilot school with broad autonomies when the state placed it in turnaround, requiring the district to appoint a new principal. Fortunately, that principal knew how to use the autonomy and resources granted by the state to lead a successful process of organizational change.

The successful urban schools we studied were not typical of others in the city. In fact, when we searched for schools where students made steady progress, despite living in high-poverty, high-minority communities, the list of candidates was short. Many who read this chapter may conclude that these schools succeeded because their principals had unusual autonomy and resources. Although those were important, we conclude that the *quality of the principal* was far more consequential. At Dickinson, which had no more autonomy or resources than most district schools, the principal worked successfully with teachers to achieve success.

These principals demonstrated crucial skills and dispositions, including a commitment to promoting a positive work environment for their teachers. They were all regarded as experienced and skilled teachers in their own right and therefore credible instructional leaders. They deftly managed resources and built systems that enabled and compelled teachers to work together on issues of instruction and school culture. Although the principals in this study were active and decisive, they did not try to run the school single-handedly but, rather, engaged teachers and other administrators in a joint mission to give their students a first-rate education. In three schools the principals created roles for teacher leaders to serve as facilitators, illustrating the enormous potential of teachers' schoolwide influence, which principals often fail to notice or quickly quash.[23]

One obvious lesson for practice is that districts and CMOs should appoint principals who are first and foremost instructional leaders. Strong management skills are essential, but they must be used in the service of better teaching and learning. Many programs to develop aspiring principals attract candidates with an interest in management but little experience as teachers. In the schools we studied, the principal's knowledge of instruction and respect for teachers were crucial to developing the key practices of hiring, evaluation, and collaborative teams. This suggests that formal preparation programs for school leaders should actively recruit expert teachers who have an interest in leading schoolwide improvement. Those candidates should then have sufficient time and ready access to observe and learn from effective school leaders before they assume administrative roles. Once appointed to head a school, new principals—like the teachers they supervise—should have ongoing supervision and support. By focusing relentlessly on both individual and collective improvement goals, these principals can foster a culture of continuous improvement, sustained support, and high expectations for all.

Methods and Protocols

METHODS

For this study, we sought a sample of schools that successfully serve high-minority, high-poverty student populations, all within a single city. We considered only schools where at least 70 percent of students were eligible for free or reduced-priced lunch. We used the state's accountability ratings as a proxy for school success. The Massachusetts Department of Elementary and Secondary Education (DESE) rates every school on a scale from 1 to 5 (with 1 designating the highest performing schools), largely based on results of the Massachusetts Comprehensive Assessment System (MCAS), administered annually to all students in district and state charter schools. The state's formula accounts for growth in student performance on the MCAS and the school's progress in narrowing proficiency gaps among subgroups of students. We realize that this definition of success is limited because it relies primarily on standardized test scores; however, we used it because it was the best proxy available for identifying schools that have a positive impact on students' learning.

We considered only elementary and middle schools in order to permit meaningful cross-case comparisons. However, because we wanted to include schools that might use different approaches to attracting, developing, and retaining their teachers, we considered traditional district schools, state charter schools, and turnaround and restart schools. To achieve variation in the sample schools' missions, policies, and human resource practices, we reviewed available reports and websites and consulted our professional networks.

Based on our analysis of documents and on advice, we drew up a proposed sample of six elementary and middle schools, all located within the boundaries of the WCSD. To recruit schools, we contacted school officials, explaining our study and requesting their participation. All agreed to participate. (For descriptive statistics for sample schools, see table 2.1.) The purposive nature of our sample allowed us to examine the practices of this set of schools and to consider the implications of our findings for others, but it did not permit causal inferences or generalizations beyond the sample.

DATA COLLECTION

Interviews

Between March and June 2014, we conducted semi-structured interviews with 142 teachers, administrators, and other staff in the six schools. Interviews lasted approximately 90 minutes with administrators and 45 minutes with teachers. At most schools, all members of the research team attended interviews with the principal and with the directors of CMOs that managed two schools. In addition, all three researchers interviewed some teachers at each school, which facilitated cross-site comparisons, improved inter-rater reliability in coding data, and ensured that each researcher had informally observed elements of every school's structures, practices, and culture.

We also purposively constructed our interview sample at each school, recruiting a wide range of teachers who varied in demographics, teaching experience, preparation, and teaching assignment. We solicited teachers' participation by email, through flyers placed in their mailboxes, and from recommendations of other teachers and administrators. In addition, we interviewed key staff members (curriculum coaches, program heads, family coordinators, etc.) when it became apparent that their work and views might inform our understanding of teachers' experiences. We granted participants assurances of confidentiality.

In each school we interviewed between 31 percent and 56 percent of the teachers, depending on the school's size, complexity, and practices used. (For descriptive statistics about the interviewees, see tables 2.2 and 2.3.) We used semi-structured protocols (see page 66) to guide our interviews and elicit comparable data across sites and across interviewers. We recorded interviews and transcribed them verbatim.

Document Collection

Although interviews were the main source of data for this study, we also gathered and analyzed many documents describing school policies and programs related to recruiting, developing, and retaining teachers, such as teacher handbooks, school policies, schedules, meeting agendas, lesson planning templates, and formats for analyzing student assessments.

DATA ANALYSIS AND VALIDITY

We wrote a structured thematic summary after each interview and then analyzed sets of thematic summaries to identify common themes and differences within and across sites. In developing thematic codes, we supplemented the etic codes drawn from the literature (e.g., "adminteach" for quotes referring to the relationship between administrators and teachers) with emic codes that emerged from the data (e.g., "demands" for quotes about teachers' professional responsibilities within the school). After achieving inter-rater reliability by simultaneously coding a subset of transcripts and then calibrating our interpretation of the codes, we coded each transcribed interview using the software Dedoose.

Based on interview data and document analysis, we created analytic matrices so that we could systematically consider our research questions about practices within and across schools. We addressed risks to validity by returning to the data to review our coding and emerging findings and by seeking rival explanations or disconfirming data. We also conducted member checks by sharing initial findings with principals from all schools and by providing all participants with links to our working papers. In each case, we invited participants' responses.

TEACHER INTERVIEW PROTOCOL

Intro: Study explanation emphasizing that we really want to learn about your experience at this school

1. Background:
   a. How did you come to be in your current position at this school?
   b. Starting with college, can you tell us what you've done?
      i. Probe for: training and employment

2. Current Teaching Assignment:
   a. What do you teach here?
   b. How did you wind up in this position?

3. Overall View of School:
   a. If another teacher would ask you, "What's it like to teach at _____?" how might you respond?
   b. What are the advantages and disadvantages of being a teacher here?

4. Hiring:
   a. How were you hired at this school (step-by-step)?
   b. Do teachers play a role in hiring other teachers? If so, how?
   c. Has the hiring process changed at this school? If so, how and why?

5. Induction:
   a. Did you have some kind of induction as a new teacher at this school? What worked and what didn't?
   b. How are new teachers inducted now? How have things changed since you got here?

6. Support:
   a. What kinds of supports are available here for teachers to improve their instruction?
   b. What works well for you? What doesn't?
      i. Probe: professional development, coaching, collaboration, evaluation

7. Evaluation:
   a. How is your teaching evaluated? Describe the process.
   b. Was it helpful? How?

8. Administration:
   a. Who do you go to for support? For what?

9. Social and Psychological Supports:
   a. What sorts of social and psychological supports does your school offer for students?
   b. What support do you get for interacting with parents and families?

10. Career Goals:
    a. How long do you expect to stay at this school? In what roles?
       i. If yes: What keeps you at this school?
       ii. If no: Why do you think you might leave?

11. Union:
    a. What role does the union or the contract play in this school?

12. More: Do you have any additional comments?

PRINCIPAL INTERVIEW PROTOCOL

Overview of Study: 6 schools—all high-poverty, high-minority, all Level 1

1. Background:
   a. How long have you been at this school? Prior experience in education? Anything else we should know about how you got here?

2. School Overview:
   a. Could you first provide an overview of its structure and programs?
   b. (Where applicable) What does it mean for your school to be a pilot/turnaround/charter school?
   c. (Where applicable) How did you go about selecting teachers when ____ was placed in turnaround?
   d. How would you describe it to a teacher or parent who might be interested in it—both its strengths and weaknesses?

3. Teachers:
   a. We'd like to get a sense of who your teachers are. Where do they come from?
   b. What formal or informal preparation do they have?
   c. What attracts them to the school?
   d. Approximately, what proportion has fewer than 10 years of experience? 5 years of experience? 0–5 years of experience? (Has that changed or remained steady?)

4. Recruitment and Hiring:
   a. Could you describe the process you use to recruit and hire teachers? (Applicants per position? Teaching demonstration? Who decides?)
   b. What challenges do you face in recruiting teachers?
   c. Are there specific demographics or subject areas that you have trouble finding/attracting? If so, how have you addressed those challenges?

5. Assignment:
   a. How do you assign teachers to a particular grade or subject?
   b. Could you describe the teachers' responsibilities, both during school hours and after school hours? Scheduled and unscheduled time?

6. Compensation:
   a. Please tell us about the pay scale for teachers.
   b. Are there additional stipends? If so, can you describe these opportunities?

7. Collaboration:
   a. Are the teachers organized by teams, grade levels, subjects? If so, what does that mean for how they do their work?
   b. What is the work of those teams?

8. Supports:
   a. What supports can a new teacher count on when getting started?
   b. What supports are available for more experienced teachers?

9. Role:
   a. Are there specialized roles for some teachers (Teach Plus, team leaders, etc.)? If so, please describe these roles.

10. Curriculum:
   a. Does the school provide a curriculum for the teachers? If so, please tell us about it.

11. Professional Learning:
   a. Do you have formal professional development? Instructional coaches? If so, please tell us about them.

12. Supervision and Evaluation:
   a. How do you supervise teachers? How do you evaluate teachers? Are these separate processes?
   b. Do students' test scores play a role in evaluating teachers?

13. Dismissal:
   a. How frequently do you dismiss or decide not to rehire a teacher? Reasons?

14. Retention:
   a. How long do teachers stay? Why do they stay? Why do they leave?
   b. Is there a type of teacher who stays or leaves?
   c. Is turnover a challenge?

15. Policy Context:
   a. Does state or local policy play a role in how you approach building your teaching capacity?

16. Union:
   a. What role if any does a teacher union play at your school?

17. More: Have we missed anything?

CHAPTER 3

Better Collaboration, Better Teaching

MATTHEW RONFELDT

Historically, teaching has been isolating work. Long ago Dan Lortie argued that teacher isolation was among the greatest obstacles to educational improvement.[1] Over the past few decades there have been increasing efforts to transform schools and classrooms into places where teachers regularly work together on improving teaching. Policy makers and practitioners have increasingly called for the creation of school-based professional learning communities (PLCs), including organizational structures that promote regular opportunities for teachers to collaborate with teams of colleagues.[2] Though it is not always the case that practitioners and policy makers see eye to eye, there seems to be mutual support for using teacher collaboration to promote instructional improvement. As a result, instructional teams (including PLCs) have become progressively common in schools across the nation.[3] In one of the largest urban districts in the United States, for example, my colleagues and I recently found that 84 percent of teachers identified as being a part of a team or group of colleagues that work together on instruction.[4] As the use of instructional teams becomes more and more common, it is critical to examine whether and how collaboration actually improves teaching and learning.

I begin this chapter with a review of the existing literature on the relationships between teacher collaboration and teaching quality.

I then summarize two of my studies that strengthen the claim that teacher collaboration in schools actually promotes instructional improvement. The first study characterizes the kinds of collaboration among in-service teachers in instructional teams across one large, urban district and considers whether schools and teachers benefit when groups of teachers engage in higher-quality collaboration. The second study focuses on preservice teacher preparation, investigating whether teachers who initially learn to teach in schools with stronger collaboration during preservice training are more instructionally effective after completing certification and becoming a teacher of record. Finally, I discuss the implications of this body of research for policy and practice.

COLLABORATION AND TEACHING QUALITY: WHAT WE ALREADY KNOW

For many decades, educational scholars have conducted mostly qualitative case studies documenting the nature of collaboration among particular groups of teachers working together in departmental teams, reading groups, and other types of instructional teams.[5] This body of work has demonstrated that the kinds and content of collaboration vary substantially across contexts, shed light on the norms and structures that promote more promising forms of collaboration, interrogated the ways that conversations among colleagues can open up or close down opportunities for teacher learning, and set the stage for today's policy focus on professional learning communities. This literature has demonstrated that instructional teams hold great promise for promoting teacher learning and instructional improvement, though typically it has not directly linked teachers' engagement in collaborative groups to their classroom practice or their students' learning.

Around the turn of this century, a number of studies began to emerge that linked teacher learning communities and instructional teams to changes in teaching practice and student learning outcomes. In their review of the literature in 2008, Vicki Vescio, Dorene Ross, and Alyson Adams identify eleven such studies and conclude that while they generally support the claim that teacher learning communities promote changes in teaching practice among participants, the studies' designs do not enable strong conclusions to be drawn about whether these changes were definitive improvements in practice.[6] For example, some studies used only teachers' self-reports that changes were beneficial as evidence for improvement. Others only observed instruction after teachers participated in learning communities, which made it impossible to conclusively attribute effects to participation in learning communities. Vescio and colleagues argue that the evidence linking teacher participation in learning communities with improvements in student achievement is more decisive.[7] The eight studies linked to student outcomes all found that student achievement was greater in schools where teachers participated in learning communities. Though teacher participation in learning communities was consistently associated with better student achievement across these studies, the evidence did not demonstrate whether teacher collaboration specifically, or some other aspect of learning communities, was responsible for improvements.

More recently, some large-scale studies looked across many schools to investigate whether teacher collaboration improves teaching and learning. Yvonne Goddard, Roger Goddard, and Meghan Tschannen-Moran found that elementary schools in which teachers reported more extensive collaboration on surveys also had better student achievement, even after controlling for a set of student and school covariates.[8] In a follow-up study, Goddard and colleagues similarly found a direct relationship between collaboration and achievement and an indirect relationship, mediated by teacher collaboration, between principal leadership and achievement.[9]

All of these studies focus on school-level correlations between average student achievement and average teacher participation in learning communities or collaboration. While these correlational studies provide initial, suggestive evidence that collaboration causes achievement to improve, other explanations are possible. First, unobserved factors could explain observed relationships. For example, better teacher retention may cause both teacher collaboration and student achievement to improve. Second, more effective teachers might nonrandomly sort into schools with better collaboration or community, or more collaborative teachers might nonrandomly sort into higher achieving schools. Finally, it is possible that stronger achievement causes teachers to collaborate, rather than the other way around.

A number of recent studies have made progress in addressing these limitations and producing estimates that are more credibly causal. Before addressing studies with experimental designs, I summarize two studies that apply innovative methods of causal inference to preexisting administrative data.[10] A contribution of both of these studies is their focus on teacher-level instructional effectiveness over time instead of student achievement aggregated to the school level. If collaboration and community are actually causing student achievement to increase, then the most likely way they would be doing so is by improving the effectiveness of teachers who are engaging in that collaboration/community. Both studies test this directly. By using teacher fixed effects approaches, they effectively compare a given teacher's performance in more supportive and less supportive settings, thus making progress in ruling out selection bias and reverse causality.

Matthew Kraft and John Papay used statewide teacher survey data to construct a measure of professional learning environments in schools that incorporates information about teacher collaboration, principal leadership, and teacher evaluation, among other features.[11] They found that, over time, teachers working in schools with more supportive teaching environments improved more than teachers working in schools with less supportive environments. Because the study used a teacher fixed effects approach, the differential sorting of more effective teachers into more supportive schools is unlikely to explain differences. However, their focus on the more general construct of "professional environment," of which teacher collaboration is only one part, obscures the specific contributions of teacher collaboration.

Using longitudinal data on elementary school teachers and an innovative teacher-school fixed effects approach, C. Kirabo Jackson and Elias Bruegmann found that a given teacher was more effective at raising student achievement in years when her grade-level teacher peers were more effective, as compared to the same teacher in the same school in years when her peers were less effective.[12] Moreover, they estimated that peer quality explained as much as one-fifth of a teacher's own effectiveness at raising student achievement. Supporting the notion that these results reflect peer learning, they found that first-year teachers benefited substantially more than more experienced teachers and that the peer effects persisted over time. Though the study suggests that teachers learn from their peers, it does not explain how. A likely explanation that the authors posit, but do not test directly, is learning through formal and informal collaboration among peers.

In Tennessee, John Papay and colleagues designed a randomized control trial to test directly whether collaboration among teacher peers can lead to instructional improvement.[13] The intervention consisted of strategically pairing teachers who scored highly in a particular dimension of the observational evaluation rubric used in the state with colleagues (target teachers) from the same school who scored lower on that same dimension. After these teacher pairs were encouraged to work together for a year on instruction, the authors found that schools which strategically paired teachers had greater achievement gains than other schools. Though target teachers benefited most, all teachers who participated in the strategic pairing demonstrated better performance. These findings offer some of the strongest causal evidence to date that encouraging teachers to work deliberately together on instruction directly improves the teaching quality of all involved. A limitation of this study is that it focused only on collaboration between pairs of teachers, when increasingly instructional teams and learning communities are being established in schools that engage groups of teachers rather than dyads.

Addressing this concern, two other recent, quasi-experimental studies provide credibly causal evidence that supporting instructional teams to engage in inquiry around student data increases student achievement.[14] The researchers designed a school-level intervention that trained instructional leaders to promote frequent teacher collaboration based on an inquiry-focused protocol. The treatment schools showed substantially greater achievement gains than the control schools. These studies build the case that collaboration causes instructional effectiveness to improve, but it is difficult to ascertain whether collaboration specifically, other aspects of the intensive intervention (e.g., trained instructional leaders, structured protocols), or both caused the observed improvement. Even if collaboration were responsible, finding such carefully orchestrated collaboration to spur improvement does not necessarily mean that more typical forms of collaboration are equally beneficial, a critique that applies also to the study by Papay and colleagues.[15]

While the literature has made great progress in establishing that teacher collaboration and community are related to student achievement and teacher effectiveness, a number of questions persist. Research on teacher collaboration has typically looked at school-level correlations between average amounts/extensiveness of collaboration in schools and average student achievement. Though studies consistently find positive and significant relationships, the likelihood of omitted variable or selection bias, among other possible concerns, prevents the drawing of causal conclusions. Studies applying innovative methods of causal inference to existing administrative data have made progress in addressing noncausal explanations, but they focus on professional environments more generally instead of collaboration specifically or infer collaboration without measuring it directly.[16] Studies using experimental and quasi-experimental designs include interventions that focus on building teacher collaboration and community and show them to make a difference; however, it is unclear whether results can be generalized to more typical, naturally occurring forms of collaboration that exist in schools today.

To address these limitations, my colleagues and I investigated naturally occurring forms of collaboration and its effects in the aggregate (at the school level) but also at the individual (teacher) level. We built on studies that have applied methods of causal inference to existing, administrative data by measuring collaboration directly rather than inferring it or considering it as part of a larger professional environment construct.

STUDY 1: THE RELATIONSHIP BETWEEN COLLABORATION QUALITY AND TEACHING EFFECTIVENESS

In this study, my colleagues and I investigated the various, naturally occurring forms of collaboration that exist among teachers in instructional teams across Miami-Dade County Public Schools, one of the largest, urban districts in the United States.[17] Our goal was to better understand the landscape of more typical forms of collaboration that exist across a district, including how collaboration quality varies for different kinds of teachers and schools. We also investigated whether collaboration quality is related to student achievement and teachers' effectiveness at raising student achievement, as measured by value-added measures (VAMs).

We sent online surveys to all teachers in the district during the two-year study, resulting in more than nine thousand survey responses. We asked teachers who reported being a part of an instructional team that worked together on instruction eighteen questions about the extensiveness and helpfulness of their collaboration in different instructional domains (e.g., discussing specific student needs, state test results). Drawing on these items, we created a general measure for the quality of collaboration across all instructional domains and a set of domain-specific measures for collaboration about students, instruction, and assessment. This allowed us to investigate whether collaboration about certain instructional topics might be more beneficial than collaboration about other topics (table 3.1). After constructing teacher-level measures, we also aggregated scores to construct school-level measures. Given that prior research examines collaboration almost entirely in terms of the amount or extensiveness of collaboration, another contribution of our work is to consider its helpfulness. Because these teacher-level measures combined information about how helpful and how extensive these collaborations were, we interpreted them to be measures of the quality of collaboration. With this in mind, we then linked collaboration measures to teacher and school effectiveness at raising math and reading achievement.

On average, teachers who participated in instructional teams found collaboration within these teams to be both extensive and helpful. Teachers felt that topics were addressed "in some depth" and that collaboration across topics was "helpful" to "very helpful." Even though teachers had generally favorable perceptions of collaboration, they found collaboration around some instructional topics

TABLE 3.1 Mean responses to survey questions about collaboration in instructional teams

When you met with your instructional team, to what extent were the following covered? *1 = not at all; 2 = a little; 3 = in some depth; 4 = in substantial depth*

Variable	Mean	SD
Reviewing formative assessments (a)	3.06	0.88
Developing instructional strategies (i)	3.06	0.83
Reviewing state test results (a)	3.02	0.94
Discussing the needs of specific students (s)	3.01	0.88
Coordinating curriculum and/or instruction across classrooms (i)	2.95	0.91
Developing curriculum and/or materials (i)	2.94	0.92
Addressing classroom management/discipline issues (s)	2.70	0.94
Reviewing students' classroom work (s)	2.51	0.97

When you met with your instructional team, how helpful did you find each of the following activities? *1 = not at all helpful; 2 = a little helpful; 3 = helpful; 4 = very helpful; 5 = essential*

Variable	Mean	SD
Developing instructional strategies (i)	3.55	1.08
Discussing the needs of specific students (s)	3.49	1.13
Developing curriculum and/or materials (i)	3.45	1.14
Coordinating curriculum and/or instruction across classrooms (i)	3.43	1.16
Reviewing formative assessments (a)	3.43	1.14
Reviewing state test results (a)	3.34	1.21
Addressing classroom management/discipline issues (s)	3.13	1.20
Reviewing students' classroom work (s)	2.97	1.21

Notes: The notation in parentheses indicate which survey items load heavily on which of the collaboration measures: (i) about instruction; (s) about students; (a) about assessment. SD stands for *standard deviation*.

to be significantly more extensive and helpful than around others. Interestingly, the kinds of collaboration they perceived to be most extensive were also those they tended to perceive as being most helpful. For instance, "developing instructional strategies" was one of the most extensively covered topics, and it was also reported to be the most helpful topic; "addressing classroom management/discipline issues" and "reviewing students' classroom work" were the least extensively covered topics and considered the least helpful. In general, this correspondence may indicate that instructional teams are selecting instructional topics well, that more attention is being paid to those topics teachers find helpful. Two possible exceptions were collaboration about formative assessments and test results; these topics were among the most extensively covered but ranked toward the middle in terms of helpfulness.

We found collaboration quality to also vary across different kinds of teachers and schools. Compared to secondary schools, teachers in elementary schools reported, on average, better collaboration quality in general and around instructional strategies/curriculum and students in particular; however, there were no significant differences between school level in terms of the quality of collaboration around assessment. Regarding variation by teacher characteristics, it is notable that teachers from historically more privileged backgrounds (white, male, highly educated) perceived their collaboration experiences to be of a lower quality than did other types of teachers. Given the self-report nature of our measures, we cannot discern whether these kinds of teachers actually engaged in less-effective collaboration or simply perceived this to be the case.

But is collaboration related to school or teacher performance? Consistent with prior research, we found that schools in which teachers reported better collaboration quality, had above-average gains in math and reading. In fact, all four collaboration quality measures were significant predictors of school-level math achievement gains, and all but collaboration around assessment were significant predictors of school-level reading achievement gains (see appendix table 1). However, we cannot conclude that these correlational results are causal in nature; among other possibilities, these findings are prone to omitted variable and selection bias.

If collaboration is in fact causing achievement to increase, then the most likely explanation for the rise in achievement rates is the improved quality of instruction among the teachers participating in this collaboration. Were this the case, then we would expect to see teachers who report engaging in higher-quality collaboration to be more effective than their peers who report engaging in lower-quality collaborations. We would also expect to see teachers improving at faster rates when working in schools with stronger collaboration. In subsequent analyses, we found evidence for this on both fronts.

Even in a school where, on average, teachers report lower-quality collaboration, some individuals within that school experience relatively higher-quality collaboration. Thus, we tested whether teachers who reported better collaboration quality also had better achievement gains than their peers. We found that teachers who reported better collaboration quality in general, and around assessment in particular, had better math achievement gains; and teachers who reported better collaboration quality around instruction had higher reading achievement gains (see appendix table 2). These findings suggest that teachers who report engaging in higher-quality collaboration are more effective than their colleagues who report engaging in lower-quality collaboration.

Next, we used a teacher fixed effects framework to look at a single teacher over time and estimate whether her instructional effectiveness increased at faster rates when she taught in schools with better average collaboration quality as compared to schools with worse average collaboration quality. Our parameters of interest—interaction terms between our measures for a teacher's collaboration quality and the years of teaching experience—all trended positive across models with both math and reading VAMs as outcomes (see appendix table 3). The results suggest that teachers' math VAM scores increased at significantly greater rates among teachers in schools with better domain-general and assessment collaboration quality; teachers' reading VAM scores increased at marginally greater rates among teachers in schools with greater domain-general collaboration quality. These findings provide some support for the claim that teachers improve at faster rates when working in schools with strong collaboration quality.

The results, then, generally support the claim that higher-quality collaboration improves the instructional effectiveness of teachers who engage in it. However, if more collaborative schools are indeed promoting instructional effectiveness, then we would expect these kinds of schools to also be especially promising sites for those who are learning to teach and who have the most to gain instructionally.

STUDY 2: LEARNING TO TEACH IN SCHOOLS WITH BETTER COLLABORATION DURING PRESERVICE PREPARATION

Similar to the first study, the second was situated in a large, urban district and drew on surveys given to all teachers in the district across three years.[18] For teachers who had completed their preservice student teaching experiences (part of initial certification) in the same district in which they were now working as a teacher of record, the survey asked them to identify the schools in which they had been placed. This allowed me to link teachers to the characteristics of the field placement schools in which they had initially learned to teach, including a measure for the quality of collaboration among teachers in those schools similar to the one I used in the prior study. Among the subset of these teachers (n=752) for whom it was possible to create VAM scores in either math or reading, I then investigated whether teachers who had initially learned to teach in schools with better collaboration quality were more effective at raising achievement after becoming teachers of record.

For the analyses I used a two-stage approach. After estimating teacher VAM scores, I used a three-level multilevel model (Time at level 1, Teacher at level 2, Current School at level 3) to estimate a teacher's VAM as a function of the characteristics of the field placement schools where they had their student teaching experiences. These models also adjusted for the characteristics of the schools in which the teachers were currently employed in order to disentangle the effects of the field placement schools from those of the current schools.

The results suggest that on the first day of class these teachers—as compared to newly hired peers who had completed their preservice preparation in less collaborative settings (by one standard deviation)—performed as though they already had at least half a year more teaching experience under their belts. Additionally, teachers who had learned to teach in schools with better prior achievement gains and lower teacher turnover rates also had better math VAM, though results were more mixed for these school characteristics. These field placement school characteristics were unrelated, though, to teachers' effectiveness at increasing reading achievement.

These results suggest that better-functioning schools—those with better collaboration, a history of prior achievement, and less teacher churn—are promising sites for preservice teaching. However, in separate analyses I found that these kinds of schools were actually less likely to be used as field placement sites. Given that all stand to gain from promoting the instructional effectiveness of preservice teachers in the pipeline for district teaching positions, an implication of this work is that district and teacher education program stakeholders need to find ways to partner in recruiting better-functioning schools to train our next generation of teachers.

COLLABORATION: A PROMISING TREND

Though educational research often concludes with a grim portrayal of schooling today, the two studies at the heart of this chapter add to a growing body of literature on a promising educational trend. For many decades, schools and districts across the country have increasingly turned to using instructional teams as a way to promote instructional effectiveness, thus seemingly benefiting schools, students, and teachers.

The results from the two studies highlighted in this chapter concur, but they also extend the existing literature in important ways. The first study describes the landscape of naturally occurring kinds of collaboration that existed among instructional teams across a large, urban district. Though teachers reported collaboration around some instructional topics to be more extensive and helpful than others, they generally evaluated collaboration in their teams quite favorably and indicated that it seemed to support their learning and development. This study demonstrates that teachers who engage in better collaboration quality outperform peers who engage in worse collaboration quality and that teachers improve at faster rates when they work in schools with better collaboration quality.

The second study indicates that teachers who initially learn to teach in schools with better collaboration quality are more instructionally effective than peers who learn to teach in schools with worse collaboration quality. All of these findings are consistent with the explanation that schools with better collaboration quality among faculty promote the instructional effectiveness of teachers. They indicate that effective schools serve as learning organizations not only for students but also for teachers and that collaboration among teachers is critical.

An overarching implication of these studies is that the increasingly common use of instructional teams to promote both teacher and student performance appears to be warranted. Of course, the findings suggest that those teachers and schools experiencing the highest-quality collaboration are benefiting most. Yet, more needs to be done to identify what characterizes higher-quality collaboration and what schools and teaching faculty can do to promote it. The first focal study in this chapter begins to consider these questions by testing whether collaboration is more beneficial around some instructional topics than others. The results suggest, however, that collaboration across a range of instructional topics (domain-general collaboration) is predictive of teacher and school effectiveness at raising achievement. This suggests that, where possible, policy makers and practitioners need to design instructional teams that collaborate across a range of instructional topics.

Time is limited, however, and instructional teams often have to make difficult choices about what topics to prioritize. Teachers in our study reported that collaboration around instructional strategies and specific student needs was more helpful than collaboration around other instructional topics. Yet, when we investigated what kinds of collaboration were associated with better achievement gains, collaboration around assessment (summative and formative) was a more consistent predictor of achievement gains than collaboration around students or curriculum and instruction.

What should we make of these mixed results? A likely, though somewhat unsatisfying, answer is that collaboration around different topics may impact outcomes. Where the goal is to raise student achievement, perhaps unsurprisingly, collaboration around assessment seems promising. Where the goal is to design instructional teams that teachers find helpful, collaboration around specific student needs or instructional strategies may hold more promise. With this in mind, members of instructional teams should think seriously about the outcomes they hope to influence when selecting the content of their collaboration.

The content, though, is only one among many features of collaboration in instructional teams that likely influences its quality. For example, the form or makeup of instructional teams no doubt makes a difference and can vary widely. For decades, scholars have explored alternative models to more typical departmental/faculty meeting formats. Catharine Lewis and Jacqueline Hurd have investigated the use of the Japanese "lesson study" to engage teams of teachers in the joint planning, observation, analysis, and refinement of specific classroom lessons.[19] Pamela Grossman, Sam Wineburg, and Stephen Woolworth detail how they supported two departments in the same school in building learning communities through an interdisciplinary reading group.[20] The Mills Teachers Scholars Group engages teachers from many districts in "inquiry groups" that deliberately study their own classrooms, collecting and analyzing classroom artifacts to learn from and improve teaching.[21]

These models differ in many ways. Some examples of lesson study included only teachers from a single department within a school. The reading group described by Grossman and colleagues engaged teachers from across departments. Inquiry groups in the Mills Teacher Scholars Group sometimes brought together teachers from many districts. Who takes responsibility for facilitating the meetings also varies across models—from departmental team leaders, to university subject matter experts, to administrators. These examples also differ in terms of how often teams meet, where they meet, and the norms of collaboration, among other features. However, despite differing in important ways, according to the available empirical and anecdotal evidence, all of these models promote high-quality collaboration.

So while there is growing consensus that collaboration in instructional teams can make a difference, there does not appear to be a single model that works better than others. This is not to suggest that practitioners and scholars will never reach consensus about which features are desirable across models and contexts. (Many have argued, for example, that collaboration must be regular and ongoing in order for it to be effective.[22]) We should continue to seek to understand the kinds of instructional teams—including the kinds of content, structure, frequency, facilitators, and norms—that promote better collaboration quality.

From a policy perspective, then, it seems unwise to mandate that schools or districts adopt a single form of teacher collaboration. An alternative might be to pursue policy which sets the expectation that schools put in place structures and allow time to make collaboration in instructional teams part of the regular work of teachers but that leaves the particulars up to each school and/or team. This recommendation seems consistent with results from Study 1 showing how collaboration that emerges naturally across a large district, taking various forms in various contexts, has promise.

Even if districts were to adopt such policy, collaboration cannot be mandated, as many argue. Certainly, requiring teachers who are opposed to any form of collaboration to collaborate would be ineffective. However, anecdotal and growing empirical evidence suggests that teachers overwhelmingly appreciate and seek out opportunities to collaborate. As for those in the minority who dislike collaboration but are required to attend departmental, faculty, and/or professional development meetings where some degree of collaboration is expected, I suspect that, given the opportunity to work in instructional teams (particularly in ones teachers can help shape) as an alternative to existing meeting requirements, even the most intractable teacher would reconsider the value of collaboration.

Whether schools and districts should employ and retain teachers who are unwilling or unable to collaborate is another matter. The growing evidence that collegial collaboration is key to how well schools function may suggest that being willing to collaborate and being skilled at collaborating should be core expectations of teachers' work. If this is the case, then these capacities should be considered in teacher recruitment, hiring, and retention decisions.

Given that both of the focal studies highlighted in this chapter are correlational in nature, we must take caution in drawing causal conclusions. The existing experimental evidence bolsters the claim that extensive teacher collaboration boosts instructional effectiveness, though it is based on studies that leverage interventions using carefully orchestrated forms of collaboration that are not typical in schools. Future research should consider ways of pairing experimental designs with interventions that use more typical and naturalistic forms of collaborative activity. A possibility might be to allow teachers or schools randomized to "collaboration" conditions to take responsibility for generating the form of collaborative activity according to the specific needs of their setting and faculty. Such an intervention could also serve as a test of the kind of policy I discuss above.

Although it seems appropriate to continue to be cautious in drawing causal conclusions, it is unusual to find a body of evidence from a group of well-designed studies that seems to point to the same general conclusion. In fact, all the studies that have linked collaboration to instructional effectiveness have found evidence of positive relationships; none, to my knowledge, has shown teacher collaboration to predict worse instructional effectiveness or student learning.

In addition to having strong empirical support, teacher collaboration (including the kinds that exist as part of professional learning communities and instructional teams) is a form of professional improvement that most, if not all, teachers, school leaders, and policy makers can get behind. Teachers in the Miami-Dade schools overwhelmingly reported the collaborations in their instructional teams as being "helpful" or "very helpful." School leaders and policy makers are increasingly promoting collaboration for early induction and ongoing teacher development. Among other advantages, this form of professional development uses existing expertise and resources and is easier to build regularly into school life, as compared with outside forms of professional development that tend to be costly, typically have little empirical support, and are often viewed as wastes of time. Teacher collaboration appears to be good for teachers and students and a strategy for instructional improvement that all stakeholders generally view as viable.

Technical Appendix

APPENDIX TABLE 1. Estimating school-level value-added in math and reading as a function of different kinds of instructional collaboration

	Math value-added		Reading value-added	
Variables	Model 1	Model 2	Model 1	Model 2
General collaboration	0.425***		0.179***	
	(0.081)		(0.050)	
Instruction collaboration		0.297**		0.127*
		(0.099)		(0.051)
Students collaboration		0.176*		0.109*
		(0.079)		(0.050)
Assessment collaboration		0.251***		0.075
		(0.069)		(0.058)
N	335	335	336	336
R-squared	0.133	0.138	0.055	0.056

Notes: *** $p<0.001$, ** $p<0.01$, * $p<0.05$, ~ $p<0.1$. Robust standard errors are clustered at the school-level (in parentheses). School response rates on surveys are used as probability weights. Only data from 2011 were used in these analyses.

APPENDIX TABLE 2. Estimating teacher-level value-added as a function of collaboration measures

	Math value-added		Reading value-added	
Variables	Model 1	Model 2	Model 1	Model 2
General collaboration (teacher level)	0.091~		0.009	
	(0.049)		(0.040)	
General collaboration (school level)	0.146*		0.111~	
	(0.070)		(0.060)	

Variables	Math value-added		Reading value-added	
	Model 1	Model 2	Model 1	Model 2
Instruction collaboration (teacher level)		0.015		0.081*
		(0.044)		(0.037)
Instruction collaboration (school level)		-0.014		0.077
		(0.064)		(0.055)
Students collaboration (teacher level)		0.040		-0.045
		(0.046)		(0.038)
Students collaboration (school level)		0.191**		0.026
		(0.070)		(0.059)
Assessment collaboration (teacher level)		0.145**		-0.043
		(0.052)		(0.044)
Collaboration assessment (school level)		0.144*		0.074
		(0.068)		(0.055)
N	542	542	674	674
Teacher characteristics	x	x	x	x
School controls	x	x	x	x

Notes: *** $p<0.001$, ** $p<0.01$, * $p<0.05$, ~$p<0.1$. Teacher-level instructional collaboration factors are school mean centered; school-level instructional collaboration factors are grand mean centered.

APPENDIX TABLE 3 Estimating teacher value-added differential returns to experience with increasing collaboration quality in schools

Variables	Math value-added		Reading value-added	
	Model 1	Model 2	Model 1	Model 2
General collaboration*experience	0.067*		0.048~	
	(0.027)		(0.025)	
Instruction collaboration*experience		0.019		0.011
		(0.026)		(0.024)

(continued)

	Math value-added		Reading value-added	
	Model 1	Model 2	Model 1	Model 2
Students collaboration*experience		0.036		0.045
		(0.026)		(0.027)
Assessment collaboration*experience		0.062*		0.029
		(0.026)		(0.024)
N	6682	6682	7880	7880
Teacher fixed effects	x	x	x	x
School controls	x	x	x	x
Year indicators	x	x	x	x

Notes: *** p<0.001, ** p<0.01, * p<0.05, ~ p<0.1. Standard errors appear in parentheses. These models include teachers from the 2010–12 academic years. Experience is entered as a quartic function, fully interacted with our measures for instructional collaboration; we present estimates only on the linear component interacted with collaboration. Models use the same 2011 school collaboration factors in 2010 and 2012, with the assumption that schools with better collaboration in 2011also have better collaboration in the subsequent and prior years.

APPENDIX TABLE 4 Estimating teacher VAM as a function of field placement school characteristics

	Math value-added		Reading value-added	
Variables	Model 1	Model 2	Model 1	Model 2
Math VAM	0.122*	0.091		
	(0.056)	(0.058)		
Reading VAM			-0.020	0.010
			(0.045)	(0.047)
General collaboration quality	0.094*	0.091*	0.008	0.046
	(0.037)	(0.040)	(0.034)	(0.035)
Stay ratio (transformed)	0.043	0.069~	-0.037	-0.038
	(0.037)	(0.038)	(0.034)	(0.034)
School-level indicators	x	x	x	x
Year indicators	x	x	x	x

Variables	Math value-added		Reading value-added	
	Model 1	Model 2	Model 1	Model 2
Teacher characteristics	x	x	x	x
Preparation features		x		x

Notes: *** p<0.001, ** p<0.01, * p<0.05, ~ p<0.1. Standard errors appear in parentheses. Each coefficient (row) comes from a separate regression model. The school VAM and collaboration quality were entered independently; the school stay ratio was entered along with other school characteristics (student race, gender, limited English proficient, exceptional student services [ESE], gifted, average absences, average suspensions, enrollment). Teacher characteristics included teacher gender, race, highest degree, and job type (instruction, ESE, other). Preparation features included whether an education major, certification area, length of student teaching (in days), and an indicator for having led or co-led teaching responsibilities while student teaching.

CHAPTER 4

The Social Side of Capability

Supporting Classroom Instruction and Enabling Its Improvement

JAMES P. SPILLANE, MEGAN HOPKINS,
TRACY M. SWEET, AND MATTHEW SHIRRELL

Though the new century is well under way, we continue to mostly rely on last-century notions about human capability. Specifically, we dwell chiefly, often exclusively, on the capability of the individual teacher or school leader—evaluating, measuring, and sometimes investing in and developing their human capital so as to improve their productivity and in turn generate higher returns to the individual, school organization, school system, and society. The empirical evidence shows that the human capital development of educational professionals is important for classroom, school, and school system productivity.

Still, in fixating on human capital we miss or risk undermining the significance of another key idea about capability that emerged toward the end of the last century: the notion of social capital. Social capital captures the idea that capability, and by extension productivity, is not simply an individual matter but also a social matter. Social capital refers to those resources for action that reside in the relations among people in a school organization, school system, community, or society; these social relations can be a source of resources, including trust, information, expertise, materials, security, obligation, incentives, and so on. Social capital is more than just the aggregate human capital of organizational or system members because it refers to resources that inhere in the relations among people rather than resources that reside in individuals. Further, social capital does not negate the importance of human capital to instructional capability in schools and school systems. Rather, social capital can help expand our understanding of human capital, in particular the development of human capital in organizations and systems. Moreover, we suspect that scholarship at the intersection of social capital and human capital will generate new insights into capability for instruction and instructional improvement in schools and school systems.

Our primary interest in this chapter is social capital—"the resources, real or potential, gained from relationships."[1] Scholars theorize that people can invest in and benefit from social capital by using their social relations to access resources that improve their capability and, in turn, their productivity.[2] Over the past three decades, research studies have documented substantial returns of social capital in schools and school systems.[3] Research suggests, for example, a positive relationship between a school's social capital and valued school processes and outcomes, including teacher commitment and student achievement.[4]

In this chapter we focus not on the returns of social capital but, rather, on understanding those factors that might help us build social capital in schools and school systems. Social relations are necessary for the generation of social capital, and social relations don't just happen by chance; thus, to understand social capital development we need to examine the factors that enable social relations, which we explore using interactions about instruction among school and school system staff. We focus on those factors associated with the presence, production, and persistence of work-related social interactions, enumerated as social ties in which school staff members share advice and/or information.[5] We do so because these interactions are a necessary prerequisite for facilitating access to social resources and therefore can help us better understand what it might take to build social capital in schools and school systems.

Using on a series of studies conducted over the past decade, we not only describe social relations but also identify those factors associated with the presence of advice or information ties in schools and school systems.[6] We begin by identifying those factors associated with intraschool interactions about instruction. Next, we turn our attention to interschool interactions, exploring those factors associated with ties among school leaders and teachers in different schools. We conclude by discussing what our work means for scholars, practitioners, and policy makers interested in social capital and its development.

INTRASCHOOL INTERACTIONS ABOUT INSTRUCTION

We studied predictors of work-related interactions among school staff in three school districts in two states. Our work suggests that several factors are predictive of advice or information ties among school staff around language arts and mathematics instruction, including characteristics of individual staff members, organizational factors, and physical proximity.

Individual Characteristics

Within schools, school leaders' and teachers' individual characteristics, such as race and gender, are positively associated with the existence of a relationship, or tie, formed around instruction. In a study of thirty elementary schools in a midsized public school district in the southeastern United States, we found that staff members of the same race and same gender were more likely to have instructional advice or an information tie than those of different races or genders.

Sociologists refer to this as *homophily,* the general finding that people prefer to interact with others who are like them—birds of a feather flock together.[7] We also found that experience matters, with more experienced teachers less likely to seek instructional advice or information from colleagues.

In a second study, this one involving twenty-eight elementary schools in two school districts (one suburban and one rural) in a midwestern state, we also found evidence that characteristics of individual teaching and administrative school staff members are associated with social interactions.[8] Building on our earlier findings, we noted that school staff with more experience were slightly less likely to either seek instructional advice and information from colleagues or to be sought out by colleagues for instructional advice and information.

Educational Infrastructure

In addition to individual characteristics, our work has found that the educational infrastructure, as represented by formal (leadership) positions and grade-level assignments, influences school staff members' instructional advice and information interactions. In both of the studies aspects of the educational infrastructure exercised a much stronger predictor of ties than individual characteristics such as gender or experience. Specifically, our quantitative analyses found that holding a formal leadership position—and a subject-specific leadership position in particular (e.g., a reading or math coach)—greatly increased the odds of school staff being sought out for instructional advice and information in that subject within their school.

Our qualitative work has built on these findings, exploring the *reasons* formal leaders are more often sought out for advice in schools. In analyses of interviews with a variety of school staff, we found that it was often the formal leaders' subject-specific expertise and specialized training, rather than their formal positions or titles, that contributed to teachers' desire to seek them out for instructional advice. Kelly, a second-grade teacher at Chamberlain Elementary in the suburban midwestern school district, explained: "If I have a question about math, well, my number one person is Mary of course, being the math coach. She's been through a lot of the training, she's had the desire and the passion for math . . . I go to her primarily." Kelly explained that she goes to Mary because of her position as "the math coach" and linked Mary's coach position with her expertise and training in mathematics. Explanations like Kelly's were commonplace in our interview data, capturing how school staff connected formal position explicitly to expertise in a school subject and, at times, also to the accompanying specialized training for the position.

Similarly, our quantitative analyses found that the more professional development a school staff member had relative to a colleague, the more likely they were to be sought out for advice or information. Teachers reporting more professional development hours were more likely to be sought out for advice and information about instruction by colleagues. At the same time, teachers who had more professional development were more likely to seek out advice and information from colleagues, suggesting that teachers with more professional development may be encouraged by school leaders to relay back to their colleagues the advice and information they gained through professional development.

Another aspect of the educational infrastructure associated with the presence of instructional advice and information ties between staff members within schools was grade-level assignment. In our work we have found that teachers teaching across multiple grade levels, such as those teaching special education or English as a second language, are less likely to provide advice or information than teachers who teach a single grade level. Moreover, teachers who teach the *same* grade are much more likely to have an instructional tie than teachers who teach different grade levels.

There are several ways in which teaching at the same grade level enables school staff interactions about instruction. First, teachers in the same grade are required to teach the same standards and curricula, potentially encouraging discussion about the instructional challenges they encounter as they plan with and implement the same curricular materials. Second, teachers teaching the same grade tend to be physically situation next to one another in the school building, and proximity may also enable interactions. Third, and perhaps most important, teachers in the same grade are more likely to participate in the same organizational routines, such as grade-level meetings, thus increasing their opportunities for advice-seeking about instruction and/or reducing any barriers (e.g., time) to making connections with colleagues. Rachel, a kindergarten teacher at Chamberlain Elementary, commented on the grade-level professional learning communities (PLC) routine, which all teachers at her school participated in weekly: "When we're planning together, if we have a question, [our math coach] is always there to help." She explained that the math coach knows "more about the curriculum. She's really good about saying . . . 'Don't miss this part' or 'This is what you really wanna have the kids get out of this.'" Rachel's account captures how the grade-level PLC routine facilitated intraschool interactions among teachers teaching the same grade and also enabled interactions with the school's math coach. All thirty-three school staff we interviewed in this school district identified participation in the grade-level PLC routine as being especially influential in shaping who they interacted with about instruction. Their accounts suggest that the importance of grade-level assignment to school leaders' and teachers' instructional interactions may be also accounted for by their participation in the same school routines, including grade-level PLCs.

Our analysis suggests that administrators keen on developing social capital should weigh decisions about leadership roles and teaching assignments. In terms of leadership assignments, administrators should think carefully about who is assigned to formal leadership positions (even part-time or zero-time teacher leadership positions that classroom teachers often hold) and if and how staff members are prepared to take on these leadership roles, as the teachers chosen for these roles are much more likely to provide instructional advice and information to their colleagues.

Our work also suggests that school leaders should strategically use professional development to promote social capital development, selecting those teachers best positioned to share advice or information about particular subjects to participate in specific professional development activities. Attention to participation in professional development is important, given that the returns from professional development are not simply the benefits of improving the information and skill of those who attend but may also be more indirect contributions to other staff members' on-the-job learning through the advice and information brought back to the school.

Decisions about grade-level teaching assignments are often based on teachers' experience or ability in working with a particular age group (e.g., primary versus upper elementary grades) or on ensuring that teachers work in grades with colleagues they get along with. Our analysis, however, finds that instructional ties are much more likely between teachers who teach the same grade level; teachers who teach multiple grades are less likely to provide or seek advice in schools. This suggests that administrators should take into account the general expertise of their teachers in assigning them to particular grades, as distributing more expert teachers across grades is more likely to ensure that their advice and information on a particular school subject is available to other staff members. Further, by selectively reassigning teachers to different grades from one year to the next, administrators may be able to create new ties around teaching among their staff over time. We recognize that there are trade-offs; administrators also have to take into account the fact that some teachers are more effective with particular grades—early versus later elementary grades—and that moving to a different grade increases a teacher's preparation time. Still, our work points to the importance of the consideration of instructional expertise in assigning teachers to grade levels within schools.

Physical Proximity

But it's not all about the educational infrastructure; the physical infrastructure also matters in shaping school staff members' interactions about instruction. We often take spatial arrangements in buildings for granted in efforts to understand work-related interactions among staff. Our exploration of the influence of physical proximity on social ties suggests that doing so is a mistake.

Our analysis of walking distances within schools finds that physical proximity influences work-related interactions among school staff. In our analysis of physical proximity and work-related ties in one of the midwestern districts we studied over four years, we found that the walking distance between school staff members' workspaces negatively predicted work-related interactions among school. That is, as the physical distance between staff *increases*, the likelihood of a them forming a tie decreases. Moreover, the effect of physical proximity on school staff interactions is independent of the other factors associated with work-related interactions, including teaching multiple grades, having a leadership position, years of experience in education, teaching the same grade, and network size.

Not content to rely solely on walking distance to measure physical proximity, we also examined whether staff members with overlapping "functional zones" were more likely to have a tie. An individual's "functional zone," the path traveled frequently during the course of the workday, captures "individual spheres of operation" in the workplace.[9] For our analyses, for example, we defined each staff member's functional zone as the paths between their workspace and two other key locations in the school, such as the principal's office and the building entrance/exit. We found that as the overlap of these functional zones between any two staff members increased, so did the likelihood of a work-related tie developing between them.

There are at least two ways physical proximity can contribute to interaction among school staff. First, the likelihood of a tie may decrease with increasing distance, because distance increases the "cost" of social interactions.[10] Clarissa, a fifth-grade teacher, explained that she had a close relationship with one of her colleagues "because we teach in the same manner, because we're next door to each other . . . Because we have that connecting door, it's just easier than across the hall." Second, distance matters because it influences exposure and thus the likelihood of chance encounters and opportunities for interaction.[11] Carol, a first-grade teacher described such a situation, when her school's first graders were doing a graphing activity: "We [other teachers in her grade level] were discussing the graph out in the hallway, and [a teacher in the same grade level] happened to walk by, and she just kind of sat down and joined us. And so then I just asked her for some feedback on how my conversation went and what I could have [done] to . . . deepen the kids' understanding."

Our analysis of the role of physical proximity in determining work-related ties in schools shows that the distance between individuals within the building matters. As with our findings on the educational infrastructure, this suggests that school administrators should be intentional about their assignment of staff members to work spaces (classrooms or offices) within their buildings. Although co-locating classrooms by grade level encourages interactions among teachers of the same grade, depending on the circumstances, administrators might also consider strategically locating teachers with certain subject area expertise throughout the building so as to increase the likelihood that other teachers are interacting with these expert teachers.

INTERSCHOOL INTERACTIONS ABOUT INSTRUCTION

As one might expect, the bulk of work-related interactions among school staff are with colleagues who are in the same building. In one study, for example, we examined interactions about language arts instruction in two school districts and found that nearly all were with colleagues who were in the same school (88 percent and 95 percent, respectively).[12] Still, interschool interactions are important because schools operate as local educational agencies (LEAs), or school districts. Although arrangements differ between and within states, the school district is the primary administrative unit for delivering education in the United States, collecting local taxes, and bearing responsibility for managing most state and federal funding.[13] Schools within a district share resources, such as funding and teachers, and rely on the same specialists to support teaching and efforts to improve it. Even under recent state and federal policy initiatives, school districts maintain a critical role in providing technical assistance to individual schools.[14] Although attention to both internal and external ties about teaching is necessary, a handful of studies have examined both intra- and interschool relations in local school districts.[15]

Similar to our intraschool findings, our research in the two midwestern school districts suggests that formal organizational arrangements supersede individual characteristics in creating ties around teaching *between* schools. More than anything else, having a formal leadership position predicts instructional advice and information seeking and providing between schools. In the schools we studied, subject-specific leaders (e.g., mathematics coach, language arts coordinator), as distinct from leaders who did not have a subject-specific position (e.g., principal), were more likely to seek out and provide instructional advice and information to staff in other schools than to staff in their own schools.

In some ways, the influential roles that subject-specific leaders played in brokering interschool relations was related to how district officials envisioned their work. Georgia, a district administrator, described how mathematics coaches were intentionally positioned to "push out" district initiatives across schools: "Our math coaches, we utilize them to impact districtwide. The curriculum will be pushed out as a district, and when I say 'district' it will come from curriculum committees, math coaches, and then be pushed out into the buildings. We have some very strong coaches who will be able to provide professional development to their peers." Georgia's comments suggest that coaches were charged with sharing information with teachers across multiple school sites and supporting interschool professional learning and development.

Again, these findings underscore the critical importance of how school districts and school leaders assign educators to leadership positions, especially subject-specific positions, recognizing that these individuals are most likely to broker relations between schools around matters of instruction (see figure 4.1).

We also found some evidence that school characteristics influence interschool interactions among school staff. Our analysis suggests that teachers in schools with similar student populations tend to share instructional advice and information more often than do teachers in schools with dissimilar populations. Specifically, in the two midwestern districts, schools that were more similar in terms of the percentages of students receiving free and reduced-price lunches were more likely to have ties among their staffs around language arts instruction. We found a similar pattern in one of these districts for mathematics learning and systemwide instructional improvement.

FIGURE 4.1 Between-school advice and information brokers in literacy and mathematics in one midwestern district, 2013

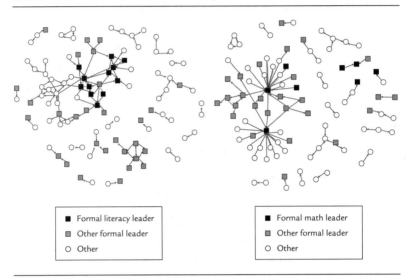

How School Subject Matters in Social
Interactions Among School Staff

In addition to language arts and mathematics instructional ties, our work also documents how the school subject matters when it comes to staff interactions about instruction, both intra- and interschool relations.[16] In one of the midwestern districts we found that interactions among elementary school staff about teaching differed depending on the school subject. Teachers and leaders communicated with more of their colleagues about teaching and learning related to language arts than about teaching related to mathematics or science. School language arts networks were on average 50 percent denser than mathematics networks and 150 percent denser than science networks, and mathematics networks were 66 percent denser than science networks. For example, at Kingsley Elementary, school staff were more likely to be connected to one another in language arts than in mathematics or science. Furthermore, the fragmentation of these advice networks increased from language arts to mathematics and science: in the science network, staff members were divided into five groups, whereas in the language arts and mathematics advice networks they comprised single groups (figure 4.2).

In terms of advice and information interactions, we found that Kingsley staff members were more likely to seek out advice about language arts than advice about mathematics and science (table 4.1). Whereas, on average, staff members across the district's schools

FIGURE 4.2 Kingsley Elementary School social network diagrams by subject, 2012

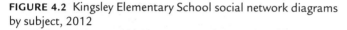

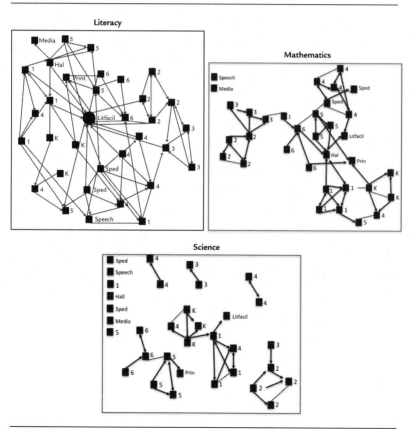

TABLE 4.1 Average centrality measures in subject matter networks, 2012

	Language arts	Mathematics	Science	Change from math to language arts	Change from science to math
In-degree	2.93	2.02	1.19	+45.0%	+69.7%
Out-degree	3.63	2.41	1.40	+50.6%	+72.1%
Betweenness	38.08	21.94	2.52	+73.6%	+770.6%

named three or four staff members as individuals they went to for advice about language arts, they named only two or three individuals in mathematics and just one or two in science. *In-degree* denotes the number of individuals seeking advice from an individual, whereas *out-degree* refers to how many others an individual seeks out for advice. So, for example, an individual with an in-degree of two has two individuals coming to them for advice; an individual with an out-degree of four seeks advice from four people.[17]

We also found substantial differences between school subjects with respect to brokering. Brokers are individuals who connect actors within the network and therefore may occupy more prominent positions in the network. On average, there was more brokering of advice related to teaching language arts than to teaching mathematics or science. Specifically, the average betweenness centrality (the measure of brokering) for language arts in one school district was 38.1, meaning that each staff member connected two other staff members about thirty-eight times. Betweenness centrality in language arts networks ranged from 7.5 to 61.0 across the fourteen schools in the district, showing that there was a large degree of variation in the degree to which individual teachers engaged in such brokering. For mathematics networks, the average betweenness centrality for school staff in the district was 21.9, ranging from 4.9 to 63.6. In science, brokering of advice was minimal overall, ranging from just 0.2 to 8.7 in the district's fourteen elementary schools.

We argue, therefore, that school leaders and system policy makers should take the school subject into consideration when investing in social capital, because the challenge of developing social capital likely differs depending on the school subject, even in elementary schools where most teachers are generalists. If school staff are less likely to seek out others for advice and information in some subjects, then the challenge of building social capital will differ by school subject. School leaders will have to work to motivate school staff to interact and create structures that enable these interactions.

THINKING SYSTEMICALLY

Our message is simple: system and school leaders can influence who talks to whom about instruction by strategically designing and redesigning their system and school-level educational infrastructure and attending to how teachers are physically located in their buildings. In doing so, they can shape interactions about teaching and learning and potentially build social capital. For example, administrators should take into account the instructional expertise of teachers in assigning them to particular grades and locations in their building. Ensuring such distribution across grades and locations in the building will more likely make the advice and information of the most expert teachers available to other staff members.

The challenge is somewhat more complex than it might appear at first blush, because system and school leaders must attend to how various components of their educational infrastructure, at both the system and school building levels, work *together and in interaction* to influence who talks to whom about teaching and learning. In this chapter we have intentionally isolated a few components of the educational infrastructure (formal position, grade-level assignment) in order to gauge their effects on interactions about instruction among school staff. But educational infrastructure includes a great many components—formal positions (mathematic lead teacher or coach), organizational routines (PLCs, grade-level meetings, instructional rounds), grade-level assignments, professional learning opportunities for teachers and school leaders, mathematics and language arts curricula, and so on. The design challenge for system and school leaders involves *strategically* and *systemically* working to ensure that these various components work together to support instruction and instructional improvement.

For example, in one of the midwestern school districts we studied, we documented how system and school leaders redesigned their educational infrastructure to support a particular vision for elementary school mathematics.[18] Our analysis captures how the school district's educational infrastructure redesign efforts to support an inquiry approach to mathematics instruction influenced interactions among school leaders and teachers and contributed to changes in teachers' beliefs about teaching mathematics. One of our key findings is that district leaders redesigned various components of the educational infrastructure not only to facilitate teacher interactions about mathematics but also to increase the likelihood that these interactions were anchored in a particular approach to teaching mathematics. District and school leaders intentionally designed and/or redesigned key components of the educational infrastructure, including system- and school-level organizational routines (e.g., the PLC routine at each grade level), a new mathematics curriculum, new mathematics teacher leader and coach positions at the school level, and professional development for mathematics leaders to support the implementation of an inquiry approach to mathematics instruction.

Our analysis shows how the different components of the infrastructure for mathematics education worked *in interaction* to shape how school leaders and teachers worked with one another on mathematics instruction and what these interactions focused on. The weekly PLC routine brought teachers together to talk about teaching and learning, the new mathematics curriculum created common instructional challenges for teachers to interact about as they worked to implement the curriculum in their classrooms, and the mathematics coaches and teacher leaders offered instructional advice during the weekly PLC meetings and more generally. Further, system-level organizational routines, including a monthly meeting of mathematics teacher leaders from each elementary school in the district, provided opportunities for district leaders to brainstorm on how best to address curriculum implementation challenges and created opportunities for mathematics teacher leaders to gain expertise for addressing these challenges in their buildings.

Our account captures how various components of the school system and school educational infrastructure do indeed influence intra- and interschool interactions about instruction among school leaders and teachers—interactions that are fundamental to developing social capital in school systems and schools. Yet these components do not function in isolation, and they should not be treated as such in practice or policy. By working to design and redesign their educational infrastructures, system and school leaders can attend to the development of social capital. Critically, they need to approach this design challenge by considering how the various components of their educational infrastructure for a particular school subject can interact to support the distribution of resources that support instruction and instructional improvement. Unfortunately, all too often in education the dominant operating approach is the silver bullet strategy—a course of action that undermines adopting a systemic approach where the primary concern is with how the various components of the educational infrastructure work in interaction rather than in isolation. It is time to change our strategy.

CHAPTER 5

Social Capital

An Untapped Resource
for Educational Improvement

CARRIE R. LEANA AND FRITS K. PIL

A century ago, the state supervisor of rural schools in West Virginia, Lyda Hanifan, described how a new school district supervisor worked closely with his teachers to really understand the 457 families in his thirty-three-square mile district. Efforts included having the teachers meet with parents and survey them regarding their needs. In addition to using the schools as a focal point for community gatherings, the teachers were encouraged to develop a deeper understanding of the history of their schools and communities. The schools became a means to improve not just the lives of the children attending them but also the broader community, as the teachers led evening classes for parents who wanted to develop an education and even brought in speakers to help improve farm yields. Student attendance improved dramatically year after year, and the communities where the schools were located benefited on a number of fronts. Hanifan coined the term *social capital* to describe the goodwill and social benefits that derived from these efforts.[1] More broadly, social capital refers to the resources embedded in the relationships among actors.[2]

Fast-forward one hundred years. Despite extensive evidence in the intervening period that social capital is a core component of school success, schools are often defined by models of individual teacher accountability, rather than by fundamental structures for learning and individual and community growth. Yet, instruction is premised on the primacy of the exchange of knowledge, a shared vision on the goals and benefits of learning, and trust and respect. These are at the heart of what make social capital such a critical component of school improvement efforts.

In this chapter we provide an overview of social capital and our research highlighting its benefits for enhancing student performance. As with all research on schools, knowing what matters and doing something about it are two very different things. So we also provide direction for policy change to facilitate and encourage the shift toward a school performance model predicated on the value of social capital.

THE THREE PILLARS OF SOCIAL CAPITAL

While the importance of social ties to the success of the educational process has long been recognized, the act of teaching has historically been a very individual and independent undertaking.[3] These norms are breaking down, however, and over the last two decades schools have increasingly been viewed as communities of professionals working together to generate, combine, and transmit knowledge.[4] Nevertheless, teachers tend to share only a limited amount of task-specific information and draw on a very small number of close ties for advice about teaching.[5] Explanations for the relatively low levels of instructionally oriented exchange include the unflattering conclusion that the best teachers want to maintain their status in an environment that offers little in the way of recognition and enhanced extrinsic rewards, as well as the proposition that less-able teachers may be unwilling to risk exposing their deficiencies and thus not engage in collaborative learning. Since the late 1990s, however, there has been an increasing emphasis in the academic literature on the value of high-quality interactions among teachers.[6]

In our own work, we emphasize the social dimensions of work as a critical factor to organizational performance in a number of contexts, ranging from auto plants to nursing homes.[7] In schools in particular, we undertook extensive large-scale studies of the social relations in urban public schools, collecting data from teachers, principals, students, and parents.[8] We asked the teachers about their relations with others teachers as well as with the leaders of their schools; we asked the parents about their views on the instructional practices in the schools; we obtained student achievement scores over time; and we had principals keep track of their activities. In our initial research in eighty-eight schools, we worked with teachers to develop a survey instrument that could assess three key dimensions of social capital: structural, relational, and cognitive.[9]

The structural dimension focuses on the content-related exchanges that occur between teachers—specifically, communication that is substantive and focused on instruction. This is often assessed by the number of interactions between pairs of teachers as well as by the percentage of all pairs of teachers within a group who could potentially be communicating with one another about instruction (e.g., the fraction of all potential pairs of teachers in a grade-level team who engage in such exchange). This interaction helps teachers understand how knowledge in use differs from formal practice. As teachers engage in reflective dialogue, and relate critical incidents and anecdotes, they enhance individual as well as collective efforts.

Complementing the structural dimension of social capital is the relational dimension, which evolves from the repeated interactions among teachers and is most prominently manifested as trust. When teachers trust one another, the structural component of social capital is characterized by richer exchanges. They are more likely to allow themselves to be vulnerable—to ask questions if they want to extend their learning, or be willing to admit when they do not know something and need help. This provides clear benefits to the school and its students, as well as to the individual teacher.

Finally, as teachers engage in rich dialogue and exchange, we see the emergence of the cognitive dimension of social capital. Teachers develop a shared understanding of the goals they wish to attain and a shared vision of what it means to be effective. This reduces the likelihood that any given teacher will feel like an outsider, and self-interested behavior becomes less prevalent as teachers become more willing to subordinate personal goals to those of the collective. Teachers feel a sense of responsibility toward one another, the agendas they have set, and efforts to facilitate and embrace collective action.

Not surprisingly, having rich communication, high trust, and a shared vision of what the collective's goals and actions should be leads to better outcomes. In our initial study in schools, we found that when teachers reported high levels of social capital in their schools, student performance on both reading and mathematics improved dramatically. Particularly for math, improvements in performance were mediated by enhanced instructional practice. In a later study, we built on our initial research and followed more than one thousand teachers in 239 grade teams.[10] We were able to link teacher reports on their social exchanges, centered specifically on math instruction, to the growth in math achievement scores of their 24,187 individual students. We found that when social capital was high in a grade-level team, student performance improved significantly. Indeed, a one standard deviation increase in team social capital improved the average performance of individual students of those teachers by an average of 5.7 percent. To put that improvement in perspective, student eligibility for free lunch for this same sample was associated with an average reduction of 7.3 percent in student achievement growth. In this regard, social capital could go a long way toward offsetting the effects of poverty. These results confirm those of our earlier research: social capital is a powerful tool for improving student learning.

SOCIAL CAPITAL IN RELATION
TO HUMAN CAPITAL

One of the earliest researchers on social exchanges and their effect on educational outcomes, James Coleman, argued that social capital should be considered a form of capital like any other: "Just as physical capital is created by making changes in materials so as to form tools that facilitate production, human capital is created by changing persons so as to give them skills and capabilities that make them able to act in new ways. Social capital, in turn, is created when the relations among persons change in ways that facilitate action."[11] In our research we show that social capital has important implications in its own right but that it also interacts in meaningful ways with other forms of capital. Looking specifically at human capital, we examined the relationship of social capital in the school, teacher human capital, and student achievement.

Here we found that teacher skill bears a nuanced relationship to social capital. The ties among teachers can take different forms. Teachers can be embedded in communities where people talk frequently, regardless of the depth of those conversations. Conversely, they can have deep conversations, but only with a limited number of people. In our study of one-thousand-plus teachers, we took a close look at the relationship between human capital and social capital. What we found was that more-able teachers (those with the strongest human capital) benefited from strong ties with other teachers, even if the number of such ties was not large. But for less-able teachers the benefits came from having denser ties—that is, being involved in a team of teachers who communicated frequently on instructional content and where there was widespread participation in such conversations. Thus, the teachers with higher levels of human capital benefited most from strong ties. Teachers with lower levels of human capital benefited most from dense ties. For these teachers, what mattered most was that conversations about instruction took place frequently and included a large number of other teachers on the team.

By linking social capital to human capital, we can also begin to understand why an individual teacher would contribute to social capital. As has been observed by many, the contributions that enrich the community of teachers can come at a cost to the individual.[12] Sharing information takes time and effort, and some degree of free riding would be expected.[13] When brought to its logical extreme, such free riding ultimately risks killing the collaboration and exchange that define the very essence of social capital. While social capital does require effort, part of what we observed in our research is that this effort centers on redirecting the nature of exchanges and conversations that often already take place. In particular, we observe that effective social capital in schools is not so much about having more conversations with peers but about shifting the nature of conversation to be more instructionally focused (e.g., questions about math concepts or effective ways to reach an individual student) rather than general talk about district policies or the state of the world. With a focus on content, teachers learn from their colleagues, develop new insights on how to teach, benefit from the camaraderie and social support that comes with shared vision and trust, and also substantively change their practice in a way that generates tangible improvements in students' outcomes.

One important conclusion is that the training teachers receive, and how it can benefit the collective, provides a useful pathway to enhancing the quality of the discourse that takes place in the school. We suspect that the historical push for continuing education is due to the economics orientation of many policy makers, who treat human capital as a resource that belongs to the organization. However, taking a more psychological perspective, aggregating individual knowledge does not explain how the collectivity of knowledge facilitates performance. Linking human capital to social capital is an important step in this direction and a way for policy makers to expand their thinking beyond dated requirements that teachers sit through a given number of professional development hours each year. In particular, professional development can provide an important pathway to developing shared vision, as well as what psychologists call "transactive memory."[14] Transactive memory is important because it provides insight regarding which of the teachers who received training can provide help ex post on particular facets of implementation. In the same vein, stability in teacher assignments in particular schools, along with professional development that is specific to the subject matter, may be better investments by school districts than general requirements for professional development hours.

THE IMPORTANCE OF EXTERNAL TIES

Despite the many benefits of social capital, there are instances where it can have significant drawbacks. Crime syndicates, for example, work directly against societal interests yet may display rich information flows, high trust, shared vision, and the collective identity associated with social capital. Studying the case of Colombian drug cartels, Mauricio Rubio terms this "perverse social capital."[15] But all forms of perverse social capital need not be based on nefarious interests. Indeed, teachers could trust one another, engage in extensive interaction, and have a shared vision and identity, but that shared vision may be one that is, at best, indifferent to student learning.

One characteristic of perverse social capital is that it tends to emerge in communities that are isolated. We have focused so far on the social capital that is developed within the school context, what academics often refer to as "bonding" social capital. While the commonality in purpose and sense of identity that such capital generates can be a source of great benefit, it also poses risks when group perspectives are too insular or parochial. The associated loyalties and bonds run the risk of becoming so strong that they crowd out external ideas and insight and discourage the exploration of perspectives from outside of the group. The risk of such insularity has been documented in a broad range of contexts, but it is especially prominent in the area of innovation. Insular design teams and firms, for example, can develop communication mechanisms and shared perspectives that lead to very successful refinement of existing products and processes. But if communication is limited only to those within the team, members often lack the ability to embrace fundamentally new and important ideas that can transform the market they depend on.

The solution is to build external ties as a means of providing a useful sounding board for ideas, sources of new perspectives, social support, and resources. Yet, despite the advantages, we see relatively little of this "bridging" social capital in school systems. For example, a few years ago New York City reorganized its principals into networks, but only a small number used their network to actively foster lateral idea and information exchange with other principals. We have, however, seen successful examples initiated by both the United Federation of Teachers and the Council of School Supervisors and Administrators, which have purposefully put into place programs to develop and foster exchange between their members across schools.

Having ties that cross school boundaries can certainly benefit the individual teacher. This is likely obvious to anyone who's used LinkedIn for a job search or online community forums to get information. But actively fostering connections to other communities of teachers, educators, and others is also helpful from an instructional standpoint. In addition to providing new perspectives that allow the teacher to question her instructional approach and develop new skills and ideas, the same external networks can provide opportunities for that teacher to influence others in her group. For example, for new teachers, participation in external networks can be a source of emotional support, a pathway toward legitimation in their new position, and a resource to the existing teachers in the school they are joining. Such resources enhance the status of the new teacher, identifying her as a productive member of the school community.

We also found evidence regarding the value of crossing status boundaries within the school. We found that the students of teachers who reported strong ties to principals and other school administrators showed higher growth in math achievement. However, the underlying dynamics driving these effects are not well understood. As with much of the traditional management research on leader-subordinate relations, in the education literature any attention to such relationships in schools has tended to focus on the principal and her leadership style rather than the interaction between principals and teachers. Yet we have heard from a number of principals that they often seek advice from the strongest teachers in the school. Efforts to involve teachers in this manner can lead to enhanced trust between teachers and administration. In addition, relatively simple matters, such as the degree of control a school administrator has, may be important to improving administrator-teacher ties.

HOW DO WE INVEST IN SOCIAL CAPITAL?

As our research has demonstrated, teacher social capital can have a powerful influence on student achievement, dwarfing the benefits of teacher education, credentialing, and other forms of human capital. At the same time, social capital can be the conduit that amplifies human capital and ensures that less-able teachers can learn from their high-performing counterparts. Not surprisingly, the most frequent question we are asked when we present our work to teachers, school administrators, and policy makers is, "How do I enhance social capital in my school?" This is a question that does not have a quick or simple answer. Building social capital takes time, nurturing it takes commitment, and both are in short supply in many districts that are pressed to deliver immediate results. Social capital is also context specific, so there is no precise recipe for success. What works best in one school may not work best in the next.

What we *can* offer, however, are evidence-based principles for building and sustaining school social capital. We organize our prescriptions around three complimentary and mutually reinforcing objectives: enhancing teacher embeddedness in the school; creating a school culture of collaboration rather than competition among teachers; and training and rewarding principals to be change agents through their external relationships.

Enhance Teacher Embeddedness in the School

Social capital takes time to build and is shaken by instability. Such instability in schools often takes the form of teacher turnover. Some schools in our large-scale research studies had annual teacher turnover rates approaching 40 percent, and the leadership in such schools was equally unstable. While some level of turnover is generally positive for a system in terms of promoting innovation and beneficial change, high levels of turnover can be detrimental for two reasons. First, while new people bring new ideas, what can be lost is a sense of history and core mission, or "institutional memory."[16] Second, several studies have shown that turnover results in decreased organizational performance.[17] In a large-scale study of more than 180 schools, Irina Shevchuk, Carrie Leana, and Vikas Mittal found that losses in human and social capital due to turnover worked synergistically in influencing the effect of teacher retention on student achievement. Essentially, when turnover resulted in social capital losses in the school, subsequent student performance declined.[18]

While these findings provide an evidence-based argument for the beneficial effects of stability in the teaching body of a school, the popular press (as well as political discourse) is rife with accusations of "dead wood" in schools and implicitly calls for more, rather than less, turnover of teachers. Moreover, highly experienced teachers seem to be the targets of such calls. Indeed, programs like Teach For America have as their implicit foundation the assumption that new college graduates with no teaching experience (or even a background in studying education) will do a better job in the classroom than those who have spent their careers as teachers. Evidence from our own research counters such assumptions. Indeed, in our research, teacher experience was the only dimension of human capital that even came close to the beneficial effects of social capital on student outcomes.

A high rate of retention preserves not only the knowledge, skills, and abilities of teachers (human capital) but also the existing structure and character of the relationships among them (social capital). Strong and dense ties among teachers within a school can serve as a source of actual and potential resources. But these resources become inaccessible once the relationships are dissolved due to turnover. And stability in the social structure of a school is a key factor affecting the creation and maintenance of its social capital. As James Coleman noted decades ago, "Disruptions of social organization or of social relations can be highly destructive to social capital."[19] By fostering stable social relations in a school, teacher retention thus facilitates the creation and maintenance of social capital. In this regard, school administrators should focus on teacher retention as an explicit policy goal.

Create a School Culture of Collaboration Rather than Competition

Most of the attention in school reform is centered on improving teacher human capital, the knowledge, skills, and abilities that individual teachers bring to the classroom, and is at the heart of policy proposals ranging from pay-for performance schemes to test-based evaluations of teacher performance. Even programs with nonpunitive aspects like "Teacher of the Year" awards implicitly assume that problems of school performance will be best remedied through a laser focus on individual teachers.

Our research findings challenge such approaches and argue for more cooperation rather than competition among teachers. Indeed, we found in our large-scale studies that the benefits of enhanced social capital on student achievement far outweigh those of human capital. A one standard deviation increase in teacher human capital (as measured by a validated test of ability) was associated with just a 2.2 percent gain in student achievement scores, while the same one standard deviation rise in social capital was associated with a 5.7 percent gain, an effect size almost three times greater.

In reviewing the empirical evidence, it is clear that social capital represents an important opportunity for school improvement. Yet, getting school administrators and policy makers to see the value of social capital is not easy. And holding them accountable for it is harder still. One way to address this impasse is to make social capital a core component in formal evaluations of administrator effectiveness. School principals could be held responsible for conducting a social capital inventory in their schools and measuring the outcomes of increases or decreases in social capital. Such an inventory might include opportunities for teacher collaboration, programs for new teacher mentoring, retention rates of teachers, and the like. Outcomes of interest might include teacher attitude surveys as well as student achievement gains. What such an inventory would *not* include, however, is so-called instructional leadership (a topic we discuss in more detail below); the role of administrators is to value and facilitate the formation and maintenance of teacher social capital, not to plan, organize, and control it. Efforts aimed at the latter are bound to fail, as they undermine the very nature of social capital, which is predicated on trust, open information exchange, and shared values. These cannot be legislated by overeager "instructional leaders," but they can be facilitated by providing resources in the form of rewards for peer-to-peer learning, school-based incentives, and, most valuable of all, time in the school day for collaboration.[20]

Another opportunity for building social capital is in the area of labor-management collaboration. It is fashionable now to lament the role of teacher unions in terms of the problems with public education in the United States. Unions are said to protect poor teachers from being remediated or dismissed from their jobs even with evidence of substandard performance. Unions are also held responsible for enforcing a tenure system that rewards longevity over competence and undermines management discretion in the selection of new teachers.

Lesser known is the beneficial effects teacher unions have had in providing much-needed stability in schools and in providing a path to building social capital. Saul Rubinstein and John McCarthy's studies of labor-management collaboration across several schools and districts are instructive in terms of both the benefits of collaboration for student learning and the ways in which such collaboration can be attained.[21] And we have found similar effects in our own work. Given this evidence, instead of being viewed as a detriment to building teacher human capital within schools (e.g., because of enforcing rules on seniority protections), unions could be more fruitfully viewed as incubators for cultivating social capital.

Train and Reinforce Principals to Network Outside of School Boundaries

One of our first research projects regarding teacher social capital included all teachers and schools in a midsized urban district.[22] We assessed teacher social capital but also focused on the role of the principal. During the course of this study, we asked each principal to keep a time diary in which they recorded all of their activities during a typical work week. We were interested in both how the principals spent their time and who they spent it with. We then looked at differences in time use and how well they predicted student achievement gains in math and literacy.

Our results were illuminating on a number of dimensions. First, there was a great deal of variability regarding the sheer amount of time principals put into their jobs. On average, they worked about 48 hours per week; but there was great variability in the amount of time worked, ranging from a low of 37 hours to a high of 61 hours per week. Moreover, the total amount of time they spent at work was unrelated to student achievement gains. This suggests that it is not the amount of time spent on the job that matters but how that time is allocated.

We separated the various activities into four different domains: (1) instructional leadership, which consisted of activities such as classroom observations, teacher development, and working on instruction and curriculum; (2) administration, which consisted of activities such as school record keeping, facilities management, and the like; (3) external relations, which included interactions with people outside the school, including community members, potential supporters, and parents; and (4) personal development. By far the largest drain on principals' time was administration, with principals spending an average of more than 27 hours (or 57 percent) of their time on these activities each week. The smallest category was personal development, on which they spent, on average, about an hour and a half (or 3 percent) of their time per week.

In studying the effects of social capital, we were most interested in the time principals spent interacting with others, whether teachers within the school or stakeholders outside the school. Here we found that principals spent, on average, about 25 percent (about 12 hours per week) of their time on instructional leadership of teachers and roughly 14 percent (more than 6 hours per week) on interactions with supporters or potential supporters outside the school. Instructional leadership can be thought of as an indicator of principals' efforts to organize and control internal social capital, while external relations is an indicator of principals' efforts to build external social capital.

Here our findings were surprising regarding the benefits of principals' activities for students. Neither administrative tasks nor instructional leadership moved the needle in terms of student achievement gains. But the opposite was true for activities aimed at building external social capital. Essentially, principals' time spent building external social capital was the *only* activity that had a significantly positive effect on student achievement gains. The lesson from these findings is simple and clear: principals can have the biggest impact on student achievement—and, in fact, the only significant impact—if they focus their time on developing relationships outside the school.

Needless to say, these findings were not well received by that portion of the education community that is invested in the value of instructional leadership by principals. But these results are, to our knowledge, the only rigorous examination of what principals actually do all day and the effects of their day-to-day activities on student learning. While there are numerous studies of "school culture" and a veritable cottage industry promoting "principal leadership," most of this research does not examine how principals actually spend their time. Indeed, when we asked principals to report on their perceptions of how they spent their time, there was a good deal of inconsistency between what they told us and their actual behavior. (The old admonition to "watch what I do, not what I say" is an appropriate lesson here in terms of guiding future researchers on more rigorous approaches to studying principal leadership.)

But our findings were quite well received by teachers who indicated repeatedly that they would like their principals to spend far more time cultivating external relations and far less time acting in the role of "line foreman" and monitoring teachers' instructional practice. In general, teachers believed that their principals could be far more effective if they spent more time with parents, community leaders, and potential sponsors, as well as "running interference" with district leadership.

In terms of policy recommendations, these findings suggest that principal selection and training ought to be geared more toward developing expertise in activities outside the school. Such external networks bring benefits in several ways. First, the principal can act as *innovator,* bringing teachers different perspectives and "best practices" from the outside, whether that be from other schools, other districts, or other types of organizations. Second, the principal can act as *ambassador* for the school, securing support and other resources from parents, community groups, and potential funders. Third, the principal can *champion* the school, impressing on district leaders the school's unique strengths as well as its needs.

CONCLUSION

Despite extensive reform efforts over the last decades, especially in schools with disadvantaged students—be it curricular reform, site-based management, varied forms of student assessment, teacher penalties and incentives, etc.—the payoffs have not been as great as one might hope.[23] Clearly, a fresh, evidence-based approach is needed. A common refrain when we visit schools is "we've tried that," with *that* being everything and anything school districts have thought of that could improve instruction, such as standardized curricula, coaches, long instructional blocks, frequent student assessment, etc. Indeed, there is a palpable sense of burnout with respect to new initiatives to improve instruction and student outcomes.

Yet, rarely heard in conversations with school administrators is a deep exploration of how a given change can enhance or adversely affect the nature of social exchange that takes place among the professionals in the school. Indeed, our findings regarding social capital help explain why efforts like teacher merit pay programs have had little effect on student outcomes when the incentives are provided to individual teachers but have a substantive effect when given to school-level groups of teachers.[24]

Social capital is key in efforts to enhance the educational process. At the same time, it is important to situate efforts in the broader context of other school reform changes. For example, there are ongoing efforts to routinize and standardize how teachers teach. We know from other contexts that such approaches can work well when organizations are dealing with well-specified products to be developed or well-articulated problems to be solved. But they have not been shown to be very effective for complex, evolving challenges, like those associated with public education. In such circumstances, collaborative approaches have been shown to be far more beneficial, as multiple individuals can bring ideas to the table to provide insight on how to address issues, resolve problems, or embrace opportunities. Teams with high levels of social capital provide solidarity, and the norms of exchange that emerge enable the collective to target ambitious goals and address setbacks and challenges.

Such an approach is sorely needed in public schools. But social capital, and the relationships that sustain it, do not emerge automatically. It requires time, active effort to encourage its development, and persistence. But its demonstrated benefits for teachers and students alike well justify the effort. Simply stated, attention to social capital in schools is long overdue.

CHAPTER 6

The Social Cost
of Leadership Churn

The Case of an Urban School District

ALAN J. DALY, KARA S. FINNIGAN, AND YI-HWA LIOU

Educational policy in the United States has remained focused on eliminating the persistent achievement gap through legislation requiring greater use of research-based evidence and increased accountability at all levels of the system. This has occurred while a growing national push has caused school and district leaders to systematically collect, interpret, and use data, particularly student test data, for decision making. Within any system, the interpretation and use of evidence for improvement takes place through formal and informal social networks, as individuals interact to co-construct, make sense, and learn as an organization.[1] These learning interactions can be significantly disrupted when a high percentage of actors leave or enter the system, which can negatively impact organizational outcomes.[2]

Recent work suggests that as many as one-quarter of the country's principals leave schools each year, with approximately half quitting their role by the third year in the position.[3] This enormous departure is particularly severe in high-poverty schools that serve our nation's most underserved populations. Although the departure of principals and teachers is extremely detrimental to progress, reform, and consistency, the discussion often overlooks the fact that central office leaders are also leaving systems at high rates. We know that educational leadership matters for educational improvement, and, further, the literature also suggests that it takes around five years for educational reforms to take hold.[4] Absent consistent leadership, there is the potential for a cascading disruptive impact of churn from the superintendent's office down to the classroom. Ultimately, students are the recipients of disjointed reforms, constant flux, and uneven progress.

While the majority of educational literature focuses on turnover as the movement out of the system, we look at both departure and arrival of actors within a given network, because there are significant and distinct costs associated with both the exit of individuals (loss of knowledge, social support, organizational memory, training and development) and the entrance of new actors (training, learning both technical and social systems).[5] In general, the limited literature on churn argues that an organization's development and improvement is dependent on the extent to which members make contributions (either actual or potential) to organizational learning, knowledge, and innovation.[6] While there may be some benefits of churn if weaker individuals leave, constant churn is disruptive to overall organizational success given the loss of fiscal, human, and social capital that it produces.

In this chapter we provide an overview of the literature on leadership stability/churn and its relationship with social capital, system performance, and complex change before turning to a discussion of the results and implications of our recent exploratory case study of a large urban district where we followed 257 district and site leaders over a three-year period.

THE COST OF LEADERSHIP INSTABILITY

While definitions of *churn* vary, the most common use of the term in education is connected with turnover as well as the intention to leave a system.[7] But few studies have examined churn by looking at the formation of new social ties, retention of existing ones, and the loss of preexisting ties at the individual level.[8]

Churn involves substantial costs in terms of training, development, and infrastructure. For example, an estimate for principal preparation programs indicates that the average cost of preparing a new leader ranges from $50,000 to over $100,000.[9] In addition, there is a wide range of other expenses involved when a leader is replaced, including human resources costs ($20,000 per senior leader), transitional training ($50,000–$85,000), onboarding ($5,500–$7,500), and professional development.[10] These studies suggest that the cost of turnover of one hundred leaders in a large school district within three years, as is the case in our study, may add up to millions of dollars. These dollar figures do not account for the additional costs to the system in terms of lost knowledge, support, expertise, and potential damage to efforts at scaling up reform.

For decades, researchers and policy makers have raised the public's attention to the critical and negative influence of high turnover rates.[11] Despite these efforts, some researchers have estimated that about 15 percent to 33 percent of leaders across a typical district vacate their positions each year.[12] Studies have also indicated that principal turnover can lead to teacher turnover, which more directly impacts student achievement.[13] In addition, superintendent turnover has been well documented, with nearly half of all superintendents leaving their positions within three years.[14]

A few studies in management have attempted to understand some of the factors associated with churn. For example, Scott Soltis and colleagues found that leaders who are most sought for relationships but receive less reward and recognition tend to leave the system.[15] In contrast, leaders who seek out others and perceive that they have the opportunity to learn and develop are more likely to stay.[16]

CHURN, SOCIAL CAPITAL,
AND SOCIAL NETWORK THEORY

To unpack and frame our understanding of churn, we draw on the theoretical literature on social capital and social networks within organizations. As Nan Lin suggests, social capital consists of "the resources embedded in social relations and social structure which can be mobilized when an actor wishes to increase the likelihood of success in purposive action."[17] At the heart of Lin's words is the idea that the quantity and quality of relationships in a social network influence the process of learning and change and are therefore important aspects to attend to when looking at relationships.[18] This perspective entails a move from a primary focus on the individual to understanding the dynamic supports and constraints of the larger social infrastructure.[19] Social network studies focus on how the constellation of relationships facilitates and constrains the flow of "relational resources" (knowledge, practices, etc.), and provide insight into how individuals gain access to, are influenced by, and leverage these resources.[20]

The concept of network structure is important for understanding how resources are exchanged among individuals and groups within an organization.[21] Social network theorists posit that dense structures facilitate a more efficient flow of ideas and information, since it takes less time and fewer steps for these resources to move from one actor to another.[22] Networks that have a dense structure generally achieve at higher levels of performance than those characterized by sparse connections.[23]

The individual network position deserves equal attention, as it indicates the degree of an actor's influence and popularity in a given network, which, in turn, affects the flow of resources across a network.[24] Actors who possess a more central network position with more ties tend to have greater influence over the network, since they are able to connect with others for diverse resources. In contrast, peripheral actors tend to be connected with less relational resources.[25] In addition to central and peripheral network positions, "brokers" are critical in how resources flow within a network; as their name suggests, these individuals link actors who are disconnected from one another.[26] Actors occupying a broker position have greater influence and power over a network both in terms of their connecting role and in their power to filter, coordinate, or distort the resources (e.g., information) that flow throughout the system. While the balance of scholarship on social networks suggests that relational ties facilitate communication and knowledge transfer at all levels of the system, little attention has been paid to the ways in which churn reduces this potential by disrupting the network.

HOW CHURN DISRUPTS A NETWORK'S ABILITY TO IMPROVE

While studies of churn have often focused on this top level of leadership or the ground level of teachers, we argue that it is critical to examine churn across the entire system of leaders. Understanding churn from a systems perspective is important, since a growing body of work suggests the nested nature of reform efforts and the importance of diffusion across a system. This idea is what animates this chapter and sets the stage for examining La Urbana Unified School District.[27]

La Urbana Unified School District employs more than 14,000 individuals across 223 educational facilities. This district serves over 130,000 preK–12 students from 15 ethnic groups (approximately 45.7 percent Hispanic, 23.9 percent white, 11.8 percent African American, 5.1 percent Indo-Chinese, and 3.3percent Asian, Native American, Pacific Islander, and multiracial/ethnic) who speak more than 60 languages. And it employs approximately 7,500 educators and almost 900 pupil services employees (bus drivers, grounds, facilities, etc.).

In the summer of 2010 (the first year of the study), the district was divided into eight "areas," each comprising up to three high school clusters (elementary and middle schools that feed the high school). These areas are loosely organized by geography, and each is served by an area superintendent who has responsibility over approximately twenty schools. As the primary point of contact, support, and input on evaluation for principals, area superintendents are formally responsible for connecting the central office to the school sites as well as coordinating articulation between schools within each area. Also in 2010, the district's governing board adopted a strategic process that set forth the explicit goal of creating a quality school in every neighborhood within five years. Approximately one year after adopting the plan, La Urbana was identified by the state board of education (SBE) as requiring corrective actions due to the failure of many of its schools to meet Adequate Yearly Progress under the No Child Left Behind Act.

At three points during the study, conducted between 2010 and 2013, the research team collected data that included the leaders' demographic information, various social aspects related to their work, and self-reported perceptions of the district's organizational learning climate (table 6.1 and table 6.2). A total of 257 unique district and site leaders (superintendent, assistant superintendent, directors, supervisors, and school principals) were included in the study at time point one (T1). Nearly all the leaders (95 percent) participated in the survey at T1. Among these 257 leaders at T1, about 29 percent were district leaders, 71 percent were school principals, and 63 percent were female. These leaders had an average of eleven years of experience serving in administration (SD = 6.5) and five years in their current position (SD = 3.9). When examining the group that stayed in the district from T1 to T3 (remainers) and the other representing

TABLE 6.1 Sample characteristics of all leaders at T1

	All leaders	Remainers	Leavers
Gender			
Female	164 (63.1%)	128 (63.1%)	36 (63.2%)
Male	96 (36.9%)	75 (36.9%)	21 (36.8%)
Role			
District leader	75 (28.8%)	48 (23.6%)	27 (47.4%)
Site leader	185 (71.2%)	155 (76.4%)	30 (52.6%)
Years in administration			
≤ 8 years	87 (33.5%)	72 (36.7%)	15 (26.0%)
8–12 years	85 (32.7%)	67 (34.2%)	18 (31.5%)
≥ 13 years	81 (31.2%)	57 (29.1%)	24 (42.5%)
Years at current position			
≤ 2 years	85 (32.7%)	62 (31.2%)	23 (46.0%)
3–6 years	77 (29.6%)	60 (30.2%)	17 (34.0%)
≥ 7 years	94 (36.2%)	77 (38.7%)	17 (34.0%)

Notes: N = 257. Numbers reported in cells are frequency, with percentages in parentheses.

TABLE 6.2 Descriptive statistics of all T1 leaders

	All leaders	Remainers	Leavers
Years of experience			
Years in administration	11.3 (6.5)	10.8 (6.1)	13.2 (7.7)
Years at current position	5.1 (3.9)	5.4 (4.0)	3.8 (3.4)
Network position			
Expertise indegree	7.0 (8.3)	6.3 (7.1)	9.7 (11.3)
Expertise outdegree	7.0 (10.1)	6.4 (7.9)	9.5 (15.4)
Expertise betweenness (%)	0.7 (2.0)	0.5 (1.0)	1.5 (3.7)

Notes: N = 257. Numbers reported in cells are mean; standard deviation in parentheses.

those who leave the district at T2 or T3 (leavers), we did not see a difference based on gender, but we do note that leavers were more likely to be district leaders than site leaders and in administration longer but in their current position a shorter amount of time.[28]

Over the course of three years, the district had a 33 percent churn rate, indicating that a third of the district and site leaders either left or entered the district during that time period. Of these leaders, 57 percent left the district within three years, and 44 percent were new to the district during the same period. Importantly, some positions were restructured or left unfilled.

On average, leaders in this district both sought out and received seven other leaders for work-related expertise (table 6.2), with incoming ties (indegree) ranging between 0 and 41 ties (SD = 8.3) and outgoing ties (outdegree) ranging between 0 and 72 ties (SD = 10.1). We note larger variation in leaders' expertise-seeking behavior than in their expertise-receiving behavior. In addition, the leaders connected to less than 1 percent of two otherwise disconnected leaders in the expertise network, with betweenness (how often a leader connects two otherwise disconnected actors) measuring at less than 18 percent (SD = 2.0). In a sense, these individuals are like brokers, linking together those in the system. It is also important note that since this is one of the first studies of its type, we can present only the data here, not a normative assessment of the amount of interaction.

Figure 6.1 illustrates the difference in leaders' network positions for those who remain. The nodes denote individual leaders, and the lines represent exchanges of work-related information, with arrows indicating the direction of nomination, whether someone nominated or was nominated as a source of expertise. The shape of the nodes represents the leader's role, and they are clustered into their district's zones, with the central office leaders in the middle and the principals and their area superintendents in the surrounding clusters.

FIGURE 6.1 Expertise network of leaders over time

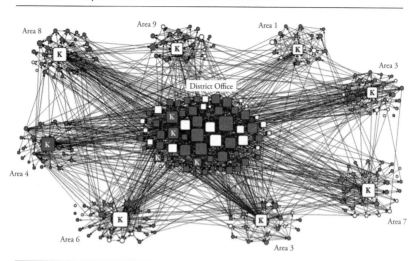

Notes: N=257. This network sociogram represents the pattern of seeking, and being re-garded as reliable, sources of expertise on a weekly basis. Nodes are sized by indegree, shaped by position (square = district leader; circle = site principals), colored by churn sta-tus (gray = remainer, white = leaver), and positioned by work area. K represents the key brokers identified by the KeyPlayer algorithm

The nodes are sized by the number of incoming ties: the larger the node, the more incoming ties a leader receives from others; the more incoming ties, the more the leader is regarded as a source of exper-tise by her peers. Central office leaders (square nodes) tend to be the most central and influential actors, as suggested by the larger sizes of many of these nodes relative to circle nodes (principals). Approx-imately 50 percent of the most central leaders (the 10 percent with the greatest number of incoming ties) left the district during the pe-riod of the study. Many of these individuals were in critical area su-perintendent positions.

One of the applications of social network analysis is in identi-fying key players, those who, if removed from the network, would cause the network to break apart into disconnected groups and indi-viduals. These leaders are critical to holding the system together, to making sure there are the connections necessary to move information through the system.

The KeyPlayer algorithm results indicate that the several leaders regarded as reliable sources of expertise are the same ones who left the district during the study's time period. For example, all but one of the area superintendents were key players and yet left the district, though some were not as central in the expertise network as others. But several less-central leaders from central office who were also identified as key players also left the district during this time. Thus, their departures caused disruption in the overall network, potentially impairing improvement efforts.

To learn more about the leaders who left the system we examined the relationship between their background as well as their network characteristics and their leaving behavior. The regression results in table 6.3 indicate that leaders who worked at the central office were more likely to leave than school site leaders. In addition, all three models demonstrate that leaders with more years of experience as an administrator and fewer years of experience in their current position were more likely to leave the district. This indicates that those leavers who might have moved to different positions across the district over the three years ended up leaving the district.

The results show some important differences with regard to the position of the leaders within the network. First, as Model 1 suggests, leaders who are sought by other leaders for their expertise (expertise indegree) are almost two times more likely to leave the district. Model 2 suggests no statistically significant association between a leader's expertise-seeking behavior (expertise outdegree) and the likelihood of leaving the district; that is, whether or not leaders actively seek expertise from others does not affect the likelihood of leaving the district. Finally, confirming the key player result, Model 3 suggests that being a broker in the expertise network (expertise betweenness) is positively associated with the likelihood of leaving the

TABLE 6.3 Logistic regression models on the likelihood of being a leaver

	Model 1			Model 2			Model 3		
	B	SE	Exp(B)	B	SE	Exp(B)	B	SE	Exp(B)
Constant	-0.42	.38	0.65	-0.13	.37	0.88	1.08	.46	2.93
Work level (site)	-1.05	.25	0.35***	-0.87	.25	0.42***	-0.98	.26	0.38***
Years in administration	0.49	.14	1.63**	0.49	.14	1.64***	0.46	.14	1.58**
Years at current position	-0.32	.15	0.73*	-0.47	.14	0.63**	-0.47	.14	0.63**
Network position									
Expertise indegree	1.86	.54	6.40**						
Expertise outdegree				0.51	.36	1.66			
Expertise betweenness							0.56	.27	1.76*
NagelkerkeR²	.19			.15			.15		
Model χ^2	55.42***			42.83***			45.12***		

Notes: N = 257 based on T1. Maximum likelihood estimation is used as the regression method in the models. Leave status coded as 1 for those who left and 0 for those who remained. *$p < .05$, **$p < .01$, ***$p < .001$.

district: those leaders who were better able to link two disconnected leaders were also more likely to leave.

FINAL THOUGHTS AND NEXT STEPS

In any given social system, brokers play a key role in maintaining the structure of relationships. Yet, as we found, it is precisely these individuals who are likely to leave the system. The loss of brokers has three potential impacts on a district. First, brokers bridge structural gaps; without them, a system loses leaders who build and support connections between otherwise disconnected actors. Second, brokers move instrumental resources, such as expertise, across a system and, as such, play critical roles in supporting the movement of ideas. And third, and particular to our study, brokers tend to occupy key administrative positions, and losing them means there is no one directly responsible for mobilizing and connecting resources, such as those most related to an overall district improvement plan.

While a system of well-connected leaders enhances the flow of expertise and increases efficiency and consistency in distributing, (re) allocating, and generating resources necessary for improvement, we found that the departure of these leaders results in a loss of institutional knowledge and fragmentation that inhibits the network's ability to effectively diffuse knowledge to all its members. This can lead to insularity within a system, to the emergence of small, cohesive, but also isolated subgroups that are not generating new ideas, which, in turn, can lead to systemic inertia.[29]

Previous studies in education have attempted to understand some of the social factors associated with churn, some, for example, suggesting that "expert" leaders who are highly sought out but do not receive reward and recognition tend to leave the system.[30] Although these experts are sought for knowledge and skills they bring to the organization, it is possible that this heavy reliance on these leaders is what pushes them out of the system, perhaps due to stress or burnout. Exacerbating this is the barrage of demands and sanctions facing underperforming systems.[31]

What can be done to prevent or break this vicious cycle? First, we found that creating opportunities for greater work-related recognition in underperforming systems as well as promoting high levels of trust and support encourages the diffusion and uptake of complex ideas and practices, providing a bit of inoculation to effects of churn. Increasing the level of trust in the system takes a concerted effort and a commitment to risk taking and vulnerability.[32] Trust has the potential to develop in systems when those who occupy upper-level positions display their own vulnerabilities and willingness to take a chance even when the outcome is not guaranteed.[33] This modeling sets the stage for other leaders in the system to also be vulnerable, to seek advice, and take a risk even when failure is a possibility. Creating and supporting systems that are risk tolerant and steeped in openness and care through modeling positive interactions can grow and even repair trust and also encourage a more efficient movement of ideas and expertise throughout a system. Creating multiple pathways for trusting social interactions may also lessen the transaction costs necessary to move resources. If a leader has the high trust connection with another leader built over time, then exchanges are easier and more efficient since the risk associated with interaction is reduced. Absent those sets of internal ties, the costs of interacting increase and become far less effective because the system has to impose external communication structures. Therefore, the creation and maintenance of high-quality trust relationships are important for supporting risk-tolerant climates as well as for reducing the costs that come from social interactions and the exchange of resources.[34]

Second, our research suggests that policy must be broadened to attend to aspects related to climate and culture, both critical in the success equation. The Every Student Succeeds Act (ESSA) includes

School Climate and Culture as one of the core components of accountability and provides districts with flexibility in how they measure accountability. While climate and culture are typically measured in relatively narrow ways (e.g., expulsion rates, student attendance) which rarely take into account other types of measures that might reflect culture, our research (indeed, this volume) underscores the importance of attending to context, particularly its interpersonal dimension. Thus, measures such as network metrics, trust, support, and churn rates are key indicators for climate and culture that have not been incorporated into traditional accountability systems. We suggest important dimensions that could be included in new accountability systems as state policy makers begin to implement ESSA, including composite measures of trust and connectedness within schools and across districts. Building more robust and socially focused indicator systems will enable districts and their leaders to be more socially responsive and to bring to the foreground the conditions that are necessary to support improvement. In addition, while the problem of churn is often conceptualized as a recruitment issue, the concern needs to also be one of retention. Creating social indicator systems will also broader accountability systems that are more cognizant of supporting the relational conditions for leaders who want to stay (and creating the conditions for teachers who want to stay as well).

Our work suggests that an overreliance on a few actors for relational resources can inhibit the distribution of expertise in the system. Importantly, we found that the sources of expertise were not equally dispersed across the systems we studied; rather, they tended to be just a few individuals, many of whom worked at the central office. Crafting policies that provide additional opportunities for leadership development that intentionally supports the diffusion of expertise across a system is well indicated. In doing so, a district will enhance its capacity and alignment to reform efforts and achieve better performance systemwide. Increased effort toward distributing expertise throughout the system through policies that incentivize the sharing of knowledge can also ease the pressure on those viewed as experts and provide opportunities to diversify the knowledge available to the system. Diffusing knowledge and expertise will also build capacity and coherence across the organization in order to support more coherent approaches to change. This will require educational leaders to develop stronger partnerships with intermediaries. Crafting policy that incentivizes and supports cross-sector partnerships to create other connection points to expertise will open up systems rather than make them overreliant on a small set of individuals. Leaders who encourage opportunities for sharing a diversity of ideas through identified brokers in the system are more likely to implement complex change.

Understanding the role of churn has never been more important, particularly as we consider issues related to improvement in educational systems and social costs. Given the relatively consistent rate of turnover, combined with the graying of the education workforce, churn will be increasingly important not just in large urban settings but across the nation. Much of the previous work does not pay close attention to the social costs of network churn as school and district leaders undertake reforms in response to accountability pressures. Our research suggests that the costs of churn extend well into the social and perceptual arenas, likely inhibiting efforts to bring about change districtwide. The introduction of ESSA provides an opportunity to promote these issues to the level of accountability policy and create the conditions that support more relational capacity in socially responsive systems.

How the Organization of Schools and Local Communities Shape Educational Improvement

ELAINE M. ALLENSWORTH

Discussions about school reform often focus on instruction, curriculum, and pedagogy. Often, the assumption is that a strong curriculum with the right pedagogy will lead to school improvement. However, learning is a social enterprise that depends on not only the curriculum and pedagogy in individual classrooms but also the ways in which teachers, school staff, and the family work together to support students through the challenges of school and help each other to provide that support in a coordinated way. Teachers' ability to deliver strong instruction depends considerably on the larger school context in which they work. In particular, it rests on the ways in which teachers and other school staff work together in the school and also on the resources and challenges of the families served by the school and the larger community.[1]

There are distinct challenges to strong instruction if teachers work in schools serving students with high rates of poverty and low levels of prior achievement; at the same time, these are the students who are most in need of vibrant instruction. Without intentional efforts to build strong collaborative relationships within the school community, individual teachers and students are left on their own to address the challenges they encounter—leading schools to re-create the inequalities that exist in the larger society. Thus, school leaders serving communities with substantial barriers to school engagement need to pay particular attention to developing school structures—norms, meetings, policies—that foster strong community-wide relationships.

RELATIONSHIPS ACROSS THE SCHOOL COMMUNITY ARE CRITICAL FOR SCHOOL IMPROVEMENT

Relationships among members of a school community—teachers, leaders, students, and families—whether strong or weak, good or bad, influence the likelihood that students will learn, teaching will improve, and school leaders will reach their goals. In 2010, my colleagues and I released the book *Organizing Schools for Improvement,* which drew on a decade of administrative and survey data examining a framework for improving student learning in schools.[2] The book details findings that elementary/middle schools strong on strategic leadership, professional capacity, parent-community ties, instructional guidance, and a student-centered learning climate were highly likely to improve, while others that weren't as strong on these five elements showed little change or fell behind. In the course of doing that study, we found that relationships across the school community formed the common thread which tied together all five domains of school organization that emerged as essential for school improvement.

The goal of the study was to understand why it was that one-quarter of the schools in Chicago improved dramatically after authority was decentralized to the local level, from 1990 to 1996, while another quarter of the schools stayed the same or got worse.[3] All of the schools in the study served low-income neighborhoods, and most served student populations that were at least 90 percent minority. In the 1990s there were myriad research studies on various facets of schools, as well as strong beliefs and knowledge based on practice, about aspects of school organization that were present in successful schools. But it was not clear how to put all of these pieces together into a scheme for school improvement. Researchers at the University of Chicago Consortium on School Research (UChicago Consortium) joined with educators and school reformers to begin thinking about key strategies for improving public schools using this large body of disconnected knowledge. Out of these early discussions, and after mounting initial surveys and field studies in schools, they developed a basic framework called the Five Essential Supports for School Improvement, or 5Essentials.[4] The research team then engaged in a ten-year study to test and refine the framework, examining different ways of measuring aspects of leadership, professional capacity, parent-community ties, instruction, and learning climate to determine in what ways each was associated with improvements in learning gains and how they worked together as an interdependent group of organizational supports.

Based on comparisons of growth in learning gains, it was clear to us that schools strong in the 5Essentials were much more likely to improve than schools that were not particularly strong in these areas, and those that were weak in the 5Essentials were very likely to show no improvements or to have declining student achievement. Looking more closely, particular combinations of organizational structures came out again and again as most strongly distinguishing the schools that improved from those that did not. Specifically, the factors that consistently showed strong connections with improvement were the ones that indicated strong relationships among adults within the school community and between students and teachers; these included measures of trust, collaboration, and inclusive leadership.[5]

Each of the five supports emerged as highly predictive of which schools improved, but out of the hundreds of variables that were included in our analyses, it was often those aspects of the school which represented strong relationships that came out as most strongly related to school improvement. For example, in the area of professional capacity, teachers' qualifications were far less important for school improvement than the professional community and the degree to which teachers took collective responsibility for the school (work orientation).[6] In fact, teacher backgrounds were only related to improvement in schools without a strong professional community or high-quality professional development.[7] In other words, schools without a collaborative learning culture among teachers seemed to need particularly highly qualified teachers to show improvement.

In the years since the original study, subsequent research has provided further evidence and nuance about the ways in which different aspects of the 5Essentials are predictive of particular student outcomes and school improvement. In Chicago, we have found that teachers tend to show better instructional practices, as measured by observations of their instructional practice on the Danielson framework and by their value added on students' test scores, in schools with more trust and commitment among school staff.[8] We also found that teachers are more likely to remain in schools where their colleagues report trusting relationships with the principal and share a sense of collective responsibility for school improvement.[9] Furthermore, principals' influence on instruction and student learning seems to work through their influence on teacher leadership and collaboration around improving the learning climate of the school.[10] As documented in other chapters in this book, a number of studies outside of Chicago have also shown similar patterns, namely that inclusive leadership and teacher collaboration are related to improvements in learning climate, instructional practice, and student achievement growth.

FAMILY COLLABORATION WITH SCHOOL STAFF MATTERS FOR SCHOOL CLIMATE AND PROFESSIONAL CAPACITY

One area of the 5Essentials that has been less studied is the role of parent-community ties, particularly the relationships that school staff have with their students' families. Students learn by making meaning of their experiences, and their experiences are often shaped by their relationships with adults—at school, at home, and outside of school. Adults help students interpret experiences so that they develop skills, mind-sets, and values that shape the foundations for their success later in life.[11] Teachers and parents often have similar goals for students, but they may work toward those goals in different and competing ways. Without intentional communication and collaboration, it can be easy to point fingers at each other when a student struggles, rather than working together to help the student succeed. That can lead everyone to feel frustrated.

In schools where teachers and parents work together to support students, teachers are more likely to feel effective and continue to teach in that school from year to year. In a study of many different factors that might be related to whether teachers left or remained in their school, parent involvement was second only to school safety in importance for teacher stability, comparing schools serving similar populations of students.[12] Furthermore, teacher-parent trust was as important as the degree to which teachers trust their principal and feel a collective responsibility among their fellow teachers and was a stronger predictor of whether teachers stayed in their school than were their reports about their professional development, their trust in other teachers, and their perception of the principal as a strong instructional leader—although all of these factors helped predict whether teachers would leave the school the following year.[13] In short, teachers tend to stay in places where they feel supported by families, colleagues, and their principal and where the climate is safe and conducive to instruction.

Family involvement also turns out to be a significant predictor of whether a school is safe and orderly in the first place. Another UChicago Consortium study examined the factors that were associated with students' and teachers' feelings of safety in school and the degree to which teachers reported problems with crime and disorder in the school.[14] The characteristics of students' home neighborhoods are strongly related to the climate of safety within schools. As might be expected, crime and poverty in students' residential neighborhoods are strongly associated with school safety. However, schools serving students from very similar neighborhoods— with similar levels of poverty and similar levels of neighborhood crime— can have very different levels of safety. Inside the school building, the mutually supportive relationships that students and their parents have with teachers are the most critical elements defining both students' and teachers' reports of crime, disorder, and safety. Much of what accounts for the large differences among schools in terms of safety are the ways in which parents, teachers, and students work together and trust each other.[15] Schools are safer when teachers view parents as supportive partners in the children's education.

CONTEXT MATTERS FOR
SCHOOL-FAMILY RELATIONSHIPS

There is an abundance of evidence that it is harder, though still possible, to create a collaborative school with strong positive relationships in neighborhoods with the most extreme levels of poverty. For parents, it is difficult to go to a parent meeting, or make it to report card pickup when their jobs have no flexibility; it's even harder when they don't have reliable transportation or are afraid of crime outside the home or around the school. There can also be cultural differences between middle-class school staff and families that serve as barriers to engagement and understanding. Further, children from poor families often face obstacles that interfere with regular attendance—chronic health problems are more common, as are other family members' illnesses,, and transportation can be unreliable, and on and on.[16] Chronic absenteeism is strongly related to low learning gains, and absences can frustrate teachers' efforts in the classroom.[17] Not only is it more difficult to build relationships with students who are not in school as often, but absences can make it seem as if students or their families do not care about school or are not willing to be partners with teachers.[18] Another obstacle is unstable housing situations, which can result in frequent transfers from school-to-school and thus impede long-term relationship building with school staff.

Even among schools serving large numbers of students who qualify for free and reduced-price lunch—the standard measure of low-income status in schools—there are large differences in the degree to which families face challenges. In Chicago, some schools serve students and families facing extraordinarily difficult circumstances. In the neighborhoods in which these students live there are, on average, four crimes for every ten residents, over half of adult males are unemployed, and a quarter or more of the students have substantiated histories of being abused or neglected. Communities with the highest levels of poverty also tend to have weak ties to social institutions—low rates of participation in religious or community groups—and fewer ties to other communities with more economic resources. These weaker relationships outside the school community are mirrored within the school community.[19]

Broadening the analysis to the entire state of Illinois, my colleagues found that schools serving larger numbers of students in poverty were much more likely to be weak on the essential supports for school improvement than schools serving fewer students in poverty. Chicago schools, in which over 85 percent of students qualify for free or reduced-priced lunch, are far less likely to have strong family-school relationships than schools in the rest of the state, with only about 6 percent of schools having very strong parental involvement.[20] Schools serving the smallest percentages of students in poverty are three times as likely as schools serving students with the highest percentages of students in poverty to be strong in at least three of the five essentials, and almost none is weak in three or more areas, compared to over a quarter of schools serving high numbers of students in poverty.[21]

Over the past twenty-five years, Chicago has seen major shifts in demographics, housing, and the economy. But it hasn't solved entrenched poverty, and the schools facing extreme disadvantage are struggling on multiple fronts. Weak partnerships between parents and school staff are just one symptom of that struggle in many of the city's schools. The 5Essentials tend to be weaker in schools serving students living in high poverty, resulting in higher teacher turnover rates, more student mobility from school to school, and more difficulty building and maintaining relationships in the school community. In Chicago, as elsewhere in the country, schools with more disadvantaged students have a more difficult time retaining teachers, and more effective teachers often move to schools with lower rates of poverty.[22] This doesn't mean that teachers are leaving students because they are poor; rather, they are leaving because the working conditions do not allow them to be as effective as they want to be.[23] Many teachers choose to work in schools serving impoverished neighborhoods because they know that there is a particularly strong need for effective teachers. But knowing how important it is to be effective in those schools can make it particularly frustrating when teaching and learning don't go as intended.

At the same time, there are examples of schools with good relationships among teachers, leaders, and parents in all types of neighborhoods. In the initial study of the 5Essentials, we wondered whether these supports were equally important in all types of schools. We divided Chicago's schools into groups based on the economic backgrounds of their students and their racial composition—the two being so closely tied that they had to be considered together. We found that schools serving students living in neighborhoods with the highest levels of poverty were the least likely to show improvement over time and the least likely to be strong on the essentials. In particular, schools serving communities with high levels of crime and violence were much less likely to have positive relationships within the school community and to have strong organizational supports. However, if schools serving the most impoverished students did have strong internal supports in at least three areas, they were just as likely to improve as the advantaged schools that had high levels of supports. More advantaged schools, in contrast, did not have to be particularly strong across the essential supports to improve; it was just critical that they not be weak.[24]

RELATIONSHIPS ARE BUILT INTENTIONALLY, BY WORKING TOWARD COMMON GOALS

What does the concept of strong, trusting relationships really mean? What fosters relationships at the teacher level and at the student level? People might assume that positive teacher-student relationships means that teachers are easygoing and likeable, that they joke around with students or ask them about their personal lives outside of school. But it turns out that students have a far different set of criteria and have very little interest in being buddies with their teachers. When we studied characteristics of high schools where students felt supported and where students received better grades than would be expected based on their test scores from the year before, we found that students rarely mentioned emotional support or personal connections. Rather, they craved clear expectations and consistently communicated goals, regular monitoring and outreach, and a willingness on the teacher's part to understand and address their individual struggles in school.[25] They defined a teacher who cares as one who has clear expectations, checks in, notices when students need help, asks if they have what they need, pushes them to do challenging work, and seeks to understand before punishing. Supportive teachers keep up with their grading and don't ignore student absences; instead, their records on grades and attendance show them who needs help and where they may need to modify or get help with their instruction. They see low grades and absences as signals that they need to reach out more actively, rather than signals that a student doesn't care. In classes where students get higher grades than expected (based on their entering test scores), we often see that teachers have very clear systems for monitoring student performance; students know where their grade stands and what they need to do to perform well. The trust that characterizes a strong relationship springs from the student understanding that the teacher is committed to helping him or her to learn and to succeed in their class and in school.[26]

In Chicago, high schools have shown tremendous improvement over the last decade in graduation rates, test scores, and college outcomes. Many have developed structures that allow school staff, families, and partners to collaborate around their goals for student achievement, using student data on attendance, grades, and behavior. In 2009, schools in Chicago started using data on early warning indicators in the ninth grade to help students have a strong transition to high school and keep them on track to graduation. Before this, conversations in schools about issues around dropout often focused on factors other than student course performance. School staff considered dropout and course failure to be problems that were outside of their control, that stemmed from students' lives outside of the school. By focusing attention on students' grades and attendance, conversations became about how students were performing in school and what school staff and parents could do to support better attendance and performance in classes, rather than trying to fix problems outside the school, such as crime and teenage pregnancy. When talking to parents, counselors can talk about what happens to the likelihood of graduating if a student misses anymore days of school or assignments. This makes it more likely that the parent will interpret the counselor's concern about the student's attendance to mean that the school practitioner cares about the student and his outcomes, instead of feeling that she is being blamed for her child's bad behavior or poor academic performance. By keeping the focus on data related to outcomes everyone cares about for the student (high school graduation, college readiness), conversations can move away from finger-pointing about who is to blame for problems at school (the student, the parent, the teacher) to making plans for improving how students are actually doing in school.[27]

In high schools that have systems for monitoring early warning data, students hear messages from their counselors and teachers about needing to "get back on track." They talk about receiving a first quarter F and being called into conferences with their on-track coordinator, teacher, and parent to develop plans for passing the class, or about how school staff would be on them if they were absent. In this way, school staff can talk to students about their performance in a way that is viewed as supportive rather than critical.[28]

As adults get together to monitor data on students (attendance, grades, behavior), they develop strategies for reaching out, for finding out what is interfering with their school work, for keeping students from falling behind. What starts out as looking at students as data points ends up being the means for strengthening relationships between teachers and students. There are a thousand reasons why students may be absent, may not be getting their work done, or may be performing poorly on tests. If nobody finds out why and helps students overcome their particular challenge, they will keep drifting further behind. If a teacher notices and helps students develop strategies to succeed, students see them as caring. This helps the student have higher performance not only in that class but in their other classes as well. The support can teach them how to be effective learners and leads their teachers to be more effective, too.

Relationships between teachers and leaders come from a strikingly analogous foundation of goals, structures, monitoring, and support. In a separate study, my colleagues and I looked at characteristics of school leaders that are associated with school improvement.[29] Among a subset of Chicago principals who are all highly rated as instructional leaders, we wondered why some of their schools showed strong and improving gains while others did not. We found that teachers crave many of the same foundational conditions that students do: to know what they are working toward, to have structures that facilitate conversations about their progress based on data, and to have supports that help them improve.

Our initial findings highlight the importance of shared leadership—trusting staff members with leadership responsibilities, giving everyone skin in the game—for fostering strong relationships between leaders and teachers. In turn, teachers feel comfortable engaging in true professional learning communities, collaborating to help each other improve. The study found that in schools not seeing strong gains, some school leaders assume that providing time for teachers to collaborate is the extent of their relationship-building role—if you provide the meeting time, the relationships will come. However, simply carving out time for collaboration is not sufficient; the time has to be in service of clear goals with a sense of collective effort and an orientation toward improvement. It's also critical that time for collaboration is structured around data—in particular, data that are clearly linked to the school's goals for student success on metrics that matter, like grades and attendance. Monitoring student data is critical to keeping conversations and effort focused on common goals and for being able to see when shared work is making progress on those goals.[30] Through this lens, collaboration time can be focused and empowering.

POLICY IMPLICATIONS

It may seem obvious that inclusive leadership, teacher collaboration, and family involvement are important for school improvement. Yet, over the years, school districts have pushed a number of policy levers to promote school improvement, none of which has specifically focused on building the organizational capacity of schools. These policies range from hiring and evaluating teachers and leaders, to threatening schools with probation or closure, to implementing new curriculum or different standards. Often schools already strong on the 5Essentials are able to use a new policy to their advantage, while for others it becomes yet another district-mandated burden on top of myriad other demands to which they respond only weakly and without any benefit for students.

School reform that is implemented without regard to organizational capacity can actually decrease the coherence of programs and instruction in the school and lead to lower levels of student achievement. Even narrow programs and policies can be used as tools for making improvements, but they need to be implemented in ways that build collaboration around shared goals among the school community, not just as another new thing for already-busy people to do. For example, a school or district leader could mandate a new literacy curriculum or a new approach to school discipline and face pushback and poor implementation, or she could bring staff, parents, and students together to discuss the new initiative and ask them to figure out approaches for implementing it and testing how it works in a way that supports existing efforts.

Time is necessary for getting people to work together, and it is influenced by district policies and priorities, such as the ways that professional development days are used or whether there is time in the school day for teachers to collaborate. However, there also need to be structures to facilitate productive collaboration and mechanisms to ensure that collaboration time stays focused on shared goals for students. These conversations can be facilitated with data on student outcomes, data that can monitor progress on shared goals and make difficult conversations less personal. This requires investments in data systems—not just systems to record data but systems for making it easy to access and use the data, quality control so that people trust the data, and investments in technology.

But we can't expect school leaders and district leaders to know how to facilitate collaboration if they haven't received any training or support in doing it. Over the last decade, there has been an increasing emphasis on preparing principals to be instructional leaders. Yet, there are many different approaches that principals can take, and not all emphasize the quality of relationships in the school. Principal preparation programs and state policies for licensure and certification could do more to provide much-needed training and supports around how to foster collaboration, build trust support shared leadership, and structure data-driven problem solving as part of that shared leadership. School leaders also benefit from interactions with other leaders working on the same issues. In Chicago, high school leadership teams that belong to the Network for College Success get together regularly, look at each other's data, and share strategies for addressing common problems. Doing so allows them to ask hard questions of each other and themselves about their practices and lets the solutions they've discovered travel.[31]

Thinking about schools as social systems requires strategic leadership that engages all stakeholders and meets the needs of students given the larger community context. That is more difficult for schools that serve more students from families which face economic instability and all of the stressors accompanying it. Leaders and staff in these schools need more time to collaborate and strategize about how to build a vibrant school climate and improve instruction than do leaders and staff in schools serving more advantaged student populations. They need to have more time dedicated to working collaboratively with families and to carefully planning structures for positive interactions. They need to have structures that make it easy to reach out to students who fall behind and supports available to help the students catch up. School improvement goes far beyond selecting a new curriculum. It takes trust, time, resources, and strategies dedicated to communication and collaboration.

CHAPTER 8

Organizing Adult Learning for Adaptive Change Management

A Systems Approach

JOSHUA P. STARR

I remember one day of my superintendency when I visited two high schools that we had identified as being in need of improvement. I was there to share with faculty and staff my plans to help them improve student achievement and to listen to their thoughts and concerns. Both schools served similar student populations. Yet, in one school the comments were mainly about how middle schools hadn't adequately prepared the students, how parents didn't value their kids' education, and how students didn't respect authority. The educators located the problem outside of their own practice and wanted me to give them more resources and remove the kids who were having the most trouble. In the other school, the faculty talked about their collective struggle to improve their practice, how they were challenging each other's belief systems about students, their desire for more professional development, and their hope for more supports to deal with issues that students were having outside of school. These educators located the problem within their own practices and recognized that they needed to learn and grow in order to meet the challenges of teaching today's high school student.

School improvement is about people coming together to solve a problem. Too many school reform efforts of the past few decades have been based in structural or technical changes without commensurate attention paid to how people respond to or enact those changes. Ron Heifetz describes this dynamic as the difference between technical and adaptive change.[1]

Problem solving often requires believing that change is necessary and that one has the capacity to bring it about by acquiring new knowledge and skills that can, in turn, shape subsequent behaviors. As we think about how to design systems at scale that promote the primacy of people-centered, adaptive change, it is essential that we first have a shared understanding of the problem we're trying to solve. All too often educators provide a solution without first identifying the specific problem of practice they are trying to address. As Jal Mehta says, and as my opening anecdote suggests, "*how* a problem or issue is defined has a considerable impact on *who* is seen as a relevant or credible advocate; conversely, the most credible advocates can shape public issues in ways that reinforce their own importance and centrality."[2]

The evidence and ideas presented in this volume are relevant to solving one of the biggest challenges of American public education today: we have an adult learning problem, not a student learning problem. Students will learn what teachers teach. But adults—teachers, support staff, building and district leaders, policy makers—need to increase their knowledge and skills in order to meet the needs of today's students and enable them to achieve higher academic standards than ever before.

This requires that school systems do two very different things: shift the distribution of average so that the typical educator increases her capacity to meet today's demands and, *at the same time,* unleash the creativity and energy of those who are ready to lead. This is a complex leadership challenge because it requires one to simultaneously embrace two potentially competing ideas. While some educators prefer structure and guidance, others are itching to break free from the district curriculum, rules, and processes and try out new ideas. In addition, some people lead in some areas and follow in others. But organizing a system to embrace and support both types of educators (not to mention those who sit in the back of professional development sessions with their arms folded or doing the crossword puzzle) is a complex leadership challenge of adaptive change management.

There are approximately 3.5 million teachers in US schools. Most of them went to a local institution of higher education for their preparation. While Todd Rose makes a compelling argument that we need to stop organizing our systems around what he calls "averagarianism"—the notion that there's a middle range of skills which describe most people—our public schools are far from that ideal.[3] The skills of most workers in any organization can be placed on a typical bell curve, and schools and school districts are no different. Some teachers are high flyers who every parent wants for their child, while others induce groans from students when they see them on their schedule. But most are somewhere in between—and herein lies the challenge for schools and districts. How does a school system create the conditions whereby the typical teacher is constantly improving her practice and, hence, improving student outcomes? And since academic standards are higher, what knowledge and skills does today's typical teacher need to have, and how should a school and a school system be organized to ensure teachers continue to improve those skills? If the problem we face is improving adult learning in order to shift the distribution of average, how do we design systems to do this?

Other chapters offer compelling evidence that school improvement rests on activating educators' capacity to teach (and learn from) each other, that the best adult learning environment is one characterized by trust and a collaborative culture. Thus, the primary responsibility of education leaders who are seeking to improve student achievement is to organize systems in which adults can learn together. This may seem a little counterintuitive for two reasons. First, today's public discourse, rife with truisms like "children first" and "focus on student needs not adult issues," suggests that we need to place sole attention on students and that the rest is a luxury or a distraction. Second, too many policy makers have been seduced by the argument that teachers just need to be held accountable for outcomes and that the unions need to be dismantled in order for student achievement to improve. But what if we assumed that teachers want to do their best for children but may not always know how? What if we assumed that teachers are unaware of how their beliefs (about their students and themselves) may be compromising their practice? Then a focus on teacher learning and adaptive change no longer seems like a diversion or so unaffordable.

A system that promotes adult learning must be coherent from the classroom to the boardroom and must be supported with commensurate policies and resources. The theory of action of such a system contends that if school and district leaders design systems that promote adult learning and organize opportunities for educators to learn with and from each other, and if teachers have ownership of that learning and it is aligned to both academic standards and student needs, then instructional practice will improve and so, too, will student outcomes.

The conditions for success that system leaders need to create in order for educators to increase their knowledge and skills so that they can serve all students at a higher level rest on the idea that increasing learning—for both students and adults—is primarily a social activity. Once we accept this premise, our focus must turn to how teachers spend their time when organized into teams and how system leaders can support and monitor such efforts.

Too much of today's conversation about teacher quality rests on the idea that the pipeline—preservice teacher or administrator training—has to be fixed so that schools get better entrants into the profession, or that if we just increase accountability for outcomes educators will rise to the occasion. While elements of both these arguments have some merit, we should also look at the factors that cause teachers to leave teaching or stagnate professionally as a way of understanding the conditions that need to be present for teachers to stay in their schools, improve, and succeed. Other sectors recognize that their entry-level employees need additional training and support in order to reach the expected level of performance. Yet, for some reason public education expects new teachers to arrive with all the skills and knowledge they need to be successful when, in fact, the opposite is true.

ATTENDING TO THE CONDITIONS FOR SUCCESS

The most important condition for improving adult learning is a safe and supportive environment where educators can take risks, speak their truths, reveal their vulnerabilities, and be actively engaged in getting better. Principals have the primary responsibility for creating that environment. Too many teachers leave the profession because they're not supported by their principals and aren't learning.[4] While it might seem obvious that a good principal, like any good boss, should be responsible for creating a supportive environment where his staff is growing, learning, and highly engaged, principals are typically only accountable for student achievement on standardized test scores, safety, and operations.

When I was superintendent of the Montgomery County (Maryland) Public Schools, we used a survey to measure employee engagement, recognizing that increased employee engagement leads to increased productivity. Everyone who supervised employees—transportation and facility managers, central office leaders, principals, and me—was accountable for ensuring that their direct reports were engaged in their work and in the life of the school or office. We know that while most people will perform at a given level if they're simply told to do certain things, their productivity increases when they feel that they're part of a team and contributing to the overall success of their organization. When their opinion and input matter, they're more likely to take on additional responsibilities, seek ways to improve their practice and their school, and thereby increase their productivity.

Using this survey to understand the context and conditions for school improvement was a systems decision. As superintendent, I had to first show that it was aligned to the district's core values. Then I had to include it in my annual budget presentation to the board of education and demonstrate that it would not increase overall spending, which I was able to do by reducing the number of standardized tests students took. Governance had to be considered, too. This was facilitated by a well-established collaborative leadership structure that included the teacher union and support professionals and principals associations as part of the executive leadership team. This team debated and eventually agreed on how to use the survey results, whether they would be part of principal evaluations, how the results would be communicated to the public, and what the overall goals and message would be.

STRUCTURES THAT PROMOTE ADULT LEARNING

In the district, principal supervisors, who were senior central office leaders, had historically assessed principal progress based solely on academic outcomes and technical measures (such as finance). But for the survey, they now had to look at both academic student outcomes and the contexts within which employees were working. Supervising processes and supervising outcomes are two very different tasks, and principal supervisors had to learn how to use these results to coach and guide as well as carry out their traditional approach to evaluation. Once survey results were in, we also needed to provide clear guidance on who and how would have access to results. Some leaders immediately shared the results with their team and started planning on how to improve, while others kept them close to the vest. In addition, results were posted on the district website as one of our School Support and Improvement Framework indicators, and supervisors were coached on how to improve their levels of employee engagement. In a school, this often means creating structures to engender collaboration and engagement. Of course, those structures were accompanied by a leadership stance that embraced teamwork and collaboration.

The most typical structure for improving adult learning within a school is a professional learning community (PLC). As common as they are, truly effective PLCs are actually hard to come by, and too often meetings have the moniker but lack the content or process. Effective PLCs rest on three ideas: (1) the group consists of professionals (2) who are actually learning something, and (3) the community enables that learning and holds each other and itself accountable for improved practice and outcomes. Professionals are expected to have a level of knowledge and expertise that they can apply to a particular situation. They take responsibility for results and recognize that they must constantly improve their practice.

Real learning—learning that leads to changes in behavior—requires deep engagement. Thus, meetings of educators should be organized around specific goals and should apply the basic principles of the improvement cycle: not only do participants need to learn new content, but they also need to apply that learning and continue to refine it based on evidence of its application's effectiveness. In a true PLC, educators are presented with a new idea or technique; they use it in their practice; and then they come back to the community to reflect and refine it. The community of colleagues is both the engine that drives improvement and the glue that holds it all together.

PLCs play another very important role in supporting adult learning and school improvement efforts more broadly as a powerful mechanism for the effective transfer of knowledge between different generations of educators. As the baby boomer generation retires, much of their knowledge and expertise will be missing in the workplace. The divide between the boomers and the millennials is striking, if not surprising, even though both are equally committed to educating and serving children. Boomers typically have deep knowledge and skills born out of years of experience, while many millennials have greater facility with technology and are more open to new and research-based ideas. Many millennials also want—even expect—to lead and contribute to overall school change efforts, while boomers weren't brought up in a system where their participation was actively encouraged. If organized properly, PLCs can be a vehicle for the intergenerational exchange of knowledge within a school and a system.

SUPPORTING AND SCALING UP EFFECTIVE PLCS

How, then, does a principal implement and support effective PLCs, and how can districts systematize them across all schools? The first, and perhaps most obvious, answer is to find the time for teachers to be together. A schedule is the black box of school transformation; it tells us not only what resources are available to meet the school's needs but what the values of the leadership are and the vision for how students should be taught and supported. The ability to schedule creatively so that human capital is maximized is not innate to all school leaders. While scheduling is a basic component of school leadership, some school leaders are much better at it than others. Similarly, some principal supervisors are better than others at coaching, supporting, and creating accountability to ensure a schedule that attends to adult learning as well as student learning.

Politics, as with most things in public education, can play a role in this. Resources in schools are limited, and the choice to schedule time for teachers to learn from each other can be seen by parents, community members, or politicians as time that would be better spent with students. (After all, don't teachers already know what to do?) It is the job of the superintendent and school board to make clear to the public why it's so important for adults to learn together and what the benefit will be for students. Yet, in order to be convinced, politicians and policy makers need more than the superintendent stating, "The research says . . . ," since there's a myriad of education research to support almost any position. So the argument must be made collectively and be supported by stakeholders. The local teacher union plays a role as well, for if teachers don't understand the benefit, or want to make it a negotiable item, then the effort to implement PLCs can be compromised.

This is why a systems approach to organizing adult learning is so important. Policies, budgets, contracts, and politics can help or hinder efforts to promote and sustain educators' learning by weakening or strengthening its interpersonal, collaborative dimension.

Assuming school leaders can carve out the time for teachers to collaborate, and all stakeholders are on board, the next strategic decision is about who should participate in PLCs. In successful PLCs, members need to have something to offer each other; perhaps it's expertise based on experience, or the ability to peer-coach, or the camaraderie born out of the collective struggle to implement a new practice. The key feature of a PLC is that educators are learning, struggling, and growing *together*.

Elementary schools PLCs are typically organized by grade level. The key questions are whether to include "specials" teachers, such as art, music, technology, instructional media specialists, and physical education, and how to include English language learner and special education teachers and reading and math specialists (or coaches), since there typically is not one per grade. At the middle and high school levels the challenge is to determine whether PLCs should be organized by grade level, subject area, or team or simply by whoever is available during a certain period of the day.

Many collaborative teams spend time making decisions about curriculum, units of study, and how to teach the standards. These are important first steps. But PLCs can also be safe places to stay if the team is uncomfortable with collective reflection on practices and results. In order to learn and grow, adults need to receive constant and honest feedback about the effectiveness of their own practices. They must look at students' formative assessments, evaluate their actual progress relative to what was expected, and then reflect on their own practices and how they affect that process. To improve their practice, teachers need to spend time understanding how their daily activities with students lead to achievement of the standard; they need to understand their belief systems, both about children and their own efficacy. This is where culture and leadership become instrumental to the ability of a school to improve through collective inquiry and to embrace the difficult work of adaptive change.

ENSURING EFFECTIVE ADULT LEARNING: THE ROLE OF THE CENTRAL OFFICE

One day during my second year as superintendent of the Montgomery County Public Schools, I was talking to a group of elementary school teachers who were participating in collaborative planning time. They shared with me that they were going through district curriculum guides and making decisions about what to teach, since the guides contained too much to cover in a year. I was struck by the fact that they were doing this, as we had been implementing the new curriculum for a few years and my assumption was that they had moved beyond making these kinds of decisions and were working on the impact of their teaching on students. This prompted me to go back and talk to Curriculum and Instruction and to the principal supervisors about how they were supporting teachers and ensuring that collaborative planning time was going beyond simply making decisions about what should be taught.

A district's central office can be instrumental in creating and maintaining effective structures for professional collaboration. Two important technical or structural areas the central office supports are determining content and monitoring and facilitating progress.

Determining Content

Students learn what teachers teach, so deciding what should be taught, how it should be taught, and how it will be assessed are among the most important tasks of PLCs. Content decisions are complex, and they should be made *with* teachers rather than for them. In order to organize effective adult learning, school systems must have absolute clarity about what students need to know and be able to do, ensure that all students will have the resources and supports they need to achieve those standards, and attend to policy and governance considerations.

Schools today are required to teach students how to meet state standards. Standards, however, can't be understood simply by reading them, inserting them in a lesson plan, or posting them on a bulletin board. I have been in too many classrooms where a standard has been written on the board as an objective and yet the lesson bears no resemblance to that standard. Every state department of education website features a detailed list of standards for every content area that delineates what students should know and be able to do. But nowhere on that site will you find the content or curriculum aligned to those standards, including scope and sequence, appropriate supporting materials, and summative and formative assessments. Those are local decisions, opportunities for schools and districts to engage in deep learning and development so that the standards address the needs of the local context. And, importantly, these decisions are best made collectively.

Mike Schrimpf describes the depth of the process that adults go through to understand the standards and the kind of instruction, differentiation, and assessment that will enable students to achieve them as the "unpacking" of standards in order to "understand what students need to know and be able to do to meet it by the end of the school year."[5] But this complex and multifaceted process cannot happen in isolation.

Monitoring and Facilitating Progress

Once it is clear what students should know and be able to do, the central office has to be transparent about how it is supervising both the results and the process by which those results are achieved (recent cheating scandals underscore the necessity of attending to both). As outcome and process results emerge, the central office needs to have a system for organizing around those results so that improvement will occur. And the tone must be set at the top: the superintendent must provide the proper support and communicate the strategy to district employees and the community.

System leaders must create the conditions for complex school improvement efforts to happen at the local level. Whether within a centrally managed system or a portfolio district with various levels of autonomy, in order for school personnel to embrace the challenge of improving their practice, the superintendent and central office leaders have to be willing to align policies, resources, metrics, and messages to support those efforts. They must have a distinct theory of action regarding how teaching and learning will improve and must be clear about who gets to make decisions about what gets taught and how. Particularly in a diverse school system, expectations around equal access to standards must be made clear, and preferably be embedded in district policy. The more that curriculum decisions are made at the school level, the tighter the monitoring and accountability mechanisms have to be in order to ensure that all students have access to high-quality curriculum, teaching, and learning.

The supervision of progress and facilitation of process are vital central office functions. Too many central offices are designed to ensure compliance, an essential element of public school administration but one that isn't necessarily focused on promoting the collaborative culture needed for improvement. State and federal regulations, board of education reports, financial and human resource concerns, and contractual obligations consume a significant amount of central office leaders' time. It's easy to get sucked into the complex technical administration of a school system and not attend to the adaptive challenges of changing adult practice.

Yet, central office leaders must serve as quality assurance agents, making sure the curriculum meets standards, teachers are instructing students in ways that will promote success, and resources are allocated according to student needs. We know that schools and districts are under pressure to show that more students are achieving at higher levels every year. Every summer, school and district leaders eagerly await state test score results to see how they're doing. And when those results are less than desired, leaders are tempted to seek solutions that they hope will cause rapid progress. While some quick fixes may have merits, they won't lead to success without attending to how the adults in the system respond to these changes. Another role of the central office, therefore, must be to facilitate adaptive change. Essential to such facilitation are clarity and consistency of message. Too many central office leaders are in silos—the literacy folks don't talk to the special education team, the English language learner department doesn't meet with the principal supervisors, and so on. And *if* they visit schools or attend principal meetings, they direct teachers and administrators from their discrete perspective, which are often legitimately different because of regulatory needs.

So while it's easy for the superintendent to say to principals, "Be bold! Ask forgiveness rather than permission. Think outside the box!" the Title I director or the special education supervisor have very different views given the enormous compliance burdens facing public schools. Invariably, when I visited schools or principal meetings, school leaders would tell me they were getting mixed messages from central office. Thus, the superintendent must ensure consistency of message among central office leaders, which, of course, requires them to commit to collaboration and engagement.

Mechanisms should also be put into place that require central office leaders to account for their work with the schools. Montgomery County Public Schools set up a system where, after each school visit, central office leaders had to record electronically what they had done at the school and with whom (a system akin to a customer service representative taking notes so that when you call the next time you don't have to rehash the problem from the beginning). Once this system was established, there was a process for central office leaders to discuss with each other what they were doing with the school, what progress the school was making, and what additional needs existed. This kind of coordinated effort, or case management approach, should look like a running conversation throughout the year. It undergirds the ability of central office leaders to supervise—through coaching, guidance, and direct observation—what's going on in the schools.

Finally, central office leaders must be expected to directly observe PLCs, collaborative planning, school leadership team meetings, or any other structure intended to bring people together to improve instruction and outcomes. They must know what excellence looks like and then know how to give feedback and coach a school leader to improve their practice.

Additional Structures to Support Adaptive Change

If improvement is expected to happen through an adaptive approach, the technical aspects must be reinforced in negotiated contracts and evaluation processes. Certainly the principals' contracts and evaluation processes must delineate expectations to ensure that interpersonal aspects of teacher learning and development are attended to, with commensurate metrics such as disaggregated staff turnover rates. If teachers of color are leaving a school at a rate that's much higher than white teachers, it's essential that the principal knows what to do to change the situation and is evaluated accordingly. As suggested earlier, other kinds of data, such as staff climate or engagement surveys or even direct observation of meetings, should be used to supervise school leaders in ways that provide support and accountability.

Another critical aspect of supporting adaptive change through contracts and evaluation processes is the role of teacher leaders. There are many formal and informal leaders within a school, and while great schools rest on both, too few systems maximize the formal role of teacher leaders—department heads, instructional coaches, staff development teachers, or team leaders, among others. Incentives for teacher leadership are essential for engendering adaptive change, and more and more contracts are reflecting the different roles teachers can play.

I believe that a key change in the roles of teachers must include teacher-to-teacher observation and evaluation. For some reason, we persist in believing that viable supervision in schools can happen with one principal and a few assistant principals directly observing and evaluating every employee. Not only does the principal or assistant principal not always have the content or pedagogical expertise to provide effective supervision to every employee, but their days are filled with a host of operational and political considerations that can distract from teaching and learning. Also, the industry standard for a supervisor to employee ratio is 1:12, but in schools it can be 1:50, making it very difficult for principals to be the "instructional leaders" they are expected to be, to observe and evaluate regularly or with the attention and care the process deserves.

Instructional leadership is not solely about being able to identify great or poor instruction and teach teachers how to improve. It's more about having a clear vision for what students should know and be able to do, relentlessly communicating the expectations for how to achieve that vision, allocating resources to improve adult practice in service of the vision, and then ensuring accountability for results. If principals have not effectively allocated their resources—time, talent, and money—in service of an instructional vision, they have to be supported and also held accountable. District hiring and evaluation practices need to reflect this new reality.

A few school systems, such as Montgomery County and Cincinnati, have well-established peer assistance and review processes that allow for colleagues to play a formal role in the evaluation and coaching of their peers; in most systems, however, members of the same bargaining unit are not allowed to evaluate each other. This approach works because, for example, a literacy coach in an elementary school is the recognized expert in literacy and is typically working directly in classes with students and teachers. As an evaluator, she will have a much more intimate view of what kinds of supports a teacher needs to improve practice and whether or not the teacher responds to those supports. While arguments are made that there needs to be a line between coaching and supervising, I'm convinced that such a distinction has been more harmful than helpful to the teaching profession.

* * *

A superintendent is the steward of a community's values. The foremost challenge of a district and school leader is to ensure that system architecture enables members of that community to increase their knowledge and skills so that all students can achieve at higher levels. This work requires deliberate attention to belief systems, culture, processes, policies, and structure. It means being abundantly clear about what students need to know and be able to do in order to succeed and what knowledge and skills adults need to help all students achieve. It calls for clear messaging about how change is expected to happen and coherent formal and informal mechanisms for monitoring and supporting change.

School improvement is a people process, as is education itself. We must create the conditions for success for educators to do their best work by learning and growing with each other. If we attend to the adaptive needs of adult learning in order to improve teaching and learning, our educators and our children will reap the rewards.

CHAPTER 9

Research-Practice Partnerships and ESSA

A Learning Agenda for the Coming Decade

WILLIAM R. PENUEL AND CAITLIN C. FARRELL

For more than a decade, the federal government has promoted policies to encourage greater use of research evidence to inform educational reform efforts. These policies have focused mainly on supporting research on the effectiveness of programs and practices using randomized controlled trials and on incentivizing or mandating the use of programs with evidence of effectiveness. They presume that the most useful research will be studies that develop unbiased evidence of program impacts through the use of experimental or quasi-experimental study designs.[1] However, most leaders in school districts and states face a variety of decisions every day for which there is little to no research.[2] If research is to influence these decisions, researchers need to be engaged more collaboratively with local leaders in joint efforts to refine understandings of problems to be tackled and identify relevant research. Studies on evidence use in a variety of fields indicate that it is through sustained interpersonal interactions that ideas and tools from research enter into practice.[3]

The Every Student Succeeds Act (ESSA) reflects a continued commitment among policy makers to the use of research evidence to inform educational reform efforts and puts a much greater responsibility on local decision makers for knowing about, using, and even developing evidence. To succeed, local leaders will need support to meet these expectations. As in all other reform efforts, making use of research will require the collaborative engagement of leaders and educators with researchers. Productive evidence use is an interactive process that is most likely to take place when there are sustained opportunities for interactions between researchers and educators.

While traditional research and development imagines a one-way path from research to practice, partnerships are a two-way endeavor, with practice informing the questions researchers ask and making research more relevant. In partnerships, researchers and educators work together to search for and test solutions to practice, blending ideas and evidence from research with the wisdom of practice. Partnerships are an infrastructure for turning the insight that reform is a social process into a systematic design for collaborative improvement that leverages the expertise and passion of both researchers and educators.

In this chapter we argue that research-practice partnerships (RPPs) that include educators from schools, districts, and out-of-school organizations are positioned to play an important role in supporting educators to incorporate evidence into their reform efforts. Using ESSA as a context, we lay out four roles partnerships can play in supporting the provisions of ESSA regarding the use of evidence, and we conclude with a set of questions for researchers, practitioners, and policy makers about increasing the field's capacity to engage in successful partnership work.

THE FEDERAL ROLE IN PROMOTING THE USE OF EVIDENCE IN EDUCATIONAL REFORM

Over the last two decades, we have seen an ongoing conversation at the federal level about how research evidence should inform local practice. In the early 2000s, the focus was on how practitioners could use findings from large-scale experimental studies with randomized control trials (RCTs), the "gold standard" of educational research.[4] The 2001 No Child Left Behind Act included more than one hundred references to "scientifically based research," with the expectation that programs funded under the law draw on such evaluation evidence in school improvement decisions.[5] There was a parallel investment from the Department of Education in the What Works Clearinghouse, with its goal of improving dissemination of research evidence from RCTs.

Recently, the debate has shifted to focus on a broader approach to understanding and scaling "what works" from education research. Both the Bush and Obama administrations invested in tiered evidence grant-making initiatives, such as the Investing in Innovation Fund (i3). In a tiered-evidence design, programs with more rigorous evidence of impact are eligible for the most funding, while programs with less rigorous or emerging evidence are eligible for smaller grants. The 2015 reauthorization of the federal Elementary and Secondary Education Act (ESEA) is an example of the push for evidence in federal education policy, one that recognizes a role for different tiers of evidence for selecting and implementing programs and practices.

Implementation of policies, like ESSA, that include provisions for research evidence will not only require technical solutions (e.g., additional administrative guidance) but also attention to the social conditions that support such efforts.[6] Policy implementation is a set of interactive, social processes occurring as actors make sense of, co-construct, and respond collectively. Therefore, we must consider the social infrastructure required to relate research and practice in new ways. We turn to research-practice partnerships, structures that are rich in relationships and committed to solving the substantial problems of education.

THE PROMISE OF
RESEARCH-PRACTICE PARTNERSHIPS

RPPs are collaborative research efforts between practitioners and researchers focused on solving critical problems facing educational leaders.[7] Rather than translating research done by others and disseminating it to practitioners, research partnerships engage in research and development activities *with* educators. Research partnerships seek to identify problems of practice, codesign solutions with practitioners, implement the design, and then study this process and its results.

All RPPs share common strands of DNA. First, RPPs are for the long term. Instead of being focused on a single study, researchers and educational leaders in RPPs sustain their work across multiple projects. Second, RPPs organize their work around a problem of practice instead of leading with gaps in existing theory or research. Third, these partnerships are mutualistic; all involved jointly negotiate and hold authority over the lines of work. This approach stands in contrast to traditional research studies where the researchers often play a central role in setting the research agenda. Fourth, RPPs develop and employ strategies to foster partnerships, which may include carefully designed rules, roles, routines, protocols, or "ways of doing business" that structure their engagement. Finally, the partnerships involve original analysis of data, where RPP participants gather data and conduct analyses to provide insight into communities' pressing questions. This analysis can both be anchored by and advance educational theory.

Outside of this shared DNA, RPPs can look quite different from one another in terms of organization and strategy.[8] In research alliance models, RPPs engage around analyses of implementation of district policies, where the researchers share findings for educational decision makers and work with them to develop solutions (e.g., University of Chicago Consortium for Chicago School Research). In design research partnerships, codesign work plays an even greater role, with researchers and district leaders codeveloping and testing strategies or tools for improving teaching and learning systemwide.[9] Still other RPPs organize as networks of schools, districts, or other institutions, such as afterschool or informal organizations, and engage in continuous improvement research to work on problems of practice.[10]

Not all partnerships fit neatly into this typology. A partnership may engage in different activities based on the goals of its work. For instance, a partnership could engage in activities that are more typical of research alliances, like integrating multiple data sets or performing independent analyses of district administrative data. The same group could also be involved in codesigning and testing strategies or tools for addressing identified needs, another feature of design research partnerships.

With recent investments by local and federal funders like the Institute of Education Sciences (IES) and the National Science Foundation, RPPs of all forms and types have multiplied.[11] Of particular note are the Regional Educational Laboratories (RELs) funded through the US Department of Education, which have devoted significant resources to the formation of research alliances and, in the 2016 competition for the next generation of RELs, promised to allocate even more to the formation of alliances and partnerships.

One claim made about RPPs is that they are an effective mechanism for supporting research use. For instance, the theory of action for IES' researcher-practitioner partnership program names improved research use as a central goal, and recent evidence lends some support to this claim.[12] Similarly, evaluation utilization scholars find that participation in the research process—a key component of work in some kinds of RPPs—is important for evidence utilization.[13] Several studies also suggest that participation in partnerships is associated with greater access to research.[14]

A key reason why RPPs may support research use is that they create opportunities for interactive social processes such as persuasion, negotiation, and sense making.[15] Research findings do not speak for themselves; engagement with research requires leaders to make sense of findings, discuss their relevance to the current district context, and design policies or programs in that particular context in light of other financial, political, or temporal constraints.[16] Within this interactive space, researchers and practitioners can sift through the range of available evidence-based programs and strategies to select programs that may work for a particular issue.[17] Partnerships, via collaborative design efforts, can create spaces to adapt these programs to fit local contexts, or they can tailor the design of a program or strategy to adapt to new, unfolding needs—a key theme emphasized in this volume. Finally, conducting local evaluations of these programs within a partnership may lead to results that are seen as more timely, credible, and central to district leaders' needs, thus making it more likely that leaders will act on the findings in their decision making.

KEY PROVISIONS REGARDING EVIDENCE USE IN ESSA

ESSA represents a significant devolution of decision-making authority from the federal government to state and local agencies. With this new authority comes the explicit expectation that local policy makers will be evidence based in their decision making.

For the first time in ESEA history, ESSA defines the four levels of evidence that constitute an evidence-based program, intervention, or activity, drawing on those set forth in the i3 stimulus program.[18] The evidence tiers are based on the strength of the research base:

- *Strong evidence* has at least one well-designed and implemented experimental study from a randomized controlled trial that shows a positive impact.
- *Moderate evidence* has at least one well-designed and implemented quasi-experimental study (e.g., a regression discontinuity analysis that shows a positive impact).

- *Promising evidence* has at least one well-designed and implemented correlational study which controls for selection bias that shows a positive impact.
- *Research-based rationale* has a body of evidence from research and evaluation to support the claim that the strategy or intervention is likely to improve student outcomes.

ESSA uses the terms *evidence* or *evidence-based* more than eighty times. This language is most notable in the regulations for the large formula and competitive grants programs. For Title I funds, for instance, school districts are to develop improvement plans for low performing schools that include "evidence-based" interventions, programs, or activities that meet the first three tiers of evidence. Further, seven of the authorized competitive grant programs (i.e., Literacy Education for All, Results for the Nation, Section 2221) similarly restrict "evidence-based" activities or interventions to the top three tiers of evidence. In these grant competitions, the US Department of Education will give priority to applications with "evidence-based" approaches, presumably by awarding more points to proposals with strong evidence than to those proposals with merely promising evidence. Other ESSA formula grant programs, including Title II (Preparing, Training, and Recruiting High Quality Teachers, Principals, and Other School Leaders) and Title IV, Part A (Student Support and Academic Enrichment Grants), encourage state and local school districts to invest in "evidence-based" interventions or programs, including afterschool and summer initiatives supported through the 21st Century Community Learning Centers program. Here, activities may qualify via the fourth tier, a demonstration "of a rationale based on high-quality research findings or positive evaluation" that also "includes ongoing efforts to examine the effects of such activity, strategy, or intervention."[19]

ESSA also includes a number of provisions that further signal a federal commitment to building the evidence base in education (table 9.1). The law authorizes the Education Innovation and Research (EIR) Grants program, which, like i3, will provide tiered grants to support the testing and replication of new strategies or programs and will require grantees to independently evaluate the effect of their grant-funded activities, thereby adding to the research base.[20]

TABLE 9.1 *Evidence provisions in ESSA*

ESSA provision	Focus
Title VIII, Sec. 8002	• Defines the four levels of evidence that constitute an "evidence-based" activity, strategy, or intervention by a state, local school district, or individual school
Title I, Sec. 1003	• Requires states to set aside a portion of their ESEA Title I, Part A funds for a range of activities to help school districts improve low-performing schools • Requires local school districts to select "evidence-based" interventions that meet strong, moderate, or promising levels of evidence in their improvement plans
Title II	• Focuses on improving the quality and effectiveness of teachers, principals, and other school leaders in preparation programs, professional learning initiatives, or recruitment efforts • Encourages states and local school districts to use their Title II funds on "evidence-based" activities (where there is available evidence)
Title III, Sec. 4611	• Authorizes the Education Innovation and Research (EIR) Grants program, a federal evidence-based education innovation fund similar to the existing i3 program
Title IV, Part A	• Student Support and Academic Enrichment Grants section encourages states and local school districts to invest their Title IV funds in "evidence-based" activities (where there is available evidence)

Competitive grant programs	• US Department of Education gives priority to applications that demonstrate strong, moderate, or promising levels of evidence for following grant programs:
	  • Sec. 2221, Literacy Education for All, Results for the Nation
	  • Sec. 2242, Supporting Effective Educator Development
	  • Sec. 2243, School Leader Recruitment of Support
	  • Sec. 4502, Statewide Family Engagement Centers
	  • Sec. 4624, Promise Neighborhoods
	  • Sec. 4625, Full-service Community Schools
	  • Sec. 4644, Supporting High-Ability Learners and Learning

Title VIII, Sec. 8601	• Allows US Department of Education to dedicate funds toward ESSA program evaluations

ESSA also allows the US Department of Education to set aside portions of Title I and Title VIII funds for program evaluations.[21]

The rollback of federal authority, combined with a commitment to interventions and strategies supported by evidence, has created serious new demands on state and local leaders. ESSA requires that state and local leaders identify and select programs or interventions that meet the standards of evidence. In the cases where there is not research that meets the top tiers, the work of using research evidence will occur in the spaces of design, adaptation, and improvement. Local decision makers will need to determine whether and how these strategies will work in their context and adapt as needed. Based on what we know from implementation research more generally, and the specific case of i3 grants more recently, it is likely that these evidence-based programs or interventions will need to be iteratively refined to meet the needs of particular communities.[22] ESSA also requires that local policy makers and practitioners become partners in contributing to the evidence base, either by evaluating the strategies in the fourth tier of evidence (research-based rationale) or through EIR grant efforts. Under ESSA, a much greater responsibility for knowing about, using, and even developing evidence is placed on local leaders, which means they will need support in meeting these expectations.

PROPOSED ROLES FOR RPPS UNDER ESSA

Research-practice partnerships are positioned to play important roles in realizing ESSA's vision for evidence-based policy making by helping leaders identify and select evidence-based programs; develop evidence-based programs through collaborative design; iteratively refine evidence-based programs through improvement science strategies; and conduct local evaluations of evidence-based programs.

Identifying and Selecting Evidence-Based Programs

RPPs can help leaders identify and select evidence-based programs that are appropriate for their context and then address the needs of their schools and districts. Under Title I, for instance, local educators must identify those programs that meet the top three evidence tiers in their action plans aimed at low performing schools.

Identifying an evidence-based program is not a simple matter of looking up evidence reports from sites like the What Works Clearinghouse or the Campbell Collaboration and selecting a program with strong evidence of impact on student learning. Nor is it as simple as accepting a claim from a publisher that the program or curriculum includes "strong evidence" for its efficacy. Identifying evidence-based programs requires knowing where to look for programs that have a strong evidence base that matches the needs of a particular program, school, district, or community. Intervention reports from the What Works Clearinghouse, which are summaries of evidence related to specific programs, typically provide little guidance on the resources required to implement programs or on the processes that educators might need to undertake to select programs based on a careful balancing of needs and resources.

A good example of an RPP model that helps with the identification and selection of programs is Communities That Care (CTC), created by the Social Development Research Group at the University of Washington. In this model, researchers work with multiagency collaboratives to assess needs and then select and implement evidence-based programs in primary prevention for adolescents. The model aims to build a culture of evidence-based decision making and a commitment to primary prevention across a community. Researchers who tested the CTC model have found that, when compared to control communities, leaders in communities that formed partnerships with researchers to implement CTC were more likely to devote resources to primary prevention than were leaders in comparison communities.[23] The researchers have also documented positive impacts on youth, with lower levels of alcohol and cigarette use and fewer delinquent behaviors compared to youth in control communities.[24] Although this example comes from outside education, schools are integral implementation partners, and the CTC model shows the benefits of partnerships for helping identify and select evidence-based programs.

Developing Evidence-Based Programs Through Collaborative Design

A few competitive grant programs in ESSA call for the development of evidence-based programs. One of them, the Supporting Effective Educator Development program, names the creation of a comprehensive center that would "identify or develop evidence-based professional development" targeting teachers of students at risk in literacy.[25] Developing new programs rooted in evidence is a labor-intensive process that takes time and extensive collaboration. It is difficult for districts and states to do on their own or for researchers to do without significant input from educators regarding the design of programs that can be implemented in schools and districts.

Some partnerships use an approach to developing interventions collaboratively with practitioners that has more realistic conditions of implementation from the start. This strategy of design-based research, first developed in the learning sciences in the early 1990s, involves the specification of a theory of how best to support learning of particular goals that is then tested in the crucible of the classroom.[26] It aims to produce not only usable innovations but also knowledge and practical principles for guiding the design of future innovations.[27]

A good example of design-based research within a partnership is a multiyear project conducted collaboratively by researchers from the Strategic Education Research Partnership (SERP) and the Minority

Student Achievement Network (MSAN), a network of eight districts focused on closing achievement gaps.[28] The challenge that MSAN members gave to SERP researchers was to design an intervention to close gaps in outcomes in algebra without isolating students of color for intervention. The district leaders also emphasized that the program should fit easily within teachers' existing routines and that the program should value teachers' expertise and contributions in the classroom.

In creating an initial version of the intervention, the team drew on research about the importance of worked examples—clear, step-by-step demonstrations of how to solve a particular problem that illustrates a class of problem types within a discipline.[29] While there is strong evidence that worked examples can help develop problem-solving strategies, they are not integrated into most mathematics texts.[30]

A design team made up of researchers and teachers developed a set of assignments with worked examples that targeted difficult mathematics concepts. Teachers piloted the assignments, and the team made subsequent revisions based on teacher input. Subsequent iteration resulted in further refinements. After several years of development and testing, the team concluded its effort with an experimental study that examined the impact of the assignments with worked examples on conceptual and procedural knowledge of algebra. The researchers found a significant main effect of the treatment, with greater gains made by low achieving students.[31]

This example illustrates the power of design-based research conducted within partnerships to design usable, effective interventions. The iterative process of design research not only resulted in successive refinements to the assignments to enhance their effectiveness, but the repeated testing in a variety of classrooms also yielded improvements that aligned better with the expressed needs of the teachers and district leaders. A focused addition to practice yielded significant gains in the long run.[32]

Iteratively Refining Evidence-Based Programs Through Improvement Science Strategies

To achieve better outcomes for students at scale, states and local agencies will need to continuously refine their programs, activities, or interventions. For instance, findings from evaluations supported under different provisions or as part of the EIR program could be leveraged to support continuous improvement efforts.

One strategy for iteratively refining a program is to employ methods of improvement research within a research-practice partnership. Improvement research is widely used in medicine to design and test strategies for improving practice using a Plan-Do-Study-Act (PDSA) cycle.[33] In these cycles, a partnership decides on a small change to be tested, defines the steps needed to test it, and determines the measures that will be used to gauge its success (Plan). It then carries out the plan (Do), analyzes data collected to see if their predictions were borne out (Study), and, finally, determines what changes need to be made for the next cycle (Act). This approach to improvement research is being more fully developed in a range of initiatives facilitated by the Carnegie Foundation for the Advancement of Teaching.[34] One such initiative involves a partnership among the Harrisonburg City Public Schools, Motivation Research Institute, Carnegie Foundation for the Advancement of Teaching, and Raikes Foundation that uses improvement research methods to test and refine a brief intervention focused on student motivation that proved successful in other settings. The team was compelled by evidence from previous studies which found that brief social psychological interventions that target students' feelings and thoughts about school can lead to large gains in achievement.[35]

Three motivation researchers worked closely with six teachers and two administrators on the effort. They first worked to identify what they perceived to be top motivational challenges to students. The group concluded that the most pressing challenge was that "students who do not believe in themselves and give up at anything that is not quick and easy for them."[36] They used a tool from improvement research called a Key Driver Diagram to name leverage points for addressing this problem. The diagram, constructed through both conversations with partners and an analysis of the literature, highlighted four key drivers: students believe they can learn, students value learning, students feel that they belong in the context, and students use effective learning strategies.

The team decided to start with "students believe they can learn" and chose an intervention focused on building growth mind-set among students that was developed by Carol Dweck's team at Stanford.[37] The intervention was developed for a different age group and lasted longer than the partnership was willing to support, so the team made three adaptations to the intervention: developed material to make it engaging for middle schoolers with limited English proficiency, shortened the intervention's length, and delivered on a handheld tablet.

Team members used a careful approach to scaling prescribed by improvement research. First, they tested the adapted intervention in one classroom with older students, mainly to establish that the content was comprehensible to them. Next, they moved the intervention to a few fifth-grade classrooms and addressed usability issues with the handheld devices through a PDSA cycle. In the process, they learned a lot from testing in the classrooms where they refined the intervention, such as the need to add follow-up activities for students who finished tasks early and to develop new material for when students saw the handheld application more than once. The testing also resulted in refinements being made to the assessment. The team is now testing the intervention in a large-scale study throughout the district.

This example shows the potential of improvement research to refine an existing evidence-based intervention. Through working in close collaboration with teachers and district leaders in what might be called a multitiered partnership, because it involves educators working at different levels of a system, a team was able to work systematically to ensure that the social psychological intervention they adapted could be reliably implemented.[38] The project also illustrates in a powerful way that even the shortest and most straightforward evidence-based programs can require significant adaptation when introduced into a new context.

Conducting Local Evaluations of Evidence-Based Programs

Under ESSA, there is a role for evaluation of federally funded activities, and some research-practice partnerships are well positioned to serve in this role. Research alliances function as independent voices in a community that documents the implementation and effectiveness of local school district policies and programs.[39] Here, educators take primary responsibility for the design and implementation of policies and programs, while researchers serve as evaluators of those policies and programs. The evaluations, however, are not undertaken as many studies are, where contractors have no ties to the community. Rather, alliances are place based and committed to an ongoing relationship with partner school districts, states, and consortia of states (as in the case of some REL alliances) to address problems of practice and to inform the search for solutions to those problems of practice.

WHAT DO WE NEED TO LEARN TOGETHER? A COLLABORATIVE LEARNING AGENDA

Though the above examples illustrate the potential for research-practice partnerships to contribute to key aspects of ESSA implementation, we are a long way from being able to claim that partnerships are a viable strategy for all educational settings. There is much for us to learn—not just about ESSA, but also about how best to form and sustain partnerships that can impact local policies, practices, and student outcomes. Here we outline a learning, not research, agenda framed by questions that we need to explore in order to increase the field's capacity to engage in successful partnership work.

Making Sense of the Evidence Base

Under ESSA, educators in both formal and informal settings will have new roles as research consumers. In some situations, this may involve selecting from programs that have demonstrated success in an RCT setting. While the application of strong evidence will likely continue to be privileged, it is also important to recognize the very limited body of knowledge that meets the criteria for the top two tiers. Therefore, educational leaders will need support in order to access, interpret, and make use of research in a range of ways. These tasks will include interpreting the results of stand-alone RCTs or quasi-experimental studies, an area where educational leaders may need support.[40] Additionally, it will require an ability to assess evidence for claims that something is "research-based" or to gauge the strength of the research base across studies. Partnerships will need to develop answers to the question, How can partners help local leaders find and interpret "bodies of evidence" relative to specific problems that go beyond single studies?

Further, decision makers at the local level will need to determine whether a research-based program, curriculum, tool, or strategy may work within their own setting given local conditions. Beyond whether a program will "work" or not, educational leaders will need information on how to implement those strategies given available resources, staffing, and previous initiatives. This requires knowledge about the applicability of a program to one's own context, considering the generalizability of findings and evidence of replication.[41] It will require strategies for implementation and plans for adapting the program to meet local conditions in order to achieve student outcome results. Partnerships may be well positioned to focus on this demand, so we need to ask, How can RPPs adapt evidence-based programs to improve reliability of implementation and equity of outcomes?

Developing Evidence-Based Programs

Another key question is, How can collaborative design processes best support the development of evidence-based programs? Traditional research and development puts researchers in control of the design process, but in RPPs educators and researchers design collaboratively. In real educational contexts, moreover, iteration must be based on both emerging evidence of impact and on changing district environments.[42] Codesign in such environments must wrestle with multiple tensions across organizational structures, such as district units or partnering institutions, and between central offices and schools.[43] At present, we do not have a range of well-tested models to draw on for organizing collaborative design of evidence-based programs. For instance, Title II provisions call on local leaders to "identify and develop" evidence-based programs for professional development for teachers, principals, and other school leaders. Although researchers have conducted experiments to test a number of different programs over the past decade, only a few have been found to be effective, and fewer still have been sustained. Recently there have been calls to develop professional learning opportunities that are better integrated into school and district infrastructures.[44] Researchers working in partnerships with districts could accomplish such a task.

GETTING BETTER AT GETTING BETTER

Collaborative design is just one important process in developing evidence-based programs. To meet the demands of practitioner timescales for rapid improvement, we need to develop faster ways to go from early-stage development to reliable impact at scale. Traditional research and development cycles take too long to generate such evidence, and by the time it is generated, it may no longer be useful for decision makers. One of the promising aspects of the Carnegie Foundation's development of improvement research methods for education is the speed and systematicity with which evidence can be generated from studying an innovation in a few classrooms and learning quickly to improve the reliability of outcomes and integrity of implementation. In ninety-day cycles, small tests of change can be undertaken and an aspect of an intervention can be refined based on evidence collected using practical measures that are targeted to studying a few outcomes. Over the course of one to two years, a comprehensive "change package" can be developed that can then be tested with large numbers of classrooms.

To implement these kinds of methods in schools and districts, we need to ask, How can networked improvement communities (NICs) support the development and improvement of specific programs and practices? At present, few researchers and educators have the capacity to form NICs. Researchers need to develop the facilitation skills to bring them about, and districts must develop mechanisms for providing time for educators to take on the new roles and responsibilities required of them. Further, in an NIC there is no clear delineating of who is a researcher and who is an educator. All work together as a network. But such a blurring of roles is counternormative.[45] To "get better at getting better," a chief aim of an NIC, we need to learn much more about how best to take on new roles in our respective organizations and about the demands they place on us.

ESSA reflects a continued commitment among policy makers to the idea that research evidence has an important role to play in supporting improvement efforts. RPPs can provide the foundation for a new, collaborative infrastructure for connecting research and practice, and programs like the Regional Educational Laboratories, as well as other grant-funding opportunities for partnerships, can help build these infrastructures. The place-based nature of RPPs is a strength, not a weakness, because the work of adapting programs to be effective in a new context requires collaboration with people who have a stake in the outcomes and responsibility for implementation of reforms. It is from these infrastructures of partnerships and processes of adaptation that others can learn to foster collaborative reform.

Improving the Interpersonal Dimension of Schools and School Systems

ESTHER QUINTERO

A s this volume's chapters make clear, improving interpersonal aspects of schools and school systems won't be quick, nor will it be easy or accomplished by simple remedies. But, as John Papay and Matthew Kraft observe, interpersonal aspects of school contexts "can improve over time, and teachers are responsive to these changes." In synthesizing the contributors' recommendations and ideas on how to improve our schools, I structure them around three broad themes: teacher collaboration, school and system leaders, and the role of system-level partnerships in reform.

TEACHER COLLABORATION

Collaborative structures, be they instructional teams or professional learning communities, provide space and opportunity for professional interactions associated with teacher learning and improvement as well as student achievement. The contributors' recommendations on how to promote high-quality interactions among teachers call attention to the *contextual* nature of collaboration, specific *models,* and organizational *conditions.*

One Size Does Not Fit All

According to Papay and Kraft, a range of collaborative models "have demonstrated benefits for teachers' instructional practice when implemented well." But "well" means different things in different contexts. Social capital is highly context specific. So, although efforts aimed at promoting collaboration among practitioners are smart policy investments, Matthew Ronfeldt disagrees with the idea that schools should be compelled to adopt a single form of collaboration; instead, he recommends policies that set the *expectation* that schools be collaborative but leave the particulars up to each school.

While there is no single model of collaboration that works better than others across contexts, research suggests that certain features are always desirable. For example, scholars have pointed out that effective collaboration must be regular and ongoing.[1] In addition, collaboration should not be "contrived"—administratively regulated, compulsory, and oriented toward implementing an idea coming from the top—since this type of cooperation fails to produce the benefits of more spontaneous, voluntary, and open-ended routines and interactions embedded in the daily work lives of teachers.[2]

Regardless of the model teams adopt, collaboration should be focused. Carrie Leana and Frits Pil note that effective social capital development means having more instructionally focused conversations. Ronfeldt recommends that when selecting the topics for collaboration, team members think deeply about their unique goals and the outcomes they hope to influence. Several contributors underscore the role of data in focusing and facilitating professional conversations. Susan Moore Johnson, Stefanie Reinhorn, and Nicole Simon cite examples of schools that "dedicated time for content teams to analyze data about students' learning in order to gauge the effectiveness of their instruction." And Elaine Allensworth contends that data can make difficult conversations feel less personal and more solution oriented, moving the conversation from "Who's to blame for a student's poor attendance?" to "What do we know about barriers standing in the way of that student's academic success?"

Effective Models

As the chapters indicate, there are many ways to go about promoting cooperation among teachers. In Johnson and colleagues' study, new and veteran teachers credited their academic content teams with reducing uncertainty about what to teach and how and their student cohort teams with focusing on behavioral issues and other student needs. By attending to both the academic and personal well-being of students, teams were able to identify those who struggled across subjects and intervene to get them back on track. Principals' active engagement in the teams' work, having dedicated times to meet, and team facilitators (teacher leaders) were factors that teachers thought contributed to the success of their teams.

Papay and Kraft highlight a promising intervention involving the pairing of teachers who have low scores in certain areas with teachers from the same school with demonstrated success in those areas. The initiative was "explicitly framed as a collaborative partnership (not coaching or mentoring)." The teacher teams were encouraged to work together throughout the year, observing each other's teaching, discussing improvement strategies, and looking at each other's evaluation results. A randomized experiment comparing the outcomes of treatment schools to control schools showed that the intervention increased teacher effectiveness.[3] Although all teachers in the treatment schools improved, lower-performing teachers experienced greater gains, what was "roughly equivalent to the difference between being assigned to a median teacher instead of a bottom-quartile teacher."

If we think of collaboration as a "way of doing" rather than an activity, we might find that many structures and routines could become venues for high-quality interactions. Take professional development (PD), for example. Research has shown that sustained PD can be leveraged to create strong collegial ties among teachers by focusing jointly on the examination of students' work and cooperative lesson planning. To the extent that these activities require ongoing dialogue among teachers, they also encourage "the emergence of group norms, reciprocity in their relationships, trust, and information-sharing among teachers—all elements of social capital."[4]

For decades scholars have examined collaborative models such as Japanese lesson study, professional learning communities, inquiry groups, and, more generally, effective teacher teams.[5] In identifying features that are effective across models, Ronfeldt recommends "pairing experimental designs with interventions that use more typical and naturalistic forms of collaborative activity." One possibility, he explains, is "to allow teachers or schools randomized to 'collaboration' conditions to take responsibility for generating the form of collaborative activity according to [their] specific needs."

Supportive Conditions

Collaboration cannot be created or maintained by just having a group of motivated teachers. Regardless of the route pursued or model chosen, certain conditions need to be in place for collaboration to work. Johnson and colleagues demonstrate that the success of teams depends in part on effective hiring and evaluation to ensure that new teachers work well with existing faculty. These three systems—hiring, evaluation, and teams—are "prominent, interdependent, and mutually reinforcing." Schools can achieve greater instructional and organizational coherence by *simultaneously* investing in intentional ways to select, assess, and support teachers.

In light of the growing evidence that effective collaboration is critical to how well a school functions, Ronfeldt observes that being willing to collaborate and being skilled at collaborating "should be core expectations of teachers' work" and should be considered in hiring and retention decisions.

Additional funding is important to supporting collaboration. Extra resources could be used to implement more thorough hiring process, expand administrative teams, and compensate teachers who take on new responsibilities as team facilitators. According to Leana and Pil, good uses for extra funding should be school based rather than individual based and incentivize and reward peer-to-peer learning. It's important, though, that funding be sustained. When turnaround schools improve, they too often become ineligible for the funds that helped them get better in the first place. Johnson and colleagues contend that "viewing turnaround as a short-term process that can be both initiated and sustained with an infusion of temporary resources is misguided . . . When school leaders use additional resources wisely to deepen and expand successful programs, they should not be expected to suddenly do without."

Given the challenge of securing resources, Ronfeldt observes that framing collaboration as a form of professional development could increase backing for such an investment, since it is likely cheaper and has stronger empirical support than conventional forms of PD, which teachers tend to view as a waste of time.

SCHOOL AND SYSTEM LEADERS

School leaders are particularly important when it comes to designing environments that are conducive to the emergence of social capital. Principals' attention to "mission and goals" or "community and trust" has subtle yet real organizational influence.[6] Principals who seek to create effective collaboration, Johnson and colleagues argue, "must convey a clear and worthy purpose before asking teachers to commit so much time to team meetings."

There are other more tangible conditions that school leaders must ensure. Time for collaboration is a basic and obvious one. But carving out such time from teachers' schedules is a complex undertaking, and principals are not always skilled at it. Many of the conditions conducive to collaboration are strongly dependent on principal leadership.

Principal Decision Making and Accountability

Johnson and colleagues recommend that principals have "substantial say in who their teachers are, how they are supported and evaluated, and how they collaborate." Principal autonomy, however, is a necessary but not a sufficient condition for orchestrating effective organizational change, since "it all depends on who the principal is and what the principal does."

Principals' active engagement in the work of teams appears to be an essential component of their success. Papay and Kraft argue that teachers need "guidance and support in creating effective team structures and flexibility in tackling the problems of practice." This suggests that school leaders need to be heavily invested in and be authentic champions of collaboration as a vehicle for improvement. Importantly, principals need to convey these beliefs to their staff.

Leana and Pil emphasize personnel stability, arguing that social capital can be threatened by excessive levels of churn and, thus, "school administrators should focus on teacher retention as an explicit policy goal." Similarly, James P. Spillane, Megan Hopkins, Tracy M. Sweet, and Matthew Shirrell advise school administrators to weigh staff decisions carefully. Since teachers chosen for leadership roles are significantly more likely to be a source of instructional advice for colleagues, leaders should ensure that staff chosen for these roles are prepared and supported. Spillane and colleagues also demonstrate that instructional ties are much more likely to develop among same-grade teachers and that teachers who teach multiple grades tend to be more isolated in schools. This suggests that administrators should take into account teachers' expertise (not just with specific age groups) when assigning them to particular grades. It is important that principals try to distribute expert teachers in ways that maximize their influence on colleagues so that exchange and learning can take place. And leaders should also consider where teachers work within their buildings. Location matters. A principal might want to assign teachers with complementary strengths to neighboring workspaces to maximize their chances of knowledge exchange.

Yet, as Joshua Starr observes, "While it might seem obvious that a good principal, like any good boss, should be responsible for creating a supportive environment where his staff is growing, learning, and highly engaged, principals are typically only accountable for student achievement on standardized test scores, safety, and operations." By and large, the contributors think this has to change. As superintendent of schools, Starr orchestrated a reform to introduce the use of a new survey to capture employee engagement and promoted its use for improvement and accountability purposes.

Along these lines, Leana and Pil recommend making social capital a central component in formal administrator evaluations, possibly holding principals "responsible for conducting a social capital inventory in their schools and measuring the outcomes of increases or decreases in social capital." Outcomes could be gathered through teacher attitude surveys as well administrative data on student achievement. As Papay and Kraft point out, even working conditions and climate surveys, which many districts and states already administer, could be used for this and other purposes to help school and district leaders "identify and target efforts toward strengthening specific organizational weaknesses in their schools." While the Every Student Succeeds Act (ESSA) includes school climate as one of the core components of accountability, climate is typically understood and measured rather narrowly. Alan J. Daly, Kara S. Finnigan, and

Yi-Hwa Liou urge us to broaden our understanding: "Measures such as network metrics, trust, support, and churn rates are key indicators for climate and culture that have not been incorporated into traditional accountability systems."

While it's true that we have a lot of data in education, it's all primarily the same kind. In order to improve, Anthony Bryk has argued, we need a different kind of data, one that reveals more about how schools *actually* work—work processes, social interactions, norms and beliefs, and, especially, *how all this comes together*.[7] Contributors to this volume make similar recommendations. Most chapters suggest using new measures for accountability purposes, although Papay and Kraft are a bit more cautious, noting that "incorporating school context surveys into accountability systems may undermine their value and lead to biased results if teachers, students and parents feel pressure to rate their school favorably."

Principal Preparation

Principals play a key role in leading and coordinating the kind of change described in this volume. To facilitate this work, Leana and Pil recommend that principal preparation be geared more toward acquiring expertise in activities *outside* the school. When principals develop external professional networks, they become sources of innovation for their schools, as well as ambassadors and champions. Moreover, as Daly and colleagues show, when leaders expand and diversify their external networks, the entire system can become more resilient by reducing dependence on a small subset of experts and by lightening the leaders' loads, making them less likely to leave the district due to burnout. Allensworth also sees value in school leaders networking outside the schools and recommends creating opportunities and structures for school leaders to interact with each other, to "get together regularly, look at each other's data, and share strategies for addressing common problems." Doing so, she contends, "allows them to ask hard questions of each other and themselves about their practices and let the solutions they've discovered travel."

There is less agreement, however, around the question of whether principals should be trained to be teachers first and managers second. How important is it that principals are effective instructional leaders? Some contributors suggest that districts appoint principals with instructional experience and that preparation focus on recruiting expert teachers with an interest in leading schoolwide reform. Starr worries that many principals and assistant principals do not always have "the content or pedagogical expertise to provide effective supervision to every employee." His solution is to support and leverage teacher leaders. And Allensworth cautions that there are many approaches to instructional leadership and that "not all emphasize the quality of relationships in the school." Accordingly, she recommends that principal preparation programs and state policies for licensure and certification "do more to provide much-needed training and supports around how to foster collaboration, build trust, support shared leadership," and so on.

Regardless of the label—"instructional leader" or "organizational change expert"—principals need to know how to create environments that prioritize strong relationships, which in turn facilitate organizational learning and coordination among school staff and between schools and families in the service of all students.

The Role of Central Office

Reforms of the kind described in these pages are only possible if a district's central office leads the charge: when policies, resources, and messages are aligned, and they have a synergistic effect. Central offices orchestrate, monitor, and support efforts to promote strong, collaborative learning cultures in schools and school systems.

In addition to securing stakeholders' buy-in and allocating sufficient resources such as time and money, the superintendent has to communicate her vision and goals to employees and the broader school community. One problem, according to Starr, is that communication within central offices isn't always ideal: "Invariably, when I visited schools or principal meetings, school leaders would tell me they were getting mixed messages from central office leaders." To remedy this, the superintendent must promote internal communication to ensure that messages going out to schools are consistent and aligned with the district's direction.

Central office leaders should observe teacher teams, leadership meetings, and any other structure intended to bring people together. To further enhance communication, mechanisms should be put in place for central office leaders to account for their work in schools and encourage discussion with fellow leaders, improved monitoring of schools' progress, and, when appropriate, support of schools' needs. According to Starr, who set up such a system when he was Montgomery County's school superintendent, "This kind of coordinated effort, or case management approach, should look like a running conversation throughout the year."

Central offices are also instrumental in augmenting and distributing formal teacher leadership through teacher contracts. Contracts can formalize roles and responsibilities of figures such as department heads, instructional coaches, staff development teachers or team leaders, among others. Contracts are powerful tools to address job descriptions and expectations, among other issues. Contract language can signal what is valued in a district and specify discrete ways to support that vision. If collaboration is a school- and districtwide priority, contracts—for teachers *and* principals—can specify schedules, as well as ground rules about how teachers will work together. Of course, this potential is maximized when management and labor have established a trusting relationship.

PARTNERSHIPS

Complex educational problems cut across organizational, political, and geographical lines and are beyond the capacity of any single organization to solve. Collaboration among stakeholders is critical to tackle these kinds of problems.[8] Two frameworks in particular can provide the necessary infrastructures for people to work together: labor-management collaborations (LMCs) and research practice partnerships (RPPs).

LMCs take place between school districts, unions, and, often times, businesses and community organizations. RPPs are between researchers and school districts and practitioners. Both forms of partnerships are attempts to redefine relationships that are conventionally in tension or simply divorced from one another. For example, RPPs challenge the subordinate role that practitioners are expected to adopt vis-à-vis researchers. LMCs contest the broadly shared view that labor-management relations ought to be adversarial. Both are long-term ventures involving diverse stakeholders with unique as well as shared interests and goals. Broadly speaking, the purpose of these partnerships is to decide jointly on the issue to be addressed and then how to tackle it.

If change depends on stakeholders' ability to work together, partnerships are bound to play an important role in educational reform. Starr describes an initiative he started as district superintendent, explaining how the on-boarding of stakeholders was instrumental to getting his proposals off the ground and how the process "was facilitated by a well-established collaborative leadership structure" that included teachers, central office leaders, and principals as part of an "executive leadership team."

Leana and Pil go even further, contending that LMCs can be effective for social capital development: "Instead of being viewed as a detriment to building teacher human capital within schools," because unions lend much-needed personnel stability, they "could be more fruitfully viewed as incubators for cultivating social capital."

RPPs are valuable because of their collaborative and place-based nature. Their goal is to investigate issues that are of local interest, blending the expertise of researchers and practitioners, and to use the resulting knowledge in a manner that makes sense to those who are both responsible for implementation and have a stake in the outcomes. William Penuel and Caitlin Farrell argue that, with the passage of ESSA, RPPs are poised to become even more indispensable. While ESSA reflects a continued commitment to the use of research evidence in educational reform, the new law "puts a much greater responsibility on local decision makers for knowing about, using, and even developing evidence." To meet these expectations successfully, "local leaders will need support." They propose several ways in which RPPs could lend such support to researchers and practitioners: by sifting through and selecting evidence-based programs together, by adapting these programs to fit local context, and by conducting iterations and evaluations of such programs. This could include selecting from multiple promising models an approach to collaboration that best fits a school's and/or district's needs, resources, and preferences.

Here again, the central office plays a critical role. Partnerships with labor and research can be key supports for a superintendent not just because they help bring stakeholders on board, but also because they bring much-needed expertise to approach change effectively.

Given the demonstrated benefits of strong school-community ties and regular teacher-parent communication, dedicating resources to these kinds of partnership efforts seems appropriate. RPPs and LMC can help accomplish some of this. Papay and Kraft suggest two mechanisms for engaging parents: first, make parent outreach a well-resourced, schoolwide priority; and second, set the expectation that teachers must communicate with parents and then support them in those efforts. Along these lines, Allensworth recommends that more resources and time be devoted to "working collaboratively with families and carefully planning structures for positive interactions."

Papay and Kraft call attention to the barriers teachers face when trying to communicate with parents, "the lack of easy access to updated parent contact information, language barriers, and the lack of noninstructional time to make contact during the school day." Leaders are responsible for reducing these barriers and for setting the expectation that it's part of the teacher's jobs to connect regularly with parents and then supporting them in that process. As Allensworth says, "Thinking about schools as social systems requires strategic leadership that engages all stakeholders and meets the needs of students given the larger community context." Partnerships of various kinds can help us get there by nurturing trust and fostering relationships among stakeholders, thereby easing the complex technical and social work of leaders.

FORWARD TOGETHER

What is clear from the chapters' findings and recommendations is that teacher collaboration is a smart and worthy policy investment. While we have promising models that could be emulated, details should be decided by schools based on their situated needs. Regardless of the approach, certain conditions must exist before effective collaboration is established. These include adequate resources, such as time and funding; hiring and evaluation mechanisms that work in synergy with the work of teams; and a broadening of teachers' professional identity to include the expectation that an effective teacher is teacher that not only gets better but also helps her colleagues get better as well.

Critical to these efforts are the school leaders. At the school level, principals play a key role in establishing collaborative environments. They should have considerable autonomy and be actively engaged in the work of teachers—not micromanaging their staff but guiding and supporting them. Principals should prioritize personnel stability and be skilled at forging relationships outside their schools. Most contributors explicitly state that we need to know more about adults' engagement in their jobs and with their organizations. This might require collecting new data, but it could also be achieved by leveraging data from existing surveys that are now routinely administered in many districts and states. Finally, all this information should be used for decision-making and accountability purposes.

At the central office level, just as the school level, attending to what teachers and principals actually do in schools is critical. Thus, the central office must establish mechanisms for collecting information and monitoring progress in schools. Such a system will also help system leaders coordinate their work and make it easier for the superintendent to monitor, support, and evaluate.

Because today's educational challenges are so complex, cooperation among stakeholders is critical. Partnerships can provide infrastructures for people to work together and can be of great support to districts and communities. They can also ensure that context and interpersonal aspects are considered when implementing reform.

Teaching in Context reminds us of the simple, but taken for granted, idea that the interpersonal dimension of teachers' work contexts is crucial for improvement. It also tells us that we need to think about the interdependent, synergistic, and systemic natures of issues. Allensworth tells us that a key motivation behind the work of the Chicago Consortium on School Research was to understand how different aspects of school organization fit *together* to produce success. To develop an actual *plan* for school improvement, it was critical for researchers to understand the system as a whole and how the various pieces interacted to produce the observed outcomes. Similarly, Johnson and colleagues premise their argument on the interdependent nature of teacher collaboration, hiring, and evaluation and the need to attend to all three systems simultaneously.

Yet, policies continue to address problems in isolation. As Spillane and colleagues lament, "The dominant operating approach is the silver bullet strategy," which discourages "adopting a systemic approach where the primary concern is with how the various components of the educational infrastructure work in interaction rather than in isolation." Starr, however, contends that leaders, particularly those at the district level, can and should connect the dots, think systemically, and make sure coordination within the district is prioritized.

Approaches to change that draw on the knowledge captured in these pages may involve doing new and additional things, doing similar things but differently, or, in some cases, stopping what we are doing. Some current policies not only overlook interpersonal and organizational aspects of school improvement, but it's very possible that they actually undermine these aspects. It will be difficult to distill this research (and the research to come) into actionable ideas, tools, and strategies. But what this all means for policy and practice isn't a question just for the researchers. Ultimately, given that the processes we are trying to influence are complex and context dependent, practitioners, policy makers, and academics need figure out what to do *together*.

NOTES

INTRODUCTION

1. Anthony Bryk and Barbara Schneider, *Trust in Schools: A Core Resource for Improvement* (New York: Russell Sage Foundation, 2002), 5.

2. To be sure, educators' relations with students as well as students' relations with each other are of vital importance to educational success. This book, however, deals almost exclusively with adults' professional relationships and how they influence school improvement.

3. For example, James P. Comer, "The School Development Program: A Psychosocial Model of School Intervention," in *Black Students: Psychosocial Issues and Academic Achievement,* ed. G. L. Berry and J. K. Asamen (Newbury Park, CA: Sage, 1989), 264–85; Linda Darling-Hammond and Velma L. Cobb, "Teacher Preparation and Professional Development in APEC Members: A Comparative Study" (report, US Department of Education, Washington, DC, 1995); Judith W. Little, "The Mentor Phenomenon and the Social Organization of Teaching," *Review of Research in Education* 16 (1990): 297–351; Judith W. Little and Milbrey W. McLaughlin, eds., *Teachers' Work: Individuals, Colleagues, and Contexts* (New York: Teachers College Press, 1993), 137–63; Dan C. Lortie, *Schoolteacher: A Sociological Inquiry* (Chicago: University of Chicago Press, 1975); Karen S. Louis, Helen M. Marks, and Sharon Kruse, "Teachers' Professional Community in Restructuring Schools," *American Educational Research Journal* 33, no. 4 (1996): 757–98; Andy Hargreaves and Michael G. Fullan, eds., *Understanding Teacher Development* (New York: Teachers College Press, 1992); Susan M. Johnson, *Teachers at Work: Achieving Success in Our Schools* (New York: Basic Books, 1990).

4. Susan J. Rosenholtz, *Teachers' Workplace: The Social Organization of Schools* (Reading, MA: Addison-Wesley Longman, 1989).

5. Alan J. Daly, ed., *Social Network Theory and Educational Change* (Cambridge, MA: Harvard Education Press, 2010).

6. Eileen M. McMahon, "Professionalism in Teaching: An Individual Level Measure for a Structural Theory" (PhD diss., Ohio State University, 2007).

7. Ibid., 6.

CHAPTER 1

1. Dan Goldhaber, "Teachers Clearly Matter, but Finding Effective Teacher Policies Has Proven Challenging," in *Handbook of Research in Education Finance and Policy,* 2nd ed., ed. Helen F. Ladd and Margaret E. Goertz (New York: Routledge, 2015),

157–73; C. Kirabo Jackson, Jonah E. Rockoff, and Douglas O. Staiger, "Teacher Effects and Teacher-Related Policies," *Annual Review of Economics* 6 (2014): 801–25.

2. Susan Moore Johnson, Matthew A. Kraft, and John P. Papay, "How Context Matters in High-Need Schools: The Effects of Teachers' Working Conditions on Their Professional Satisfaction and Their Students' Achievement," *Teachers College Record* 114, no. 10 (2012): 1–39; Matthew A. Kraft, William H. Marinell, and Darrick Yee, "School Organizational Contexts, Teacher Turnover, and Student Achievement: Evidence from Panel Data," *American Educational Research Journal* 53, no. 5 (2016): 1411–99; Helen F. Ladd, "Teachers' Perceptions of Their Working Conditions: How Predictive of Planned and Actual Teacher Movement?" *Educational Evaluation and Policy Analysis* 33, no. 2 (2011): 235–61.

3. For more detail on the study's sample, see Matthew A. Kraft, John P. Papay, Megin Charner-Laird, Susan Moore Johnson, Monica Ng, and Stefanie K. Reinhorn, "Educating amid Uncertainty: The Organizational Supports Teachers Need to Serve Students in High-Poverty, Urban Schools," *Educational Administration Quarterly* 51, no. 5 (2015): 753–90; Susan Moore Johnson, Stefanie K. Reinhorn, Megin Charner-Laird, Matthew A. Kraft, Monica Ng, and John P. Papay, "Ready to Lead, but How? Teachers' Experiences in High-Poverty Urban Schools," *Teachers College Record* 116, no. 10 (2014): 1–50; Megin Charner-Laird, Monica Ng, Susan Moore Johnson, Matthew A. Kraft, John P. Papay, and Stefanie K. Reinhorn, "Teachers' Instructional Teams in High-Poverty, Urban Schools: Boon or Burden?" (working paper, Project on the Next Generation of Teachers, Cambridge, MA, n.d.).

4. Susan Moore Johnson, *Teachers at Work: Achieving Success in Our Schools* (New York: Basic Books, 1990); Susan Moore Johnson, "Having It Both Ways: Building the Capacity of Individual Teachers and Their Schools," *Harvard Educational Review* 82, no. 1 (2012): 107–22; Judith Warren Little, "Norms of Collegiality and Experimentation: Workplace Conditions of School Success," *American Educational Research Journal* 19, no. 3 (1982): 325–40; Judith Warren Little and Milbrey W. McLaughlin, eds., *Teachers and Work: Individuals, Colleagues, and Contexts* (New York: Teachers College Press, 1993); Dan C. Lortie, *Schoolteacher: A Sociological Inquiry* (Chicago: University of Chicago Press, 1975).

5. See, for example, Eric A. Hanushek, John F. Kain, and Steven G. Rivkin, "Why Public Schools Lose Teachers," *Journal of Human Resources* 39, no. 2 (2004): 326–54.

6. Richard M. Ingersoll, "Teacher Turnover and Teacher Shortages: An Organizational Analysis," *American Educational Research Journal* 38, no. 3 (2001): 499–534; John P. Papay, Andrew Bacher-Hicks, Lindsay C. Page, and William H. Marinell, "The Challenge of Teacher Retention in Urban Schools: Evidence of Variation from a Cross-Site Analysis" (working paper, 2015), https://ssrn.com/abstract-2607776.

7. For the financial costs of teacher turnover, see Gary Barnes, Edward Crowe, and Benjamin Schaefer, "The Cost of Teacher Turnover in Five School Districts: A Pilot Study," National Commission on Teaching and America's Future, 2007, http:// nctaf.org/wp-content/uploads/2012/01/NCTAF-Cost-of-Teacher-Turnover-2007 -full-report.pdf; Sarah E. Birkeland and Rachel E. Curtis, *Ensuring the Support*

and Development of New Teachers in the Boston Public Schools: A Proposal to Improve Teacher Quality and Retention (Boston: Boston Public Schools, 2006); and Anthony Milanowski and Allan Odden, *A New Approach to the Cost of Teacher Turnover* (Seattle: School Finance Redesign Project, Center on Reinventing Public Education, 2007); For the costs in student achievement, see Matthew Ronfeldt, Susanna Loeb, and James Wyckoff, "How Teacher Turnover Harms Student Achievement," *American Educational Research Journal* 50, no. 1 (2013): 4–36.

8. Johnson, Kraft, and Papay, "How Context Matters."

9. Gerald Grant, *Hope and Despair in the American City* (Cambridge, MA: Harvard University Press, 2009); Jonathan Kozol, *Death at an Early Age: The Destruction of the Hearts and Minds of Negro Children in the Boston Public Schools* (New York: Penguin Books, 1967); Jonathan Kozol, *Savage Inequalities* (New York: Crown, 1991).

10. Nicole S. Simon and Susan Moore Johnson, "Teacher Turnover in High-Poverty Schools: What We Know and Can Do," *Teachers College Record* 117, no. 3 (2013): 1–36.

11. Richard M. Ingersoll. "Teacher Turnover and Teacher Shortages: An Organizational Analysis," *American Educational Research Journal* 38, no. 3 (2001): 499–534

12. Johnson, Kraft, and Papay, "How Context Matters."

13. Jason A. Grissom, "Can Good Principals Keep Teachers in Disadvantaged Schools? Linking Principal Effectiveness to Teacher Satisfaction and Turnover in Hard-to-Staff Environments," *Teachers College Record* 113, no. 11 (2011): 2552–85; Donald Boyd et al., "The Influence of School Administrators on Teacher Retention Decisions," *American Educational Research Journal* 48, no. 2 (2011): 303–33.

14. Anthony S. Bryk et al., *Organizing Schools for Improvement: Lessons from Chicago* (Chicago: University of Chicago Press, 2010).

15. Johnson, Kraft, and Papay, "How Context Matters."

16. Ladd, "Teachers' Perceptions."

17. Kraft, Marinell, and Yee, "School Organizational Contexts."

18. Matthew A. Kraft and John P. Papay, "Can Professional Environments in Schools Promote Teacher Development? Explaining Heterogeneity in Returns to Teaching Experience," *Educational Evaluation and Policy Analysis* 36, no. 4 (2014): 476–500.

19. Matthew Ronfeldt et al., "Teacher Collaboration in Instructional Teams and Student Achievement," *American Educational Research Journal* 52, no. 3 (2015): 475–514.

20. Charner-Laird et al., "Teachers' Instructional Teams."

21. Kraft, Marinell, and Yee, "School Organizational Contexts."

22. Ronfeldt et al., "Teacher Collaboration"; Min Sun, Susanna Loeb, and Jason Grissom, "Building Teacher Teams: Evidence of Positive Spillovers from More Effective Colleagues," Education Evaluation and Policy Analysis, 2016, http://epa.sagepub.com/content/early/2016/08/31/0162373716665698.abstract; C. Kirabo Jackson and Elias Bruegmann, "Teaching Students and Teaching Each Other: The Importance of Peer Learning for Teachers," *American Economic Journal: Applied Economics* 1, no. 4 (2009): 85–108.

23. Charner-Laird et al., "Teachers' Instructional Teams."

24. Lortie, *Schoolteacher.*

25. Andy Hargreaves, *Changing Teachers, Changing Times: Teachers' Work and Culture in the Postmodern Age* (New York: Teachers College Press, 1994).

26. Charner-Laird et al., "Teachers' Instructional Teams," 30.

27. John P. Papay, Eric S. Taylor, John H. Tyler, and Mary E. Laski, "Learning Job Skills from Colleagues at Work: Evidence from a Field Experiment Using Teacher Performance Data" (Working Paper No. w21986, National Bureau of Economic Research, Cambridge, MA, 2016).

28. Kraft et al., "Educating amid Uncertainty."

29. Robert Rosenthal and Lenore Jacobson, "Pygmalion in the Classroom," *Urban Review* 3, no. 1 (1968): 16–20.

30. Stephen W. Raudenbush, "Magnitude of Teacher Expectancy Effects on Pupil IQ as a Function of the Credibility of Expectancy Induction: A Synthesis of Findings from 18 Experiments," *Journal of Educational Psychology* 76, no. 1 (1984): 85.

31. Will Dobbie and Roland G. Fryer Jr., "Getting Beneath the Veil of Effective Schools: Evidence from New York City," *American Economic Journal: Applied Economics* 5, no. 4 (2013): 28–60.

32. Kraft, Marinell, and Yee, "School Organizational Contexts."

33. Anne T. Henderson, Karen L. Mapp, Vivian R. Johnson, and Don Davies, *Beyond the Bake Sale: The Essential Guide to Family-School Partnerships* (New York: The New Press, 2007).

34. Elisa Nadworny, "What One District's Data Mining Did for Chronic Absence," National Public Radio, 2016, http://www.npr.org/sections/ed/2016/05/30/477506418/what-one-districts-data-mining-did-for-chronic-absence.

35. Matthew A. Kraft and Shaun M. Dougherty, "The Effect of Teacher-Family Communication on Student Engagement: Evidence from a Randomized Field Experiment," *Journal of Research on Educational Effectiveness* 6, no. 3 (2013): 199–222; Matthew A. Kraft and Todd Rogers, "The Underutilized Potential of Teacher-to-Parent Communication: Evidence from a Field Experiment," *Economics of Education Review* 47 (2015): 49–63; Peter Bergman, "The More You Know: Evidence from a Field Experiment on Parent-Child Information Frictions and Human Capital Investment" (unpublished manuscript, Department of Economics, University of California, Los Angeles, 2012).

36. Boyd et al., "The Influence of School Administrators"; Bryk et al., "Organizing Schools"; Grissom, "Can Good Principals Keep Teachers?"

CHAPTER 2

1. Steven G. Rivkin, Eric A. Hanushek, and John F. Kain, "Teachers, Schools, and Academic Achievement," *Econometrica* 73, no. 2 (2005): 417–58; Jonah E. Rockoff, "The Impact of Individual Teachers on Student Achievement: Evidence from Panel Data," *American Economic Review* 94, no. 2 (2004): 247–52; Susan Moore Johnson and Sarah E. Birkeland, "Pursuing a 'Sense of Success': New Teachers

Explain Their Career Decisions," *American Educational Research Journal* 40, no. 3 (2003): 581–617; H. F. Ladd, "Teachers' Perceptions of Their Working Conditions: How Predictive of Planned and Actual Teacher Movement?" *Educational Evaluation and Policy Analysis* 33, no. 2 (2011):235–61.

2. Elaine Allensworth, Stephen Ponisciak, and Christopher Mazzeo, *The Schools Teachers Leave: Teacher Mobility in Chicago Public Schools* (Chicago: Consortium on Chicago School Research, University of Chicago, 2009).

3. Nicole S. Simon and Susan Moore Johnson, "Teacher Turnover in High-Poverty Schools: What We Know and Can Do," *Teachers College Record* 117, no. 3 (2015): 1–36.

4. Susan Moore Johnson, Matthew A. Kraft, and John P. Papay, "How Context Matters in High-Need Schools: The Effects of Teachers' Working Conditions on Their Professional Satisfaction and Their Students' Achievement," *Teachers College Record* 114, no. 10 (2012): 1–39.

5. For a full explanation of this concept, see Susan Moore Johnson, *Teachers at Work: Achieving Success in Our Schools* (New York: Basic Books, 1990), 1–28.

6. Donald Boyd et al., "The Influence of School Administrators on Teacher Retention Decisions," *American Educational Research Journal* 48, no. 2 (2011): 303–33; Anthony S. Bryk et al., *Organizing Schools for Improvement: Lessons from Chicago* (Chicago: University of Chicago Press, 2010); Johnson, Kraft, and Papay, "How Context Matters."

7. See Morgaen L. Donaldson, "Principals' Approaches to Cultivating Teacher Effectiveness: Constraints and Opportunities in Hiring, Assigning, Evaluating, and Developing Teachers," *Educational Administration Quarterly* 49, no. 5 (2013): 838–82; and Allensworth, Ponisciak, and Mazzeo, *The Schools That Teachers Leave.*

8. For articles and working papers based on prior studies, visit www.projectngt.gse.harvard.edu.

9. Edward Liu and Susan Moore Johnson, "New Teachers' Experiences of Hiring: Late, Rushed, and Information Poor," *Educational Administration Quarterly* 42, no. 3 (2006): 37.

10. James Coleman, "Social Capital in the Creation of Human Capital," *American Journal of Education* 94 (1988): S95–S120.

11. We use pseudonyms for the names of all places and individuals.

12. Liu and Johnson, "Experiences of Hiring."

13. Jessica Levin and Meredith Quinn, "Missed Opportunities: How We Keep High-Quality Teachers out of Urban Classrooms," The New Teacher Project, 2003, http://eric.ed.gov/?id=ED481608.

14. Marisa Cannata and Mimi Engel, "Does Charter Status Determine Preferences? Comparing the Hiring Preferences of Charter and Traditional Public School Principals," *Education Finance and Policy* 7, no. 4 (2012): 455–88; Marisa Cannata, "Understanding the Teacher Job Search Process: Espoused Preferences and Preferences in Use," *Teachers College Record* 112, no. 12 (2010): 2889–934.

15. Carol Dweck, *Mindset: The New Psychology of Success* (New York: Ballantine, 2006).

16. Thomas Toch and Robert Rothman, *Rush to Judgment: Teacher Evaluation in Public Education* (Washington, DC: Education Sector, 2008); Daniel Weisberg et al., *The Widget Effect: Our National Failure to Acknowledge and Act on Differences in Teacher Effectiveness,* 2nd ed. (New York: The New Teacher Project, 2009).2008

17. Darrel Drury and Justin Baer, *The American Public School Teacher: Past, Present and Future* (Cambridge, MA: Harvard Education Press, 2011); Matthew Ronfeldt et al., "Teacher Collaboration in Instructional Teams and Student Achievement," *American Educational Research Journal* 52, no. 3 (2015): 475–514.

18. Jennifer O'Day, "Complexity, Accountability, and School Improvement," *Harvard Educational Review* 72, no. 3 (2002): 293–329.

19. Jonah E. Rockoff, "The Impact of Individual Teachers on Student Achievement: Evidence from Panel Data," *American Economic Review* 94, no. 2 (2004): 247–52.

20. Megin Charner-Laird et al., "Gauging Goodness of Fit: Teachers' Assessments of Their Instructional Teams in High-Poverty Schools," *American Journal of Education* (forthcoming).

21. Ibid.

22. See http://www.doe.mass.edu/edeval/.

23. Susan Moore Johnson et al., "Ready to Lead, but What Role Will They Play? Teachers' Experiences in High-Poverty Urban Schools," *Teachers College Record* 116, no. 10 (2013): 1–50.

CHAPTER 3

1. Dan Lortie, *Schoolteacher: A Sociological Perspective* (Chicago: University of Chicago Press, 1975).

2. Thomas G. Carroll, "Teaching for the Future," in *Building a 21st Century U.S. Education System*, ed. Bob Wehling and Carri Schneider (Washington, DC: National Commission on Teaching and America's Future, 2007), 46–58; Laura Hamilton et al., *Using Student Achievement Data to Support Instructional Decision Making* (Washington, DC: National Center for Education Evaluation and Regional Assistance, Institute of Education Sciences, 2009), http://ies.ed.gov/ncee/wwc/publications/practiceguides; "Standards for Professional Learning," National Staff Development Council, 2001, http://learningforward.org/standards/learning-communities#.UogfCGTk_R0.

3. *The MetLife Survey of the American Teacher: Collaborating for Student Success* (New York: MetLife, 2010), http://files.eric.ed.gov/fulltext/ED509650.pdf.

4. Matthew Ronfeldt et al., "Teacher Collaboration in Instructional Teams and Student Achievement," *American Educational Research Journal* 52, no. 3 (2015): 475–514.

5. Anthony S. Bryk et al., *Organizing Schools for Improvement: Lessons from Chicago* (Chicago: University of Chicago Press, 2010); Pam Grossman, Sam Wineburg,

and Stephen Woolworth, "Toward a Theory of Teacher Community," *Teachers College Record* 103, no. 6 (2001): 942–1012; Judith Warren Little, "Locating Learning in Teachers' Communities of Practice: Opening up Problems of Analysis in Records of Everyday Work," *Teaching and Teacher Education* 18, no. 8 (2009): 917–46; Milbrey W. McLaughlin and Joan E. Talbert, *Professional Communities and the Work of High School Teaching* (Chicago: University of Chicago Press, 2001); Louise Stoll et al., "Professional Learning Communities: A Review of the Literature," *Journal of Educational Change* 7, no. 4 (2006): 221–58; Vicki Vescio, Dorene Ross, and Alyson Adams, "A Review of Research on the Impact of Professional Learning Communities on Teaching Practice and Student Learning," *Teaching and Teacher Education* 24, no. 1 (2008): 80–91.

6. Vescio, Ross, and Adams, "A Review of Research."

7. Ibid.

8. Yvonne L. Goddard, Roger D. Goddard, and Meghan Tschannen-Moran, "A Theoretical and Empirical Investigation of Teacher Collaboration for School Improvement and Student Achievement in Public Elementary Schools," *Teacher College Record* 109, no. 4 (2007): 877–96.

9. Yvonne L. Goddard et al., "Connecting Principal Leadership, Teacher Collaboration, and Student Achievement" (paper, American Educational Research Association Annual Meeting, Denver, May 2010).

10. C. Kirabo Jackson and Elias Bruegmann, "Teaching Students and Teaching Each Other: The Importance of Peer Learning for Teachers," *American Economic Journal: Applied Economics* 1, no. 4 (2009): 85–108; Matthew A. Kraft and John P. Papay, "Can Professional Environments in Schools Promote Teacher Development? Explaining Heterogeneity in Returns to Teaching Experience," *Educational Evaluation and Policy Analysis* 36, no. 4 (2014): 476–500.

11. Kraft and Papay, "Can Professional Environments in Schools Promote Teacher Development?"

12. Jackson and Bruegmann, "Teaching Students and Teaching Each Other."

13. John P. Papay et al., "Learning Job Skills from Colleagues at Work: Evidence from a Field Experiment Using Teacher Performance Data" (Working Paper No. 21986, National Bureau of Economic Research, Cambridge, MA, February 2016), http://www.nber.org/papers/w21986.

14. Ronald Gallimore et al., "Moving the Learning of Teaching Closer to Practice: Teacher Education Implications of School-Based Inquiry Teams," *Elementary School Journal* 109, no. 5 (2009): 537–53; William M. Saunders, Claude Goldenberg, and Ronald Gallimore, "Increasing Achievement by Focusing Grade-Level Teams on Improving Classroom Learning: A Prospective, Quasi-Experimental Study of Title 1 Schools," *American Educational Research Journal* 46, no. 4 (2009): 1006–33.

15. Papay et al., "Learning Job Skills."

16. Kraft and Papay, "Can Professional Environments in Schools Promote Teacher Development?"; Jackson and Bruegmann, "Teaching Students and Teaching Each Other."

17. Ronfeldt et al., "Teacher Collaboration."

18. Matthew Ronfeldt, "Field Placement Schools and Instructional Effectiveness," *Journal of Teacher Education* 66, no.4 (2015): 304–20.

19. Catherine Lewis and Jacqueline Hurd, *Lesson Study Step by Step: How Teacher Learning Communities Improve Instruction* (Portsmouth, NH: Heinemann, 2011).

20. Grossman, Wineburg, and Woolworth, "Toward a Theory of Teacher Community."

21. For information about the Mills Teacher Scholars Group, see http://millsscholars.org/. Anna Richert and Claire Bove. "Inquiry for Equity: Supporting Teacher Research," in *Handbook of Reflection and Reflective Inquiry* (New York: Springer US, 2010), 319–32.

22. Judith Warren Little, "Organizing Schools for Teacher Learning," in *Teaching as the Learning Profession: Handbook of Policy and Practice,* ed. Linda Darling-Hammond and Gary Sykes (San Francisco: Jossey-Bass, 1999), 233–62.

CHAPTER 4

1. Nan Lin, *Social Capital: A Theory of Social Structure and Action* (New York: Cambridge University Press, 2001).

2. James S. Coleman, "Social Capital in the Creation of Human Capital," supplement, *American Journal of Sociology* 94 (1988): S94–S120; Janine Nahapiet and Sumantra Ghoshal, "Social Capital, Intellectual Capital, and the Organizational Advantage," *Academy of Management Review* 23, no. 2 (1998): 242–66.

3. Anthony S. Bryk and Barbara Schneider, *Trust in Schools: A Core Resource for Improvement* (New York: Russell Sage Foundation, 2002); Alan J. Daly et al., "Relationships in Reform: The Role of Teachers' Social Networks," *Journal of Educational Administration* 48, no. 3 (2010): 359–91; Frank A. Kenneth et al., "Focus, Fiddle, and Friends: Experiences That Transform Knowledge for the Implementation of Innovations," *Sociology of Education* 84, no. 2 (2011): 137–56; Nienke M. Moolenaar et al., "Linking Social Networks and Trust at Multiple Levels: Examining Dutch Elementary Schools," in *Trust and School Life: The Role of Trust for Learning, Teaching, Leading, and Bridging*, ed. Dimitri Van Maele et al. (Dordrecht, Netherlands: Springer, 2014), 207–28.

4. Yvonne L. Goddard, Roger D. Goddard, and Megan Tschannen-Moran, "A Theoretical and Empirical Investigation of Teacher Collaboration for School Improvement and Student Achievement in Public Elementary Schools," *Teachers College Record* 109, no. 4 (2007): 877–96; Carrie R. Leana and Frits K. Pil, "Social Capital and Organizational Performance: Evidence from Urban Public Schools," *Organization Science* 17, no. 3 (2006): 353–66.

5. We measured social ties by asking school staff to complete online surveys which asked, among other things, who they go to for advice and information about instruction in core subjects. We used these data to map out the advice and information ties among school staff—who is connected to whom and how.

6. See www.distributedleadership.org.

7. James P. Spillane, Chong M. Kim, and Kenneth A. Frank, "Instructional Advice and Information Seeking Behavior in Elementary Schools: Exploring Tie Formation as a Building Block in Social Capital Development," *American Educational Research Journal* 49, no. 6 (2012): 1112–45.

8. James P. Spillane, Megan Hopkins, and Tracy Sweet, "Intra- and Inter-School Interactions About Instruction: Exploring the Conditions for Social Capital Development," *American Journal of Education* 122, no. 1 (2015): 71–110.

9. Felichism W. Kabo et al., "Proximity Effects on the Dynamics and Outcomes of Scientific Collaborations," *Research Policy* 43, no. 9 (2014): 1469–85; Felichism W. Kabo et al., "Shared Paths to the Lab: A Sociospatial Network Analysis of Collaboration," *Environment and Behavior* 47, no. 1 (2015): 57–84.

10. David Marmaros and Bruce Sacerdote, "How Do Friendships Form?" *Quarterly Journal of Economics* 121, no. 1 (2006): 79–119.

11. Mario L. Small, "Weak Ties and the Core Discussion Network: Why People Regularly Discuss Important Matters with Unimportant Alters," *Social Networks* 35, no. 3 (2013): 470–83; Mario L. Small and Christopher Sukhu, "Because They Were There: Access, Deliberation, and the Mobilization of Networks for Support," *Social Networks* 47, no. 1 (2016): 73–84.

12. Spillane, Hopkins, and Sweet, "Intra- and Inter-School Interactions."

13. Michael W. Kirst and Frederick M. Wirt, *The Political Dynamics of American Education* (Richmond, CA: McCutchan, 2009).

14. Douglas E. Mitchell, Robert L. Crowson, and Dorothy Shipps, *Shaping Education Policy: Power and Process* (New York: Routledge, 2011).

15. Cynthia E. Coburn and Jennifer L. Russell, "District Policy and Teachers' Social Networks," *Educational Evaluation and Policy Analysis* 30, no. 3 (2008): 203–35; Alan J. Daly and Kara S. Finnigan, "Exploring the Space Between: Social Networks, Trust, and Urban School District Leaders," *Journal of School Leadership* 22, no. 3 (2012): 493–530; Julie M. Hite, Ellen J. Williams, and Steven C. Baugh, "Multiple Networks of Public School Administrators: An Analysis of Network Content and Structure," *International Journal of Leadership in Education* 8, no. 2 (2005): 91–122; Julie M. Hite et al., "The Role of Administrator Characteristics on Perceptions of Innovativeness Among Public School Administrators," *Education and Urban Society* 38, no. 2 (2006): 160–87.

16. James P. Spillane and Megan Hopkins, "Organizing for Instruction in Education Systems and School Organizations: How the Subject Matters," *Journal of Curriculum Studies* 45, no. 6 (2013): 721–47.

17. At the school level, out-degree centrality in language arts (the average number of advisers per staff member) ranged from 2.6 to 4.6, compared to a range of 1.6 to 3.1 in mathematics and 0.8 to 2.1 in science.

18. Megan Hopkins and James P. Spillane, "Conceptualizing Relations Between Instructional Guidance Infrastructure (IGI) and Teachers' Beliefs About Mathematics Instruction: Regulative, Normative, and Cultural-Cognitive Considerations," *Journal of Educational Change* 16, no. 4 (2015): 421–50; James P. Spillane, Matthew Shirrell,

and Megan Hopkins, "Designing and Deploying a Professional Learning Community (PLC) Organizational Routine: Bureaucratic and Collegial Structures in Tandem," *Les Dossiers des Sciences de l'Education* 35 (2016): 97–122; James P. Spillane, Megan Hopkins, and Tracy Sweet, "Teacher Interactions and Beliefs About Mathematics Instruction: School District Educational Infrastructure and Change at Scale" (under review).

CHAPTER 5

1. Lyda Hanifan, "The Rural School Community Center," *Annals of the American Academy of Political and Social Science* 67 (1916): 130–38.

2. Carrie Leana and Harry Van Buren, "Organizational Social Capital and Employment Practices," *Academy of Management Review* 24 (1999): 538–55.

3. Andy Hargreaves, "Contrived Collegiality: The Micro-Politics of Teacher Collaboration," in *The Politics of Life in Schools: Power, Conflict, and Cooperation,* ed. J. Blasé (Newbury Park, CA: Sage, 1991); R. Warren, "Context and Isolation: The Teaching Experience in an Elementary School," *Human Organization* 34 (1975): 139–48.

4. See, for example, Milbrey McLaughlin and Joan Talbert, *Professional Communities and the Work of High School Teaching* (Chicago: University of Chicago Press, 2001); and A. Bryk and B. Schneider, *Trust in Schools: A Core Resource for Improvement* (New York: Russell Sage, 2002).

5. James Spillane, *Distributed Leadership* (New York: Jossey-Bass, 2006).

6. See Bryk and Schneider, *Trust in Schools;* McLaughlin and Talbert, *Professional Communities;* Anthony Bryk et al., *Organizing Schools for Improvement: Lessons from Chicago* (Chicago: University of Chicago Press, 2009). For our work in this space, see Carrie Leana and Frits Pil, "Social Capital and Organizational Performance: Evidence from Urban Public Schools," *Organization Science* 17 (2009): 353–66; Frits Pil and Carrie Leana, "Applying Organizational Research to Public School Reform: The Effects of Teacher Human and Social Capital on Student Performance," *Academy of Management Journal* 52 (2009): 1101–24. Our work focuses on the importance of social capital to a community of teachers and schools more generally, including the ties between teachers and principals and the external ties between school employees and the community. Some work has looked at ties between teachers and students: Elizabeth Saft and Robert Pianta, "Teachers' Perceptions of Their Relationships with Students: Effects of Child Age, Gender, and Ethnicity of Teachers and Children," *School Psychological Quarterly* 16 (2001): 125–41; and Christopher Murray and Keith Zvoch, "The Inventory of Teacher-Student Relationships: Factor Structure, Reliability, and Validity Among African American Youth in Low-Income Urban Schools," *Journal of Early Adolescence* 31 (2011): 493–525. Other work has focused on ties among school leadership: Jorge Lima, "Social Networks in Teaching," in *Social Geographies of Educational Change,* ed. F. Hernandez and L. Goodson (London: Kluwer, 2004), 29–46; and Spillane, *Distributed Leadership.* Still other work has focused on ties between

schools and parents: Erin Horvat, Elliot Weininger, and Annette Laureau, "From Social Ties to Social Capital: Class Differences in the Relations Between Schools and Parents Networks," *American Educational Research Journal* 40 (2003): 319–51.

7. See, for example, Carrie Leana, Eileen Appelbaum, and Iryna Shevchuk, "Work Process and Quality of Care: Encouraging Positive Job Crafting in Childcare Classrooms," *Academy of Management Journal* 52 (2009): 1169–92; Carrie Leana, Jirs Meuris, and Cait Lamberton, "More Than a Feeling: The Role of Empathetic Care in Promoting Safety in Healthcare" (working paper, Center for Healthcare Management, University of Pittsburgh, 2016); Frits Pil and Takahiro Fujimoto, "Lean and Reflective Production: The Dynamic Nature of Production Models," *International Journal of Production Research* 45 (2007): 3741–61; Frits Pil and John Paul MacDuffie, "What Makes Transplants Thrive: Managing the Transfer of Best Practice at Japanese Auto Plants in North American," *Journal of World Business* 34 (2000): 372–91.

8. Our work has been conducted in several midsized and large urban school districts, including Pittsburgh, Nashville, Providence, and New York City. Carrie Leana and Frits Pil, "Social Capital and Organizational Performance: Evidence from Urban Public Schools," *Organization Science* 17 (2009): 353–66; Frits Pil and Carrie Leana, "Applying Organizational Research to Public School Reform: The Effects of Teacher Human and Social Capital on Student Performance," *Academy of Management Journal* 52 (2009): 1101–24; Carrie Leana, "The Missing Link in School Reform," *Stanford Social Innovation Review* 9 (2011): 30–35.

9. These dimensions were first articulated in abstract fashion by Janine Nahapiet and Sumantra Ghoshal, "Social Capital, Intellectual Capital, and the Organizational Advantage," *Academy of Management Review* 23 (1998): 242–66.

10. Pil and Leana, *Applying Organizational Research.*

11. James Coleman, *Foundations of Social Theory* (Cambridge MA: Harvard University Press, 1990), 304.

12. Indeed, almost two decades ago, Hansen and colleagues argued that strong relations not only take time to build, but require effort to maintain. See Morten Hansen, Joel Podolny, and Jeffrey Pfeffer, "Social Networks in Organizations—Capital or Liability?" (working paper, Harvard Business School, Cambridge, MA, 1999). In the same vein, Portes and Landolt suggest that the social resources claimed *from* the collective by some teachers need to be provided *to* the collective by others, a nontrivial burden to the contributors to the collective. See Alejandro Portes and Patricia Landolt, "The Downside of Social Capital," *American Prospect* 94 (1996): 18–21.

13. Free riding happens when people take from a collective without giving back. Economists define this as a classic market failure. In the context of social capital, free riding would occur when an individual takes information and advice from others without making any corresponding contributions to collective knowledge.

14. This refers to the idea that as individuals learn together, they not only develop an understanding of the material they are being taught but also a sense of how knowledge is distributed among others undergoing training.

15. Mauricio Rubio, "Perverse Social Capital—Some Evidence from Colombia," *Journal of Economic Issues* 31 (1997): 805–16.

16. For a general discussion, see Carrie Leana and Denise Rousseau, *Relational Wealth: The Advantages of Stability in a Changing Economy* (New York: Oxford University Press, 2000).

17. Leana, Appelbaum, and Shevchuk, "Work Process and Quality of Care"; Jason Shaw, Michelle Duffy, Jonathan Johnson, and Daniel Lockhart, "Turnover, Social Capital Losses, and Performance," *Academy of Management Journal* 48 (2005): 594–606; Gregory Dess and Jason Shaw, "Voluntary Turnover, Social Capital, and Organizational Performance," *Academy of Management Review* 26 (2001): 446–56; Michele Kacmar et al., "Sure Everyone Can Be Replaced . . . . but at What Cost? Turnover as a Predictor of Unit-Level Performance," *Academy of Management Journal* 49 (2006): 133–44.

18. Iryna Shevchuk, Carrie Leana, and Vikas Mittal, "Teacher Retention and School Performance: The Role of Organization- and Task-Specific Forms of Human and Social Capital" (working paper, Center for Healthcare Management, University of Pittsburgh, 2009).

19. Coleman, *Foundations of Social Theory,* 320.

20. In our research, we have found that teachers are about twice as likely to go to their peers for answers for instructionally related questions as to experts, coaches, or school administrators. This suggests that peer-to-peer learning is already taking place. What we are advocating is the recognition and fostering of it by school administrators.

21. Saul Rubinstein and John McCarthy, "Union-Management Partnerships, Teacher Collaboration, and Student Performance," *Industrial and Labor Relations Review* 69, no. 5 (2016): 1114–32.

22. Leana and Pil, *Social Capital and Organizational Performance.*

23. For a well-written critique and call for more scientific evidence to back up school reform efforts, see Barbara Schneider and Venessa Keelser, "School Reform 2007: Transforming Education into a Scientific Enterprise," in *Annual Review of Sociology,* ed. D. S. Massey and K. Cook (Palo Alto, CA: Annual Reviews, 2007).

24. Matthew G. Springer et al., "Team Pay for Performance Experimental Evidence from the Round Rock Pilot Project on Team Incentives," *Educational Evaluation and Policy Analysis* 34, no. 4 (2012): 367–90; Karthik Muralidharan and Venkatesh Sundararaman, "Teacher Performance Pay: Experimental Evidence from India" (working paper, National Bureau of Economic Research, Cambridge, MA, 2009).

CHAPTER 6

The study discussed in this chapter was supported through a research award from the W. T. Grant Foundation (Grant No. 0174). All opinions and conclusions expressed in this article are those of the authors and do not necessarily reflect the views of the W. T. Grant Foundation. The first and second authors contributed equally to this chapter.

1. Chris Argyris and Donald Schön, *Organizational Learning II: Theory, Method and Practice* (Boston: Addison Wesley, 1996); Cynthia Coburn, "Shaping Teacher Sensemaking: School Leaders and the Enactment of Reading Policy," *Educational Policy* 19, no. 3 (2005): 476–509; Leigh Parise and James Spillane, "Teacher Learning and Instructional Change: How Formal and On-the-Job Learning Opportunities Predict Change in Elementary School Teachers' Practice," *Elementary School Journal* 110, no. 3 (2010): 323–46.

2. Zuzana Sasovova, Ajay Mehra, Stephen Borgatti, and Michaela Schippers, "Network Churn: The Effects of Self-Monitoring Personality on Brokerage Dynamics," *Administrative Science Quarterly* 55 (2010): 639–68.

3. *CHURN: The High Cost of Principal Turnover* (Hinsdale, MA: School Leaders Network, 2014).

4. Karen Seashore-Louis, Kenneth Leithwood, Kyla Wahlstrom, and Steven Anderson, *Learning from Leadership: Investigating the Links to Improved Student Learning* (Alexandria, VA: Educational Research Service, 2010).

5. Kara Finnigan, Alan Daly, and Yi-Hwa Liou, "How Leadership Churn Undermines Learning and Improvement in Low-Performing School Districts," in *Thinking and Acting Systemically: Improving School Districts Under Pressure,* ed. Alan Daly and Kara Finnigan (Washington, DC: American Educational Research Association, 2016), 183–208; *CHURN;* Sasovova et al., "Network Churn."

6. William King, ed., *Knowledge Management and Organizational Learning,* Annals of Information Systems No. 4 (Dordrecht, Netherlands: Springer, 2009).

7. Susan Aud et al., *The Condition of Education 2011,* NCES 2011-033 (Washington, DC: National Center for Education Statistics, 2011); *CHURN;* Terence Mitchell et al., "Why People Stay: Using Job Embeddedness to Predict Voluntary Turnover," *Academy of Management Journal* 44 (2001): 1102–21.

8. Daniel Halgin and Stephen Borgatti, "An Introduction to Personal Network Analysis and Tie Churn Statistics Using E-NET," *Connections* 32 (2012): 37–48; Sasovova et al., "Network Churn."

9. Lee Mitgang, *The Making of the Principal: Five Lessons in Leadership Training* (New York: The Wallace Foundation, 2012).

10. Richard Feinberg and Nina Jeppeson, "Validity of Exit Interviews in Retailing," *Journal of Retailing and Consumer Services* 7, no. 3 (2000): 123–27; Mitgang, *The Making of the Principal.*

11. Tara Béteille, Demetra Kalogrides, and Susanna Loeb, "Stepping Stones: Principal Career Paths and School Outcomes," *Social Science Research* 41, no. 4 (2012): 904–19; Ed Fuller and Michelle Young, *Tenure and Retention of Newly Hired Principals in Texas,* Texas High School Project: Leadership Initiative Issue Brief 1 (Austin: Department of Educational Administration, University of Texas, 2009).

12. Béteille, Kalogrides, and Loeb, "Stepping Stones"; Jeanne Ringel et al., *Career Paths of School Administrators in Illinois: Insights from an Analysis of State Data* (Santa Monica, CA: Rand, 2014).

13. Béteille, Kalogrides, and Loeb, "Stepping Stones."

14. Jason Grissom and Stephanie Andersen, "Why Superintendents Turn Over," *American Educational Research Journal* 49 (2012): 1146–80.

15. Scott Soltis, Filip Agneessens, Zuzana Sosovova, and Guiseppe Labianca, "A Social Network Perspective on Turnover Intentions: The Role of Distributive Justice and Social Support," *Human Resource Management* 52 (2013): 561–84.

16. Ray Friedman and Brooks Holtom, "The Effects of Network Groups on Minority Employee Turnover Intentions," *Human Resource Management* 41 (2002): 405–21; Kevin Mossholder, Randall Settoon, and Stephanie Henagan, "A Relational Perspective on Turnover: Examining Structural, Attitudinal, and Behavioral Predictors," *Academy of Management Journal* 48, no. 4 (2005): 607–18.

17. Nan Lin, *Social Capital: A Theory of Social Structure and Action* (New York: Cambridge University Press, 2001), 24.

18. See, for example, Colleen McGrath and David Krackhardt, "Network Conditions for Organizational Change," *Journal of Applied Behavioral Science* 39 (2003): 324–36.

19. Rob Cross, Stephen Borgatti, and Andrew Parker, "Making Invisible Work Visible: Using Social Network Analysis to Support Strategic Collaboration," *California Management Review* 44 (2002): 25–46.

20. Alain Degenne and Michel Forsé, *Introducing Social Networks* (London: Sage, 1999).

21. Cross, Borgatti, and Parker, "Making Invisible Work Visible"; Seokwoo Song, Sridhar Nerur, and James Teng, "An Exploratory Study on the Roles of Network Structure and Knowledge Processing Orientation in the Work Unit Knowledge Management," *Advances in Information Systems* 38 (2007): 8–26.

22. Ronald Burt, *Structural Holes: The Structure of Competition* (Cambridge, MA: Harvard University Press, 1992); Mark Granovetter, "The Strength of Weak Ties," *American Journal of Sociology* 78, no. 6 (1973): 1360–80.; Mark Granovetter, "The Strength of Weak Ties: A Network Theory Revisited," in *Social Structure and Network Analysis*, ed. Peter Marsden and Nan Lin (Beverly Hills, CA: Sage, 1982), 105–30.; Robert Putnam, "Bowling Alone: America's Declining Social Capital," *Journal of Democracy* 6, no. 1 (1995): 65–78.

23. Ray Reagans and Ezra Zuckerman, "Networks, Diversity, and Productivity: The Social Capital of R&D Teams," *Organization Science* 12, no. 4 (2001): 502–17.

24. Stanley Wasserman and Katherine Faust, *Social Network Analysis: Methods and Applications* (New York: Cambridge University Press, 1994).

25. Stephen Borgatti and Martin Everett, "Models of Core Periphery Structures," *Social Networks* 21 (1999): 375–95; Robert Cross and Andrew Parker, *The Hidden Power of Social Networks: Understanding How Work Really Gets Done in Organizations* (Boston: Harvard Business Review Press, 2004).

26. Ronald Burt, *Structural Holes: The Structure of Competition* (Cambridge, MA: Harvard University Press, 1992); Ronald Burt, "The Network Structure of Social Capital," in *Research in Organizational Behaviour* 22 (2000): 345–423.

27. Alan Daly and Kara Finnigan, "A Bridge Between Worlds: Understanding Network Structure to Understand Change Strategy," *Journal of Educational Change* 11 (2009): 111–38; Alan Daly et al., "Misalignment and Perverse Incentives: Examining the Politics of District Leaders as Brokers in the Use of Research Evidence," *Educational Policy* 28 (2014): 145–74; Finnigan, Daly, and Liou, *Thinking and Acting Systemically*, 183–208.

28. More details regarding the procedures, variables, data analysis, and additional descriptive statistics follow.

Procedure: In collecting the data, we asked leaders to complete an online survey once a year (spring) for three years. We collected information about individual characteristics (gender, job title, workplace, etc.) as well as social networks. In this chapter we focus on these leaders' self-assessed frequency of seeking reliable work-related expertise ties (expertise network) to examine this instrumental or work-related network. We used a bounded approach and included all the members of the leadership team (district and school administrators), as this strategy, coupled with high response rates, provides more valid results. [John Scott, *Social Network Analysis* (London: Sage, 2012)] We drew on the literature regarding district improvement processes and practices, evidence use in education, and previous network studies and piloted our network questions with practicing administrators in order to better validate the items.

Measures, dependent variables: We were interested in the system's leavers (coded as 0) and the remainers (coded as 1).

Measures, independent variables: We asked participants to "check the interaction frequency of those administrators to whom you turn to for reliable source of expertise related to your work" on a four-point interaction frequency scale ranging from 1 (within the past two months) to 4 (one or two times a week). We extracted frequent interactions, defined as every week or two to one or two times a week.

We calculated three network measures related to individual centrality in the expertise network: indegree, outdegree, and betweenness using the UCINET 6.0 social network software package. [Stephen P. Borgatti, Martin G. Everett, and Linton C. Freeman, *UCINET for Windows: Software for Social Network Analysis* (Cambridge, MA: Analytic Technologies, 2002)] *Indegree* of a leader refers to the number of incoming ties around expertise a leader receives from other leaders. *Outdegree* refers to the number of outgoing ties around expertise a leader sends to other leaders. *Betweenness* centrality measures how likely a leader is to possess a broker position in connecting otherwise disconnected leaders in the network. [Stanley Wasserman and Katherine Faust, *Social Network Analysis: Methods and Applications* (New York, Cambridge University Press, 1994)]

Measures, control variables: We controlled work level (district or site) and years of experience (in administration and in the current position).

Data analysis: First, we presented descriptive statistics. Second, we constructed a network sociogram to illustrate the expertise network structure of the leaders with a focus on distinguishing the leavers from the remainers. We used the NetDraw social network software to generate the sociogram that contained information such as nodes (individual leaders), ties (connections between leaders for, in this case, the source of expertise), and actor attribute of work level (e.g., district or site leaders). Third, we ran KeyPlayer analysis to identify a set of actors who play a central role in connecting other actors. We used fragmentation criterion for the expertise network based on the calculation of actor level betweenness to identify the top number of key actors that would cause the most fragmentation of the network if removed.

Finally, we employed binary logistic regression analyses to test the likelihood of a leader leaving the district as well as the likelihood of a leader remaining in the position (indegree, outdegree, and betweenness). Given the difference in the number of leaders who remain and those who leave, we used a normalized weighting strategy retaining the sum of the weights to be 1. In doing so, we were able to obtain unbiased estimates and correct significant levels. All models were significant, explaining 15 percent to 19 percent of the variance in predicting the likelihood of being a leader as opposed to a remainer ($p < .001$).

29. Michael Hannan and John Freeman, "Structural Inertia and Organizational Change," *American Sociological Review* 49, no. 2 (1984): 149–64.

30. Soltis et al., "A Social Network Perspective."

31. Kara Finnigan, Alan Daly, and Jing Che, "Systemwide Reform in Districts Under Pressure: The Role of Social Networks in Defining, Acquiring, and Diffusing Research Evidence," *Journal of Educational Administration* 51 (2013): 476–97; Kara Finnigan, Alan Daly, and Tricia Stewart, "Organizational Learning in Schools Under Sanction," *Education Research International* (2012), doi: 10.1155/2012 /270404.

32. Kara Finnigan and Alan Daly, "Mind the Gap: Learning, Trust, and Relationships in an Underperforming Urban District," *American Journal of Education* 119 (2012): 41–71.

33. Alan Daly, "Rigid Response in an Age of Accountability," *Educational Administration Quarterly* 45, no. 2 (2009): 168–216.

34. Finnigan and Daly, "Mind the Gap."

CHAPTER 7

1. Milbrey McLaughlin and Joan Talbert, *Reforming Districts: How Districts Support School Reform* (Washington, DC: Center for the Study of Teaching and Policy, 2003); Charles M. Payne, *So Much Reform, So Little Change: The Persistence of Failure in Urban Schools* (Cambridge, MA: Harvard Education Press, 2008).

2. Anthony S. Bryk et al., *Organizing Schools for Improvement: Lessons from Chicago* (Chicago: University of Chicago Press, 2010).

3. Ibid., 19.

4. The initial conceptualization of the 5Essential Supports appeared in a 1995 guide provided to schools from Chicago's Central Office, *Pathways to Achievement*, http://annenberginstitute.org/sites/default/files/product/276/files/SIGuide_Chicago .pdf). In 1998 I joined the team that studied the framework.

5. Ibid., 113–26.

6. Ibid., 109–12.

7. Ibid., 120.

8. Jennie Y. Jiang and Susan E. Sporte, *Teacher Evaluation in Chicago: Differences in Observation and Value-Added Scores by Teacher, Student and School Characteristics* (Chicago: University of Chicago Consortium on School Research, 2016).

9. Elaine Allensworth, Stephen Ponisciak, and Christopher Mazzeo, *The Schools Teachers Leave: Teacher Mobility in Chicago Public Schools* (Chicago: University of Chicago Consortium on Chicago School Research, 2009).

10. James Sebastian, Haigen Huang, and Elaine Allensworth, "The Role of Teacher Leadership in Principals' Influence on Classroom Instruction and Student Learning." *American Journal of Education* (forthcoming); Karen S. Louis, Kenneth Leithwood, Kyla L. Wahlstrom, and Stephen E. Anderson, *Investigating the Links to Improved Student Learning: Final Report of Research Findings* (St. Paul: University of Minnesota Center for Applied Research and Educational Improvement, 2010).

11. Jenny Nagaoka, Camille A. Farrington, Stacy B. Ehrlich, and Ryan D. Heath, Foundations *for Young Adult Success: A Developmental Framework* (Chicago: University of Chicago Consortium on Chicago School Research, 2015).

12. Matthew Steinberg, Elaine Allensworth, and David W. Johnson, *Student and Teacher Safety in Chicago Public Schools: The Roles of Community Context and School Organization* (Chicago: University of Chicago Consortium on Chicago School Research, 2011), 33–38.

13. Relationships with school leaders, parents, and other teachers significantly predicted teacher mobility, controlling for differences in school composition, structure, changes in student enrollment, and teachers' background characteristics. Allensworth, Ponisciak, and Mazzeo, *The Schools Teachers Leave.*

14. Steinberg, Allensworth, and Johnson, *Student and Teacher Safety.*

15. Ibid., 33–38.

16. S. B. Ehrlich, Julia A. Gwynne, Amber Stitziel Pareja, and Elaine M. Allensworth, *Preschool Attendance in Chicago Public Schools: Relationships with Learning Outcomes and Reasons for Absences* (Chicago: University of Chicago Consortium on Chicago School Research, 2014).

17. Douglas D. Ready, "Socioeconomic Disadvantage, School Attendance, and Early Cognitive Development: The Differential Effects of School Exposure," *Sociology of Education* 83, no. 4 (2010): 271–86; Robert Balfanz and Vaughan Byrnes, *Meeting the Challenge of Combating Chronic Absenteeism: Impact of the NYC Mayor's Interagency Task Force on Chronic Absenteeism and School Attendance and its Implications for Other Cities* (Baltimore: Everyone Graduates Center, Johns Hopkins University School of Education, 2013); Elaine M. Allensworth, Julia A. Gwynne, Paul Moore, and Marisa de la Torre, *Looking Forward to High School and College: Middle Grade Indicators of Readiness in Chicago Public Schools* (Chicago: University of Chicago Consortium on Chicago School Research, 2014).

18. Steinberg, Allensworth, and Johnson, *Student and Teacher Safety,* 41–42.

19. Bryk et al., *Organizing Schools for Improvement,* 175.

20. Joshua Klugman, Molly F. Gordon, Penny Bender Sebring, and Susan E. Sporte, *A First Look at the 5Essentials in Illinois Schools* (Chicago: University of Chicago Consortium on Chicago School Research, 2015).

21. Ibid.

22. Donald Boyd et al., "Who Leaves? Teacher Attrition and Student Achievement" (Working Paper No. w14022, National Bureau of Economic Research, Washington, DC, 2008); Eric A. Hanushek, John F. Kain, and Steven G. Rivkin, "Why Public Schools Lose Teachers," *Journal of Human Resources* 39, no. 2 (2004): 326–54; Allensworth, Ponisciak, and Mazzeo, *The Schools Teachers Leave.*

23. Nicole S. Simon and Susan Moore Johnson, "Teacher Turnover in High-Poverty Schools: What We Know and Can Do," *Teachers College Record* 117, no. 3 (2013): 1–36.

24. Bryk et al., *Organizing Schools for Improvement.*

25. Elaine Allensworth et al., *Free to Fail or On-Track to College: Setting the Stage for Academic Challenge; Classroom Control and Support* (Chicago: University of Chicago Consortium on Chicago School Research, 2014).

26. Ibid. We interviewed sixty students over the course of their eighth- and ninth-grade years about their experiences in their math and English classes, observed their classroom experiences, and interviewed their math and English teachers. Using data on all students who attended Chicago schools for the grades 8 and 9 in the same year (about 22,000 students), we calculated the degree to which students' grades in ninth-grade were higher or lower than expected, given their eighth-grade test scores, grades in their eighth-grade classes, demographic characteristics, and economic backgrounds. We aggregated these values for each ninth-grade English and math class; doing so allowed us to compare the degree to which students received higher or lower grades in particular classes and link those values to the observations and interviews.

27. Elaine Allensworth, "The Use of Ninth Grade Early Warning Indicators to Improve Chicago Schools," *Journal of Education for Students Placed at Risk* 18, no.1 (2013): 68–83; Melissa Roderick, Thomas Kelley-Kemple, David W. Johnson, and Nicole O. Beechum, *Preventable Failure: Improvements in Long-Term Outcomes When High Schools Focused on the Ninth Grade Year: Research Summary* (Chicago: University of Chicago Consortium on Chicago School Research, 2014); Marcia Davis, Liza Herzog, and Nettie Legters, "Organizing Schools to Address Early Warning Indicators (EWIs): Common Practices and Challenges," *Journal of Education for Students Placed at Risk* 18, no. 1 (2013): 84–100.

28. Allensworth, "The Use of Ninth Grade Early Warning Indicators."

29. Amber S. Pareja, Holly Hart, and Molly Gordon, "How Do Successful School Leaders Lead Efforts to Improve Instruction and Learning?" (under review).

30. Ibid.

31. Allensworth, "The Use of Ninth Grade Early Warning Indicators."

CHAPTER 8

1. Ron Heifetz, Alexander Grashow, and Marty Linsky, *Diagnose the Adaptive Challenge: Understanding the Human Dimension of Change* (Boston: Harvard Business Press, 2009).

2. Jal Mehta, *The Allure of Order* (New York: Oxford University Press, 2013), 32.

3. Todd Rose, *The End of Average* (New York: Harper Collins, 2015).

4. Lucinda Gray and Soheyla Taie, *Public School Teacher Attrition and Mobility in the First Five Years: Results from the First Through Fifth Waves of the 2007–08 Beginning Teacher Longitudinal Study*, NCES 2015-337(Washington, DC: National Center for Education Statistics, 2015); Donald Boyd et al., "The Influence of School Administrators on Teacher Retention Decisions," *American Educational Research Journal* 48, no. 2 (2011): 303–33.

5. Mike Schrimpf, "Unpacking Standards to Improve Instruction," *Kappan Common Core Writing Project* (blog), 2016, http://www.kappancommoncore.org/unpacking -standards-to-improve-instruction/.

CHAPTER 9

1. Mark Dynarski, "Advancing the Use of Scientifically Based Research in Forming Policy: A Response to Mahoney and Zigler," *Applied Developmental Science* 27 (2006): 295–97.

2. Thomas B. Corcoran, Susan Fuhrman, and C. L. Belcher, "The District Role in Instructional Improvement," *Phi Delta Kappan* 83, no. 1 (2001): 78–84.

3. Damien Contandriopoulos, Marc Lemire, Jean-Louis Denis, and Emile Tremblay, "Knowledge Exchange Processes in Organizations and Policy Arenas: A Narrative Systematic Review of the Literature," *Milbank Quarterly* 88, no. 4 (2010): 444–83.

4. Grover J. Whitehurst, "The Institute of Education Sciences: New Wine, New Bottles" (paper, American Educational Research Association, Chicago, April 2003).

5. Meredith I. Honig and Cynthia E. Coburn, "Evidence-Based Decision-Making in School District Central Offices: Toward a Research Agenda," *Educational Policy* 22, no. 4 (2008): 578–608.

6. Nienke M. Moolenaar and Alan J. Daly, "Social Networks in Education: Exploring the Social Side of the Reform Equation," *American Journal of Education* 119, no. 1 (2012): 1–6.

7. Cynthia E. Coburn, Wiliam R. Penuel, and Kimberley E. Geil, *Research-Practice Partnerships: A Strategy for Leveraging Research for Educational Improvement in School Districts* (New York: William T. Grant Foundation, 2013).

8. Ibid.

9. Paul A. Cobb et al., "Design Research with Educational Systems: Investigating and Supporting Improvements in the Quality of Mathematics Teaching and Learning at Scale," in *Design-Based Implementation Research: Theories, Methods, and Exemplars,*

ed. William R. Penuel et al. (New York: National Society of the Study of Education Yearbook, 2013), 320–49.

10. Bronwyn Bevan et al., *Enriching and Expanding the Possibilities: Research-Practice Partnerships in Informal Science Education* (San Francisco: Research + Practice Collaboratory, 2015).

11. W. R. Penuel et al., "Conceptualizing Research-Practice Partnerships as Joint Work at Boundaries," *Journal of Education for Students Placed at Risk* 20, no. 1–2 (2015): 182–97.

12. "Researcher-Practitioner Partnerships in Education Research," Institute of Education Sciences, https://ies.ed.gov/funding/ncer_rfas/partnerships.asp.

13. Kelli Johnson et al., "Research on Evaluation Use: A Review of the Empirical Literature from 1986 to 2005," *American Journal of Evaluation* 30, no. 3 (2009): 377–410.

14. William E. Bickel and William W. Cooley, "Decision-Oriented Educational Research in School Districts: The Role of Dissemination Processes," *Studies in Educational Evaluation* 11, no. 2 (1985): 183–203.

15. Nabil Amara, Mathieu Ouimet, and Rejean Landry, "New Evidence on Instrumental, Conceptual, and Symbolic Utilization of University Research in Government Agencies," *Science Communication* 26, no. 1 (2004): 75–106; Damien Contandriopoulos et al., "Knowledge Exchange Processes in Organizations and Policy Arenas: A Narrative Systematic Review of the Literature," *Milbank Quarterly* 88, no. 4 (2010): 444–83.

16. *Using Science as Evidence in Public Policy* (Washington, DC: National Research Council, 2012).

17. Cynthia E. Coburn and Mary K. Stein, eds., *Research and Practice in Education: Building Alliances, Bridging the Divide* (Lanham, MD: Rowman & Littlefield, 2010).

18. Every Student Succeeds Act [ESSA], Pub. L. 114-95, Sec. 8002 (2015).

19. ESSA, Pub. L. 114-95, Sec. 8002 (2015).

20. ESSA, Pub. L. 114-95, Sec. 4601 (2015).

21. ESSA, Pub. L. 114-95, Sec. 1003, 8601 (2015).

22. Anthony S. Bryk et al., *Learning to Improve: How America's Schools Can Get Better at Getting Better* (Cambridge, MA: Harvard Education Press, 2015); Milbrey Wallin McLaughlin, "Implementation as Mutual Adaptation: Change in Classroom Organization," *Teachers College Record* 77, no. 3 (1976): 339–51; Donald J. Peurach, "Innovating at the Nexus of Impact and Improvement: Leading Educational Improvement Networks," *Educational Researcher* 45, no. 7 (2016): 421–29.

23. Eric C. Brown et al., "Prevention Service System Transformation Using Communities That Care," *Journal of Community Psychology* 39, no. 2 (2011): 183–201.

24. J. David Hawkins et al., "Early Effects of Communities That Care on Targeted Risks and Initiation of Delinquent Behavior and Substance Use," *Journal of*

Adolescent Health 43, no. 1 (2008): 15–22; J. David Hawkins et al., "Results of a Type 2 Translational Research Trial to Prevent Adolescent Drug Use and Delinquency: A Test of Communities That Care," *Archives of Pediatrics and Adolescent Medicine* 163, no. 9 (2009): 789–98.

25. ESSA, Pub. L. 114-95, Sec. 2242 (2015).

26. Ann L. Brown, "Design Experiments: Theoretical and Methodological Challenges in Creating Complex Interventions in Classroom Settings," *Journal of the Learning Sciences* 2, no. 2 (1992): 141–78; Paul Cobb et al., "Design Experiments in Educational Research," *Educational Researcher* 32, no. 1 (2003): 9–13.

27. Carl Bereiter, "Principled Practical Knowledge: Not a Bridge but a Ladder," *Journal of the Learning Sciences* 23, no. 1 (2014): 4–17; Daniel C. Edelson, "Design Research: What We Learn When We Engage in Design," ibid., 11, no. 1 (2002): 105–21.

28. Julie L. Booth et al., "Design-Based Research Within the Constraints of Practice: AlgebraByExample," *Journal of Education for Students Placed at Risk* 20, no. 1–2 (2015): 79–100.

29. Robert K. Atkinson et al., "Learning from Examples: Instructional Principles from the Worked Examples Research," *Review of Educational Research* 70, no. 2 (2000): 181–214.

30. Harold E. Pashler et al., *Organizing Instruction and Study to Improve Student Learning* (Washington, DC: National Center for Education Research, US Department of Education, 2007).

31. Booth et al., "Design-Based Research."

32. William R. Penuel, Jeremy Roschelle, and Nicole Shechtman, "The WHIRL Co-Design Process: Participant Experiences," *Research and Practice in Technology Enhanced Learning* 2, no. 1 (2007): 51–74.

33. Donald M. Berwick, "The Science of Improvement," *Journal of the American Medical Association* 299, no. 10 (2008): 1182–84.

34. Bryk et al., *Learning to Improve.*

35. David Yeager and Gregory M. Walton, "Social-Psychological Interventions in Education: They're Not Magic," *Review of Educational Research* 81, no. 2 (2011): 68–71.

36. Kenneth E. Barron, Chris S. Hulleman, R. Bruce Inouye, and Thomas A. Harkta. "Using a Networked Improvement Community Approach to Design and Scale Up Social Psychological Interventions in Schools" (presentation, National Center on Scaling Up Effective Schools Conference, Nashville, 2015), slide 11.

37. David Paunesku et al., "Mind-Set Interventions Are a Scalable Treatment for Academic Underachievement," *Psychological Science* 26, no. 6 (2015): 784–93.

38. Sam Severance, Heather Leary, and Raymond Johnson, "Tensions in a Multi-Tiered Research Partnership," in *Proceedings of the 11th International Conference of the Learning Sciences,* ed. Joseph L. Polman et al. (Boulder, CO: International Society of the Learning Sciences, 2014).

39. Melissa Roderick, John Q. Easton, and Penny Bender Sebring, *The Consortium on Chicago School Research: A New Model for the Role of Research in Supporting Urban School Reform* (Chicago: Consortium on Chicago School Research, 2009).

40. William R. Penuel et al., "Findings from a National Study on Research Use among School and District Leaders," in *Technical Report No. 1* (Boulder, CO: National Center for Research in Policy and Practice, 2016).

41. C. Matthew Makel and Jonathan A. Plucker, "Facts Are More Important Than Novelty: Replication in the Education Sciences," *Educational Researcher* 43, no. 6 (2014): 304–16.

42. Joshua L. Glazer and Donald J. Peurach, "School Improvement Networks as a Strategy for Large-Scale Education Reform: The Role of Educational Environments," *Educational Policy* 27, no. 4 (2013): 676–710.

43. Raymond Johnson et al., "Teachers, Tasks, and Tensions: Lessons from a Research-Practice Partnership," *Journal of Mathematics Teacher Education* 19, no. 2 (2016): 169–85.

44. National Research Council, *Science Teachers' Learning: Enhancing Opportunities, Creating Supportive Contexts* (Washington, DC: National Academies Press, 2015).

45. Coburn, Penuel, and Geil, "Research-Practice Partnerships."

CONCLUSION

1. Judith Warren Little, "Organizing Schools for Teacher Learning," in *Teaching as the Learning Profession: Handbook of Policy and Practice*, ed. Linda Darling-Hammond and Gary Sykes (San Francisco: Jossey-Bass, 1999), 233–62.

2. Andy Hargreaves, *Changing Teachers, Changing Times: Teachers' Work and Culture in the Postmodern Age* (New York: Teachers College Press, 1994).

3. John P. Papay, Eric S. Taylor, John H. Tyler, and Mary E. Laski, "Learning Job Skills from Colleagues at Work: Evidence from a Field Experiment Using Teacher Performance Data" (Working Paper No. w21986, National Bureau of Economic Research, Cambridge, MA, 2016).

4. Adam Gamoran, Ramona Gunter, and Toma Williams, "Professional Community by Design: Building Social Capital Through Teacher Professional Development," in *The Social Organization of Schooling* (New York: Russell Sage Foundation, 2005), 111–26.

5. Catherine Lewis and Jacqueline Hurd, *Lesson Study Step by Step: How Teacher Learning Communities Improve Instruction* (Portsmouth, NH: Heinemann, 2011); Pam Grossman, Sam Wineburg, and Stephen Woolworth, "Toward a Theory of Teacher Community," *Teachers College Record* 103, no. 6 (2001): 942–1012; Anna Richert and Claire Bove, "Inquiry for Equity: Supporting Teacher Research," in *Handbook of Reflection and Reflective Inquiry* (New York: Springer US, 2010), 319–32; Vivian Troen and Katherine C. Boles, *The Power of Teacher Teams: With Cases, Analyses, and Strategies for Success* (Thousand Oaks, CA: Corwin Press, 2011).

6. Jonathan Supovitz, Philip Sirinides, and Henry May, "How Principals and Peers Influence Teaching and Learning," *Educational Administration Quarterly* 46, no. 1 (2009): 31–56.

7. Anyhony S. Bryk et al., *Learning to Improve: How America's Schools Can Get Better at Getting Better* (Cambridge, MA: Harvard Education Press, 2015).

8. Eric Trist, "Referent Organizations and the Development of Interorganizational Domains," *Human Relations* 36, no. 3 (1983): 269–84.

ACKNOWLEDGMENTS

The work that inspired this book began in the spring of 2014. I had been acquainting myself with scholarship on topics such as the role of school organization in instructional improvement, the importance of the interpersonal dimension of school reform, and the influence of social capital in teacher development and effectiveness. It felt like a vast and rich field, one that I still don't presume to know in its entirety, but one that resonated strongly with me as a sociologist.

Several things struck me about this scholarship from the beginning. I was surprised at how little known the work seemed to be beyond academic circles. I also noted how much new research there was and how sophisticated and diverse it was, as well as how much these studies had in common in terms of their assumptions, principles, and overall approaches. I couldn't help but wonder how the world of education policy could be enriched by this knowledge. All of this convinced me that the field might really benefit from a synthesis of this work, one that brought together interrelated studies that would speak to policy makers and practitioners more directly.

I had experience inviting scholars to share their work by writing for the blog of the Albert Shanker Institute. But my goal this time was to have a *sustained* focus on the interpersonal and relational dimensions of school improvement. In the summer of 2014 the Institute launched the blog series *The Social Side of Education Reform*, which currently features more than thirty columns written by twenty-plus contributors. Working with these talented researchers, forging relationships with them, getting to know their work and helping them to disseminate it more broadly has been a most rewarding professional experience. I acknowledge everyone who contributed to the series, particularly the early collaborators who joined in without hesitation when all these ideas were still a bit nebulous, as well as the practitioners and leaders whose knowledge and perspectives are essential to bringing about change.

My biggest thanks go to the volume's contributors, most of whom I had the privilege of working with on the blog series. It's been my distinct pleasure and honor to work with each of you.

I am indebted to the team at the Harvard Education Press, especially to Caroline Chauncey, who has been there for me throughout the entire process and from whom I've learned so much.

This volume would not have materialized without the support of my colleagues at the Albert Shanker Institute. I am particularly grateful to Leo E. Casey for always giving me the space and freedom to explore and work on ideas that didn't always yield immediate results or products.

Several organizations have provided financial support for the broader initiative connected to this book. I am thankful to the National Public Education Support Fund, to the Campaign for Grade-Level Reading, and to the Spencer Foundation for their generous support.

Finally, I thank my husband, César Talón, for the innumerable ways, big and small, he supported this work. César, you are so talented and so kind to me; I couldn't have done any of this without you. I am also grateful to my father, Manuel Quintero Peña, for his unconditional love and for making me laugh and to my late grandmother, Concepción Peña García, who passed away many years ago but remains a source of inspiration in my life.

ABOUT THE EDITOR

Esther Quintero is a senior fellow at the Albert Shanker Institute, where she conducts and synthesizes research that can inform education issues such as equity, systemwide reform, and improving the teaching profession. Specifically, she focuses on understanding schools as organizations, social capital as a lever for educational improvement, and the sociology of the classroom. In July 2014 Quintero launched the *Social Side of Education,* a research campaign and blog series focusing on the social and relational aspects of improving teaching where established and emerging scholars (and, increasingly, practitioners) share their research and expertise in accessible ways. She is also coinvestigator in an Institute of Education Sciences–funded project that will develop an instrument to capture rich evidence of teachers' professional activity and the contexts in which it occurs. Other areas of interest to Quintero include social inequality, the sociology of gender and race, and group processes. She holds a BA from the University of Seville (Spain) and a PhD in sociology from Cornell University.

ABOUT THE CONTRIBUTORS

Elaine M. Allensworth is the Lewis-Sebring Director of the Consortium on Chicago School Research, where she conducts studies on what matters for student success and school improvement. Her research on early indicators of high school graduation has been used to create student tracking systems used in Chicago and districts across the country. In addition to studying educational attainment, she conducts research in the areas of school leadership and school organization. Allensworth is a coauthor of *Organizing Schools for Improvement: Lessons from Chicago* (University of Chicago Press, 2010), which provides a detailed analysis of school practices and community conditions that promote school improvement. She has been the principal investigator on research grants from funders such as the Institute of Education Sciences, the National Science Foundation, and the Bill & Melinda Gates Foundation. She has briefed members of Congress and their staffers on Consortium research findings through private meetings, briefings, and congressional testimony.

Alan J. Daly is chair and professor in the Department of Education Studies at the University of California, San Diego, and is also the founding executive editor of the Sage journal *Educational Neuroscience*. His research and teaching are influenced by his sixteen years of public school experience in a variety of instructional and leadership roles. His research primarily focuses on the roles of leadership, educational policy, and organization structures and the relationship between those elements on the educational attainment of traditionally marginalized student populations. In his work, Daly draws on his theoretical and methodological expertise in social network theory and analysis, and he has multiple publications and a book on the topic, *Social Network Theory and Educational Change* (Harvard Education Press, 2010). He is the coauthor of *Using Research Evidence in Schools* (Springer, 2014, with Kara Finnigan) and the author of *Thinking and Acting Systemically: Improving School Districts under Pressure* (AERA, 2016).

Caitlin C. Farrell is the director of the National Center of Research in Policy and Practice (NCRPP) at the University of Colorado Boulder. She specializes in research on policy implementation and K–12 educational reform, with a particular focus on organizational theory. She uses qualitative methods to explore the links between educational policy and the conditions that foster successful reform, such as examining evidence use at the classroom, school, and system levels. Prior to joining NCRPP, Farrell served as a postdoctoral fellow at the University of California, Berkeley, where she studied research-practice partnerships between school districts and research organizations. Earlier, she was an elementary school teacher in the New York and Washington, DC, public school systems. She holds a bachelor of arts from Dartmouth College, a master of science in teaching from Pace University, and a doctor of philosophy in urban education policy from the University of Southern California.

Kara S. Finnigan, an associate professor of educational policy at the University of Rochester, has conducted research and evaluations of educational policies and programs at the local, state, and federal levels for more than twenty years. Her work focuses on K–12 schools in urban contexts with an emphasis on how policies impact students of color and from low socioeconomic backgrounds. She has written extensively about low-performing schools and accountability, district reform, principal leadership, and school choice. Finnigan's research blends perspectives in sociology and political science; employs qualitative and quantitative methods, including social network analysis and GIS mapping; and examines the impact of federal and state policies at the local level. She recently published *Using Research Evidence in Education: From the Schoolhouse Door to Capitol Hill* (Springer, 2014) and *Thinking and Acting Systemically: Improving School Districts Under Pressure* (AERA, 2016).

Megan Hopkins is an assistant professor of education studies at the University of California, San Diego, and a 2016 National Academy of Education/Spencer Postdoctoral Fellow. Her research takes a sociological approach to teacher learning and development and uses mixed methods to explore how formal policies and organizational structures, as well as district and school norms and individual beliefs, shape teachers' learning opportunities within and between education systems.

Susan Moore Johnson is the Jerome T. Murphy Research Professor in Education at the Harvard Graduate School of Education, where she served as academic dean from 1993 to 1999. A former high school teacher and administrator, Johnson has an ongoing research interest in the work of teachers and the reform of schools and school systems. She studies, teaches, and consults about teacher policy, organizational change, and administrative practice. Since 1998, Johnson has directed The Project on the Next Generation of Teachers, which examines how best to recruit, support, develop, and retain a strong teaching force. She is the author or coauthor of seven books and many articles.

Matthew A. Kraft is an assistant professor of education and economics at Brown University. His research and teaching interests include the economics of education, education policy analysis, and applied quantitative methods for causal inference, with his primary work focusing on efforts to improve educator and organizational effectiveness in K–12 urban public schools. He has published on topics including teacher labor markets, coaching and professional development, teacher evaluation systems, teacher-parent communication, school working conditions, and social-emotional skills. He is the recipient of the William T. Grant Scholars Award, the Palmer O. Johnson Memorial Award, and the Spencer Dissertation Fellowship. Prior to earning his doctorate from the Harvard Graduate School of Education, Kraft taught middle and high school humanities in Oakland and Berkeley, California.

Carrie R. Leana is the George H. Love Professor of Organizations and Management at the University of Pittsburgh, where she holds appointments in the Graduate School of Business, the School of Medicine, the Graduate School of Public Affairs, and the Learning Research and Development Center. She has published two books and more than a hundred papers on such topics as employment relations, authority at work, and human and social capital. Leana is a fellow of the Academy of Management, a Fulbright Senior Scholar, and a resident scholar at the Rockefeller Foundation's Bellagio Center, among other honors. She serves on the board of directors of the Albert Shanker Institute and has written extensively about social capital in public schools. Her current research examines the effects of financial insecurity on work performance.

Yi-Hwa Liou is an assistant professor in the Department of Educational Management at the National Taipei University of Education. Her research interests primarily focus on bringing the network research method to understanding several complex areas of organization-level research, such as organizational dynamics and learning, leadership and development, and data-informed decisions. Liou is currently conducting a longitudinal study of social network change in a school district leadership team and its alignment effort around improvement. She has published her work in various peer-reviewed journals.

John P. Papay is an assistant professor of education and economics at Brown University. His research focuses on teacher policy, the economics of education, and teacher labor markets. He has published on teacher improvement, teacher evaluation, teacher working conditions, teacher compensation, school improvement, high-stakes testing, and program evaluation methodology. His current work examines the conditions that support or constrain teacher professional growth. Papay is a research affiliate with The Project on the Next Generation of Teachers at Harvard University. A former high school history teacher, he earned his doctorate in quantitative policy analysis from the Harvard Graduate School of Education.

William R. Penuel is a professor of learning sciences and human development in the School of Education at the University of Colorado Boulder. His current research examines conditions needed to implement rigorous, responsive, and equitable teaching practices in STEM education. With colleagues from across the country, he is developing and testing new models for supporting implementation through long-term partnerships between educators and researchers. Currently, Penuel is a leader in a partnerships with Denver Public Schools and in a partnership with a national association of state science coordinators, and both partnerships are focused on implementing the vision of science education outlined in a *Framework for K–12 Science Education*. Penuel is currently the principal investigator for the National Center for Research in Policy and Practice, which is focused on how school and district leaders use research. As a co-PI of the Research+Practice Collaboratory, he is developing resources to help people build and sustain research-practice partnerships.

Frits K. Pil is a professor of business administration and a research scientist at the University of Pittsburgh. He has published extensively on the dynamics of organizational innovation, learning, and change. He studies both for-profit and public-sector organizations, examining where knowledge originates, where it resides, and how it is transferred and leveraged within and across organizational boundaries. His recent work on innovation and organizational improvement efforts explores the interplay between local and systemic performance improvement efforts and the role of knowledge diversity, social architecture, and organizational design.

Stefanie K. Reinhorn is an educational consultant working with schools and districts on instructional improvement. She is a faculty co-chair for the Instructional Rounds Institute at Harvard Graduate School of Education and teaches in the Teacher Leadership Graduate Program at Brandeis University. Reinhorn earned her doctorate at Harvard Graduate School of Education, where she continues as a research affiliate with The Project on the Next Generation of Teachers. Her research focuses on leadership practices, teacher evaluation, and teacher working conditions in urban schools. She was formerly an elementary school teacher, a middle school math teacher, and an instructional coach in urban, suburban, and international schools.

Matthew Ronfeldt is an assistant professor of educational studies at the University of Michigan School of Education. His scholarship seeks to understand how to improve teaching quality, particularly in urban and underserved settings, and his research sits at the intersection of educational practice and policy and focuses on teacher preparation, teacher retention, teacher induction, and the evaluation of teachers and preparation programs. Ronfeldt is currently a co–principal investigator on projects supported by the Spencer Foundation, the Gates Foundation, and the Joyce Foundation. He received his doctoral degree from Stanford University School of Education, where he was also an Institute of Education Sciences postdoctoral fellow. Before that he taught middle school math and science for eight years.

Matthew Shirrell is an assistant professor of education administration in the Department of Educational Leadership at George Washington University. His research focuses on the intersection of policy, school working conditions, school leadership, and teacher retention.

Nicole S. Simon is director of strategic initiatives at the City University of New York's John Jay College of Criminal Justice. She is responsible for developing pathways into John Jay from New York City high schools and community colleges and then out into careers. She is currently collaborating with K–16 and industry partners to develop a pipeline into the field of cyber security. Simon earned her doctorate at Harvard Graduate School of Education, where she remains a research affiliate with The Project on the Next Generation of Teachers. She served as a Harvard Presidential Public Service Fellow at the Boston Public Schools and as a Radcliffe/Rappaport Policy Fellow at the Massachusetts Department of Education. Prior to her doctoral work, she was the founding director of Early College Awareness Programs at the Urban Assembly School for Law and Justice, a Brooklyn public school.

James P. Spillane is the Spencer T. and Ann W. Olin Professor in Learning and Organizational Change at the School of Education and Social Policy at Northwestern University and also a professor of Human Development and Social Policy, professor of Learning Sciences and faculty associate at Northwestern's Institute for Policy Research. His work explores the policy implementation process at the state, district, school, and classroom levels, focusing on intergovernmental and policy-practice relations. He also studies organizational leadership and change and distributed leadership in schools. Spillane has published extensively on issues of education policy, policy implementation, school reform, and school leadership. Recent projects include studies of relations between organizational infrastructure and instructional advice seeking in schools and the socialization of new school principals.

Joshua P. Starr is the chief executive officer of PDK International. Before PDK International, he was superintendent of the Montgomery County Public Schools in Maryland and superintendent of schools in Stamford, Connecticut. Beginning his career teaching special education in Brooklyn, Starr became a central office leader in urban/suburban districts in the New York metropolitan area. He then served in the New York City Department of Education under Chancellor Joel Klein, first as deputy senior instructional manager in the Office of Programs, overseeing services for English language learners, special education, gifted and talented, instructional technology, and early childhood and then as director of school performance and accountability. Starr holds a bachelor's degree in English and history from the University of Wisconsin, a master's degree in special education from Brooklyn College, and a doctorate in education from the Harvard Graduate School of Education.

Tracy M. Sweet is an assistant professor in the Measurement, Statistics and Evaluation program in the Department of Human Development and Quantitative Methodology at the University of Maryland. Her research interests include social network modeling and educational applications.

INDEX